# EMERGENCY PREPAREDNESS

A **PRACTICAL GUIDE** FOR **PREPARING** YOUR **FAMILY**

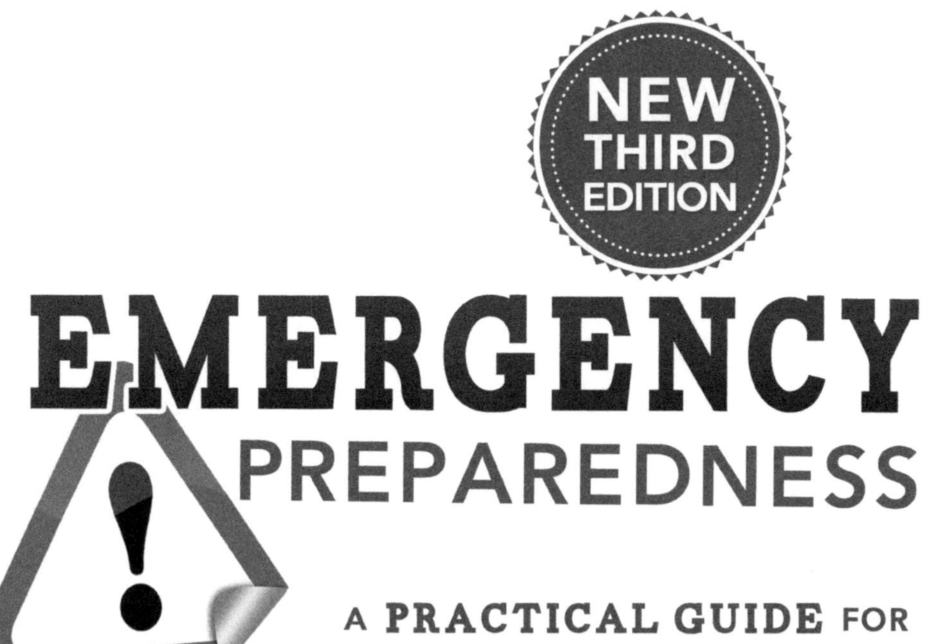


EVAN GABRIELSEN

PLAIN SIGHT PUBLISHING
An imprint of Cedar Fort, Inc.
Springville, Utah

Paperback ISBN 13: 978-1-4621-4749-6
eBook ISBN 13: 978-1-4621-4834-9

Published by Horizon Publishers, an imprint of Cedar Fort, Inc.
2373 W. 700 S. Suite 100, Springville, UT, 84663
Distributed by Cedar Fort, Inc., www.cedarfort.com

Library of Congress Cataloging Number: 2024936350

Gabrielsen, Evan M.
Emergency preparedness : a practical guide for preparing your family / Evan M. Gabrielsen.
— Third edition.
pages cm
Includes index.
ISBN 978-1-4621-4749-6
1. Survival—Handbooks, manuals, etc. 2. Emergencies—Handbooks, manuals, etc. 3. Families—Handbooks, manuals, etc. 4. Emergency management—Handbooks, manuals, etc. I. Title.
GF86.G33 2013
613.6'9—dc23

Cover design by Shawnda Craig
Cover design © 2024 by Lyle Mortimer
Edited and typeset by Evelyn Coleman

Printed in the United States of America

10 9 8 7 6 5 4 3 2 1

Printed on acid-free paper

To Terisa, who contributed immeasurably with suggestions, critiques, editing, and boundless encouragement.

# Contents



## PART 1:
## Emergency Preparedness Skills and Principles

# PART 2:
## Responding to Emergencies

## PART 3:
## Emergency Preparedness as a Way of Life

# Introduction to the Third Edition

Good for you! Just opening this book shows that you are willing to take responsibility for your own survival. As you will see, attitude is half the battle. The other half is doing something about it, and here is where this book can help.

Since the first edition of this book was published in 1999, just prior to the Y2K scare, the world has changed. A grim morning in September 2001 changed our perspective of what threats we might face; evidence of a warming climate makes us brace for hotter temperatures and ever more powerful storms and wildfires; a pandemic taught us about the transmission of infection though the connectivity of the world, and we learned the fragility of supply chains. Technology continues to advance, as well. We have experienced the ubiquity of personal computing, witnessed the replacement of payphones and landlines with cell phones, and seen the rise of LED lighting. Meteorologists predict the paths of large storms days in advance, a huge improvement from January 1888, when the Schoolhouse Blizzard hit the Great Plains so unexpectedly that it caught and killed hundreds of children between their schools and home. Satellite surveillance of weather systems is continuous. We now get most of our weather and news (and all information, really) from a handy little invention called the Internet, though the bias, quality, and accuracy must all be watched closely. Our whole world revolves around phones so capable, we call them "smart." It is remarkable that in the east coast Superstorm Sandy of October 2012, people messaged each other about losing power; social media was more reliable than the power grid. And yet, when the power grid goes down, our phone batteries run down, and our access to all of that helpful information is cut off. In the twenty-five years since this book was published, have preparedness principles also changed? The answer is: not that much.

What is important? Where do you start? This book was created to be a practical, common-sense answer to those questions. This book distills the important information from many sources and describes it in an accessible and practical way. This is not an advanced, exhaustive book; this is a book of fundamentals to help you make a solid start. It is not a survival manual for when society collapses; it is a guide to making preparedness a way of life, so you can ride out the little—and big—emergencies of life. This book summarizes, organizes, and focuses the important principles of each topic in a balanced, common-sense, everyday way.

The first part, "Emergency Preparedness Skills," includes basic topics and skills that are applicable to most emergencies. The second part, "Responding to Emergencies," begins with case studies of actual, representative disasters and discusses how to prepare for, survive, and respond to an array of specific common emergencies. The third and last part, "Emergency Preparedness as a Way of Life," is about making emergency preparedness a low-key, but regular part of your life. After you have read the information here, you will be better equipped to decide which of the many advanced sources you can use to tailor your preparation to your needs. You can benefit from reading this book in any order. If you have a specific interest or worry, start there. Pick up a pencil and underline things or make notes in the margins. This is a practical guide and workbook. If you like it, share it with your friends and family; preparedness is team sport.

In this book we have intentionally avoided the hysterical. Yes, we might sell more books if the title was, "BUY THIS BOOK OR DIE IN THE APOCALYPSE!" but it is not helpful to scare or bully anyone into preparedness. When panic is the driver, the result may be incomplete; and when the emotion passes, the let-down could damage the resolve to keep going. Instead, this book is built on the "slow and steady" philosophy of Aesop's tortoise. Emergency preparation is not about doom and gloom, it is ultimately hopeful: by preparing, we gain some control over events that seem uncontrollable; by preparing, we become "survivors," a mental attitude that experts say is more important than any gear we could collect; by preparing, we banish fear and panic. And we enable ourselves to help family, friends, and neighbors: humanity is fundamentally good, and in so many situations, neighbors help neighbors through the worst of the rough patches.

Reading this book does not guarantee survival, but it might make you more aware of principles that can minimize your exposure to emergencies; applying the advice provided here can ease some of the difficulties disasters put into our lives. There are no promises, mostly because your situation and experience are unique to you.

Basic principles found in the first edition of this little book are still fundamentally sound: make preparation a low key, but ever-present part of your life; work at it day by day, make a plan, prepare a short-term emergency kit, learn some camping and cooking skills, pay attention to forecasts and warnings, collect some skills and maybe some supplies. With these principles, a family can take on earthquakes, floods, superstorms, tsunamis, nuclear meltdowns, and, yes, hypothetical zombie attacks, without expecting someone else to do for us what we have the time, the sense, and the resources to do for ourselves.

So, after twenty-five years, this is still a practical guide, and it still urges common-sense planning, using fundamental principles. It still affirms that any preparation is better than no preparation, so you aren't immobilized by the impossibility of perfection. And it still counsels:

Do one thing today.

# PART 1
# EMERGENCY PREPAREDNESS SKILLS AND PRINCIPLES

# Do One Thing Today

## The Most Potent Advice

*Emergency preparedness.* The phrase evokes images of calamity, of privation, of wheat in the basement and guns in the closet. It represents uncertainty; it causes fear. Many people avoid emergency preparedness because to acknowledge it makes disaster seem certain. Others avoid it because it is complex, intimidating, and overwhelming. There are so many things to be done, so much to be organized, so much to be learned. Where do you start?

The chapters in this book end with the same phrase:

"Emergency preparedness: do one thing today."

This is the most potent advice in the entire book. It is more potent than telling you how much water to store, or how to secure your water heater, or why earthquakes do the damage they do. It is more potent than an emergency kit list or a first aid kit description. Why is it such useful advice? Here are nine reasons:

### 1. "The journey of a thousand miles begins with one step."

*—Lao Tse*

"Do one thing today" restates a universal principle: by the yard it's hard; by the inch it's a cinch. Henry Ford said, "Nothing is particularly hard if you divide it into small jobs." This universal principle enables ordinary people to accomplish extraordinary projects by doing a little bit at a time. It works for things other than emergency preparedness. It works for self-improvement. It works for engineering and construction projects. It works for writing books about emergency preparedness. It just works.

## 2. "Don't let life discourage you; everyone who got where he is had to begin where he was."

*—Richard L. Evans*

"Do one thing today" gives you a starting point. Complex tasks, like emergency preparedness, do not always have a clear beginning and end. The prospect of the task can be overwhelming and discouraging. But the principle of "do one thing today" gives you permission to start anywhere you are comfortable, just as long as you start.

## 3. "We cannot do everything at once, but we can do something at once."

*—Calvin Coolidge*

"Do one thing today" breaks the paralysis of procrastination, gets you moving, gives you momentum. And once you are moving, forward progress is easier to sustain. Once you are moving, the things that intimidate you don't seem so insurmountable. It's easier to face the bear than to worry about facing the bear.

## 4. "Have no fear of perfection. You'll never reach it."

*—Salvador Dali*

"Do one thing today" gives you permission to be imperfect and incomplete. You only have to be a little better than you were. This realization releases you from a potentially disabling obsession of perfection. You don't need to compare yourself with anyone else or some imagined standard. You only need to do what you can immediately see to do. You can start with a single thing. And then, as you do the simple things, it will become clear to you what the next goals should be.

## 5. "Perseverance is more prevailing than violence; and many things which cannot be overcome when they are together, yield themselves up when taken little by little."

*—Plutarch*

Most worthwhile undertakings in this life are long-term projects where perseverance is more important than speed. "Do one thing today" is the mantra of the person who is in it for the long term. It acknowledges that emergency preparedness is not a fad of the week but an attitude for life.

## 6. "He is educated who knows how to find out what he doesn't know."

*—Georg Simmel*

"Do one thing today" is better than knowledge. If taken to heart, it supplies the motivation that will lead to knowledge.

## 7. "Diligence is the mother of good luck."

*—Benjamin Franklin*

"Do one thing today" is more effective than "do it all once and forget it." Emergency preparedness requires regular attention. If you constantly review and improve your supplies, you'll know what you have, and what you need. This knowledge will allow you to be resourceful instead of panicky. If you constantly review and improve your preparedness, it is easier to stay current on rotation and replacement schedules. As you continue to review and improve, you'll naturally tailor your efforts to changing needs and risks.

## 8. "Willful waste brings woeful want."

*—Thomas Fuller*

"Do one thing today" is cheaper than one-shot preparedness. You'll tailor your purchases to your own needs better than a pre-packed kit would. You'll be able to shop sales. You'll be more aware of opportunities. You will be more organized and orderly. Panic-buying is never cheap.

## 9. "Do one thing today" really works.

## Scheduled Disasters, Convenient Emergencies, and Other Myths

All right, let's get started: everyone get out your calendar and find the entry that shows the next earthquake. What? It's not on there? Okay then, how about the next tornado? Hmm. Does anyone's calendar show a date for their next house fire? No? Hazardous material incident? No? What's the problem here? Surely it makes sense to schedule disasters and emergencies so we can get ready for them. But we can't predict the future; we cannot schedule disasters. Even worse, disasters occur when they occur, not when it is convenient for us.

Some might say, "Well, we can read conditions and determine that disasters are going to come. We pay attention to the news; we'll get some warning of social problems and wars and things like that." Okay, but earthquakes, tornados, hazardous material spills, dam failures, floods, avalanches, power outages, and so on all occur without having the common courtesy to warn us first, on local news stations or otherwise. Even in those cases when we get some advance notice, like hurricanes, droughts, volcanic activity, epidemics, and social disorder, by the time the situation becomes clear, it is often too late to do serious preparing. Others might say, "The Bible gives us signs of impending calamities. The faithful will have warning." But this is the same Bible that gives us the parable of the ten virgins and the message that when the bridegroom comes, those without oil in their lamps will be left behind. Some might even say, "Oh, the government will take care of me, and the schools will take care of my children," or, "My church or neighbors will take care of me."

If you haven't realized it yet, realize it now: preparedness is about taking personal responsibility for yourself and your family. While many people can help in small ways, you can't depend upon others to take care of your family if you don't. The lesson is clear: we have to prepare before the disasters strike. We have to remain prepared all of the time.

What does it mean to be prepared all of the time? It means having the right knowledge, gear, and attitude on hand. It means everyone in your household must know what to do, since some of them may have to face an emergency alone. It means:

1. You learn: knowledge is the most versatile commodity. It's portable, infinitely updatable, never out of style. Learn what emergencies you

can expect in your area. Learn their causes and effects. Learn how to protect yourself from them. Learn fire safety, learn how to store water and food, and learn first aid. Learn basic skills like safely starting a fire, cooking over a fire, cooking one-pot meals, cleaning up with a minimum of water, and so on.

2. Having some concrete plans for what you'll do in an emergency reduces the chances for panic. It also gives you the survivor's attitude that experts say is so important in weathering a crisis.

3. You establish a core of preparedness supplies. The best first step here is a basic, short-term emergency kit. A kit that contains supplies enabling your family to be self-sufficient for several days will help you through anything that requires an evacuation and through the first days of most other emergencies as well. There are any number of pre-assembled kits that can be quite complete, but you should always familiarize yourself with the contents, and adapt them to your own family's specific needs.

4. Once you have a solid core of supplies, you can add items that are useful for your specific hazards. You could add an alternate source of heat if you live in a colder climate. You could add special kits for your kids' backpacks, your office, or your car. You could begin a program of long-term food storage to carry you through emergencies like unemployment or long-term recovery from an area devastation

5. Finally, always being prepared means that you regularly update your preparedness: replace stored clothes as you outgrow them, rotate and replenish food and water to make sure they're ready when you need them, replace stored fuels and batteries as they expire or become outdated, and so on. Updating is something that should become a low-key, but constant, part of your life.

People who have alternate types of lighting and heating won't be paralyzed by a power outage. People who have emergency gear and food on hand don't have to risk the mob scene at the stores. People who have emergency heating may be able to avoid frozen and broken pipes in an extended cold snap. People who have emergency kits already assembled can evacuate more quickly, assured that they have the most important things. People who have some water and water purification stored can keep their families healthy if the water supply becomes contaminated or unavailable.

The short and painful truth is this: we don't know when our lives will be shaken up by a disaster. Although this seems to be a disadvantage about the way the world works, there are actually a number of positives associated with the unknowability of trouble:

- If everyone knew exactly when the next disaster was going to hit, many would still postpone their preparation until it was too late. Then, in addition to the disaster, we would have runs on stores, riots, and chaos. At least we're spared that roller-coaster ride.
- Not knowing when an emergency will occur requires that we be ready all of the time. Those who are prepared can live in this world with less fear of it.
- Being prepared, especially with some sort of food storage, can be a less expensive way to live.
- The lifestyle of preparation provides the perspective that life is more than just THIS INSTANT. A longer view of life can enable the weathering of all of life's ups and downs with equanimity.
- The lifestyle of preparation is full of life-lessons for children. Frugality, saving for a rainy day, anticipating consequences of decisions—these are valuable lessons of maturity.
- If you are prepared yourself, you can assist friends, family, and neighbors. If not, you'll be so busy keeping your own family going that you won't be able to help anyone else who might need it.

Does constantly being prepared mean that you have to become a raving fanatic or camouflage-wearing bunker-builder? No, it just means thinking ahead and visualizing living your life after a disaster. And it means doing a little bit all of the time rather than a lot all at once and then nothing.

Emergency preparedness:
Do one thing today.

(Then do another thing tomorrow.)

# The Single Most Important Thing You Can Do

## Create a Family Emergency Plan

Get organized for emergencies by creating a family plan. There is no "correct" outline or content for a family plan. It is simply a collection of information and plans you have made with your own family. When you make your family plan, remember:

- Identify the most likely emergency situations in your area and get ready for those first. Near Salt Lake City, for example, storm-related power failures, house fires, hazardous material spills, and earthquakes are the most likely scenarios. Your area may have different hazards: local authorities and news stations can help you identify likely emergencies.
- Keep your plan short; no one can remember a lot of details, and you might forget things in a disaster.
- Write the plan down and post it where it can be seen: inside a closet door or on the refrigerator. You may also want small cards with key information like phone numbers and such that you give to each member of the family for backpacks, purses, wallets, and so on.
- Involve everyone in the family, including small children. Helping in the planning will help them remember the plan and will help them deal better emotionally with a disaster.

Your plan might include some of the following elements:

## A Reunion Plan

First, identify the daily routines of everyone in the family. Where do you spend your time? At work, at school, at friends' houses, at the store, at the church? Discuss how you will get from each location to home in an emergency. Select a primary reunion location, like your home; then select a secondary reunion location out of the immediate area, in case you are not able to get home. Secondary locations might include churches, schools, or public buildings that everyone knows.

How will you get to the reunion location? What routes will you use, if passable? It would be a good idea to walk or drive each of the routes looking for anything that might be a hidden hazard or make roads impassable like bridges, large power lines, and so on. Who will pick children up from school? What will you do if driving is not possible? If driving is not possible and it's too far to walk or the conditions make getting home unsafe, are there any nearby relatives, friends, or public shelters you can go to?

Considering the emergency plans and policies that schools have in place is important. Most schools will not allow anyone who is not on an approved list to pick up your child, even in an emergency. Many schools have plans in place so they can hold children at the school if needed. Some schools may have release policies. All schools want parents to know what is in their emergency response plans, so a quick phone call to the school will provide all of the relevant information here. And don't forget to read through the emergency plan at your place of work.

If children can walk home, plan a detailed route so that parents will know where to look for them. Avoid main traffic arteries, or routes that have many electrical or water hazards. Practice walking the route with the children so they are familiar with it. You should also consider where the children will go if the parents are not home when they arrive. Coordinate with neighbors or relatives.

Each person in the family should also have a "get home bag" that includes good shoes and socks, a small bottle of water, a high-energy snack, medications you may depend on, a photo of the family (for identification and comfort), and the ever-versatile bandanna (see chapter 35).

## A Communication Plan

Even though you have a plan for getting back together, you will still want to contact your family to let them know you are all right. And no matter how thorough your planning, an emergency may require you to change your plans. Although cell phones are nearly ubiquitous, many disasters will make it difficult for you to contact each other directly: in Superstorm Sandy, high winds knocked out power lines, and storm-surge flooding knocked out power—including cell phone nodes—to a large part of the coastal area. Communications by phone were impossible in the local area for some time. In an emergency, it may be easier to make long distance calls than local ones. Identify a friend or relative outside of the immediate area or city (preferably outside the state) whom you can each call to relay messages. This contact person can act as a message board. Talk to your out-of-state contact in advance about what kind of information they should calmly extract—and write down—from each family member when they call: where they are, what time they called, where they are going, what route they will use, when they will call again, and so on. If cell phone calls are not going through, try sending a text, which uses less bandwidth, and it might make it through. Identifying two or three different contact people is a good idea, in case one of them is not home. In addition to the out-of-state contact, make a list of other neighbors and family you might call. Include parents' work numbers, nearby neighbors and family members, clergy, and day care. (It's a good idea to also include medical insurance plan information on this list). Make sure everyone has a copy of the phone numbers (update frequently) and knows when and how to use them. This list should be written down, and not simply programmed into a cell phone, which becomes useless when the battery runs out after a few hours.

## A "Get Ready" Plan

You already know a lot of things you could and should do to be more prepared for emergencies. Make a list and set some goals, with specific dates. You could have goals on:

- **Learning**: Check out emergency preparation sites on the Internet (see Additional Resources). Go to the library and see what resources they have. Take first-aid and CPR classes. Learn about local hazards and how to prepare from your police and fire departments and your utility companies.

- **Training**: Train everyone who is old enough to know how—and when—to turn off the utilities. Figure out your home fire escape plan; train and drill often. Have a "lights-out" practice.
- **Kits**: Put together a basic short-term emergency kit (see chapter 3). It doesn't have to be perfect—just get a start with what you have. Assemble a simple first aid kit (see chapter 5). Put together a car kit: your car is most likely to be somewhere near you in an emergency. Create mini-kits for pockets, purses and backpacks.
- **Organization**: Organize all of your information on emergency preparedness into one place; put it in a binder. Assemble copies of your important papers and then put the originals in a safe place, like a safe deposit box at a bank. Make a written, video or photo inventory of your household contents, and put a copy in a safe place. This will speed resolution of insurance claims.

• • •

The reason a family plan is the most important thing you can do is that it begins the discussion of what scenarios you want to prepare for and starts you thinking about how to get ready. You don't have to make a perfect family plan. Start with just one of the elements here and then add to it a little at a time. Your plan could even include elements that aren't listed here, like long-term food storage or street safety training. The most important part of your plan is what your own family needs right now.

Emergency preparedness:
Do one thing today.

<table>
<tr><td colspan="2">Sample Family Plan Outline</td></tr>
<tr><td colspan="2">Primary Reunion Location Home  Plan Updated: June 1, 2023</td></tr>
<tr><td>If Mom and Dad Aren't Home<br>Johnson's: 123 Cedar<br>(123)456-7890</td><td>If Can't Get to the House<br>Church: 123 Main St.<br>(by the south door)</td></tr>
<tr><td>Dad Work<br>ABC Co. 123 Park<br>(123)456-7890<br>Cell: (123)456-7890</td><td>Mom Work<br>State U. 123 Center<br>(123)456-7890<br>Cell: (123)456-7890</td></tr>
<tr><td>Dad's Route Home<br>West on Park. South on I-100 Freeway. West on Main. South on Walnut</td><td>Mom's Route Home<br>West on University. North on I-100 Freeway. West on Main. South on Pine. East on Spruce</td></tr>
<tr><td>Dad's Backup Location<br>John Smith. 456 Park. (123)456-7890</td><td>Mom's Backup Location<br>Dr. Jones. 456 Center (123)456-7890</td></tr>
<tr><td>Bobby's School<br>ABC Elementary. 123 Walnut.<br>(123)456-7890<br>Pickup by Dad or Mrs. Johnson</td><td>Patty's School<br>ABC Middle. 123 Spruce<br>(123)456-7890<br>Pickup by Mom or Mrs. Brown</td></tr>
<tr><td>Bobby's Route Home<br>South on Ash. East on Alder. South on Walnut</td><td>Patty's Route Home<br>South on Pine. West on Maple. South on Walnut</td></tr>
<tr><td>Bobby's Backup Location<br>Johnson's: 123 Cedar (123)456-7890</td><td>Patty's Backup Location<br>Brown's 456 Spruce (123)456-7890</td></tr>
<tr><td colspan="2">Out of State Contact: Grandma in California (123)456-7890 or (123)456-7890</td></tr>
<tr><td>Fire Escape Plan: ✓Yes</td><td>Where Meet? By Johnson's fence</td></tr>
<tr><td colspan="2">Fire Practices & Smoke Alarm Tests: ✓Jan ✓Apr Jul Oct</td></tr>
<tr><td colspan="2">Water Turnoff: ✓Dad ✓Mom ✓Patty ✓Bobby</td></tr>
<tr><td colspan="2">Gas Turnoff: ✓Dad ✓Mom Patty Bobby</td></tr>
<tr><td colspan="2">Electricity Turnoff: ✓Dad ✓Mom Patty Bobby</td></tr>
<tr><td>Emergency Kits: Front closet</td><td>Emergency Kit Check up:<br>✓Apr Oct</td></tr>
</table>

| Goals for This Year: 1. Secure bookshelves 2. Teach Bobby and Patty how to turn off gas and electrical 3. Have a 24-hour practice (warm weather) |
|---|
| Other Phone Numbers:<br>Aunt Mary (Aunt) (123)456-7890<br>Mr. Williams (Bishop) (123)456-7890<br>Mrs. Adams (Dad's Supervisor) (123)456-7890<br>Mrs. Petersen (Mom's Supervisor) (123)456-7890<br>Gonzalez (Neighbor) (123)456-7890<br>Hill (Neighbor) (123)456-7890 |

## Emergency Plans for Seniors

Making emergency plans for seniors requires some additional considerations. We think of disasters as earthquakes, floods, blizzards—things that affect a wide area. But for elderly adults living independently, there is an additional set of personal crises that can threaten their safety and independence: strength and mobility limitations, slips and falls, medication imbalance, crime, and even minor power outages that can affect medical equipment. If your family includes a senior outside of your immediate neighborhood, there are things you all can do right now to reduce vulnerability and keep in touch in an emergency.

### Identify Emergency Scenarios

The first planning step for seniors is the same as for everyone else: identify the emergencies you are preparing for, both personal and community. Review chapter 10 and make a written list of possible natural disasters you might experience. This list will be the first page of your plan.

For seniors, this includes consideration of your living situation: do you live independently in your own residence? Do you live independently in a senior community? Do you live in a care facility? Also objectively evaluate your health, strength, and mobility, all of which can change over time.

If you live in a care facility, or a senior apartment or condominium community, your assessment should include a discussion with the administration or care staff. Ask what they are prepared for and how you might support that with your own preparedness efforts. Find out how they will notify you of a facility-wide emergency: are there alarms? Will staff go door to door? Is there a gathering place in case of evacuation? Also ask how you can alert them of any personal-scale emergencies.

If you live in your own home, assess its safety for your activities of daily living. Look for electrical fire risks, such as damaged cords, cords running under carpets, or overloaded circuits. Evaluate the kitchen to make sure clutter and fire risks around stoves and ovens are minimized. Make sure smoke and carbon monoxide alarms work, and fire extinguishers are in good repair. Review instructions for operating extinguishers. Clean up clutter. Look for furniture that could topple in an earthquake. Check stairs, halls, and especially bathrooms for slip and fall hazards. Throw rugs can be especially hazardous trip risks. Repair loose handrails, and install non-slip surfaces and grab bars, if necessary. Don't forget to check outside. Look for loose railings, hazards and obstacles along walking surfaces, or nearby trees or power lines that could damage the house. The insurance company can tell you if your residence is in a flood plain or a wildfire zone, and the age of the home can give some indication of the level of earthquake it is designed to withstand. You may be able to correct some deficient items during your home hazard hunt, but likely there will be some others that will be more involved projects. Make a written list of things you want to fix; this list will be another page in your plan.

## Identify & Consult with Your Support Team

Make a written list of people who can help you prepare and whom you may need to contact in an emergency. Write down the list and relevant contact information; don't depend upon lists in phones and other devices that may run out of batteries. The list may include:

- Doctors, pharmacists, nurses, aides, other caregivers
- Administrators of your facility
- Lawyers, accountants, financial advisors, insurance agents
- Regular service providers, such as in-home care, meal services, plumbers, electricians, trusted small repair contractors and the like
- Family and friends
- Clergy
- Neighbors
- Emergency pet care (some shelters do not allow pets)

Also identify an out-of-state person that both you and the family can check in with if a widespread emergency makes long distance calling easier than local. This written list will be another page in your preparedness plan.

Call each person on this list (a good application of "do one thing today!") and identify your specific needs and enlist their support in both preparing for and responding to emergencies. For doctors and medical providers, you might ask about building up emergency supplies (a thirty-day supply is a good target) of medications or equipment and consumable supplies. For lawyers and financial advisors, you might ask about important papers to have in order, and copies to file in an off-site location (be cautious about who you allow to get involved with your financial affairs.) For family in the area, neighbors, and friends, you might try to establish several people who can check on you—by phone or in person—in case of a disaster, or who can watch for a distress signal from you. If you need transportation to a shelter, is there someone who can help with that? You could invite someone close at hand to learn how to operate and maintain any medical equipment you depend upon. You might recruit someone to care for your pets in case you need to evacuate, since some public shelters will not accept animals.

Ask questions, develop answers collaboratively, and write down any decisions you make. This will form another page of your plan. Pick four key contacts to list on the plan, along with contact information:

1. The first person you would call for assistance
2. The first family member your nearby team should contact
3. The first person nonlocal family members could call to check on you
4. Your out-of-state communications contact

Your plan should also include a summary page of recent and relevant medical history that lists the condition, medications and dosages, the prescribing doctor, and pharmacy contact information.

## Make a Plan to Prepare for Evacuation Emergencies

Many types of emergencies require you to leave your home and go to another shelter. If you reside in a facility, the evacuation and shelter destination should be part of the facility's planned response. If you live in your own home, members of your support team may offer some alternatives to public shelters. There may be someone close who can shelter you if your home is not safe. You may need more distant options if your neighborhood is not safe (think floods, wildfires, hazardous material accidents.) Depending on the type and location of the emergency, public shelters may be established by the community or organizations such as the American Red Cross. If you drive, be sure to follow suggested routes exactly. If you don't drive, you will need to arrange a ride from someone on your team.

When evacuating, you will want to have an emergency kit ready to grab at a moment's notice. Refer to chapters 3 and 4 for descriptions of the contents of different types of kits, but you may need special adaptations for your situation. Make your own written list of what you want in your kit. In addition to the general items like a change of clothes, a blanket, and a small amount of water and food for your specific diet, you will need a supply of your medications, whatever mobility equipment you use (walkers, wheelchairs, canes, all labeled with your name), and extra medical and hygiene supplies. Include a battery-powered radio (with an earphone jack and earphones), a flashlight, extra batteries for hearing aids, extra glasses, and an extra phone charger. Add copies of your medical history and support team contact list, some earplugs (public shelters may be noisy), and items to entertain yourself in the shelter. You may be able to collect these items all at once, but more likely you will need to accumulate them over a few days or weeks. Use your list to remind you of items to purchase on your next shopping trip. Be sure to get a study container or duffle bag to put all of this in, and store it where it is easy to grab on your way out the door.

## Prepare to Shelter in Place

Many types of emergencies do not require you to leave your residence. This means your home is not in immediate danger and you can stay in your residence with all of its resources. See chapter 3 for information on a short-term emergency kit that can support you for several days on your own. You can store more water in your own home (plan on one gallon per person per day for three to four days), and more food for yourself. Store foods compatible with your diet and be sure to store tools to open food containers, such as can-openers or scissors. Store ready-to-eat foods since you may not have power or utilities. Store food and supplies for your pets. You can store foods with shorter shelf lives if you are disciplined about rotating supplies regularly. Store flashlights, LED lanterns, and extra batteries. Because of fire risks, do not depend solely on candles for your emergency lighting. As with the evacuation kit, use the information in this book to make a list of items you would like to have on hand if you will be on your own for a few days. Collect what you can right away and use the list to complete your kit when possible.

## Consult with Your Support Team Regularly and Update Plan as Needed

Distribute the plan information to key, trusted members of your support team. Invite their assistance to complete tasks, and update the plan as your residential or health situations change. Conduct a hazards assessment at least yearly. Check in with your contact persons. If you find that there is someone on the list that is not as available as you would like, consider making a change. Practice parts of your plan. Can you open the food and water containers? Is the ready-to-eat food edible and tasty? How would you do overnight without electricity?

In an emergency, stay calm and work your plan. Don't panic if everything doesn't work exactly as planned. You have enough alternatives to fall back on, and your support team will be helpful. And after an emergency, critically evaluate your plan: what worked? What didn't? Get input from all members of your team, update the plan, and redistribute.

Emergency preparedness:
Do one thing today.

# Short-Term Emergency Kits

## Ten Key Principles of Short-Term Emergency Kits

Large-scale disasters frequently overwhelm first responders and government organizations for a short time. The bigger the event, the longer it will take for public resources to get to everyone. First responders often must use triage principles to prioritize their efforts. The case studies described in chapter 11, and a quick review of recent and current disasters underscore the principle that each person, each family, must be responsible for their own safety and response. A large disaster could cut off utilities, public services, roads, bridges, and access to stores and gas stations for three days or more. Officials urge each household to prepare themselves by gathering a supply of essential items (see table at end of chapter) to support your household for several days. Follow these ten guidelines to maximize the effectiveness of your emergency kit.

1. The most important emergency tool is your brain. It is portable, expandable, and infinitely adaptable. Fill it with information and protect it from panic.
2. Tailor your kits to the needs of your family. Include items that are important to your family, not someone else's. Include food you'll eat, clothes you'll wear, and games your family finds fun.
3. Emergency kits don't have to be expensive. Build them now with supplies on hand and then upgrade gradually. Shop at discount stores and watch for sales.

4. Your survival supplies must be gathered into a single location before an emergency occurs. Pack contents in waterproof, nonbreakable containers. Store everything in backpacks, duffle bags, or roller suitcases. Put the kits in a convenient location that everyone knows.
5. Include multiple solutions to problems. For example: store water as well as water purification tablets. Or store battery-powered flashlights as well as chemical light sticks.
6. Plan for comfort as well as survival. Technically, you could survive on much less than you will have in your kit, but what could you add to reduce the emotional impact of a stressful situation? Adequate light, warm food, and a good night's sleep all reduce stress.
7. Your kits should be portable in case you have to evacuate on short notice. Keep a list of non-kit items you want to grab if you have time and space.
8. Don't forget Spot and Fluffy's needs.
9. If you borrow from a kit for those daily emergencies (this is allowed; an emergency is an emergency), make it a priority to replace the item. Put a list of what's in the kits in the top, to make it easier to inventory. Check and update the kits every six months. An easy time to remember is when you set the clocks back in the fall and forward in the spring. (Those are good times to change the batteries in your smoke detectors too.) Check the food, replace the water, rotate the batteries. Do the clothes still fit growing children? Is there any insect or water damage?
10. Involve everyone in getting the kits together. And involve everyone by practicing with them. If you want to know what should go in your family's survival kit, try living out of it for twenty-four hours. Or try cooking a meal without your stove. If the lights went out tonight, how would you cope? Could you entertain yourselves without TV? How much water do you use if the taps are shut off?

Only you can prepare yourself for emergencies. Preparedness is no more complicated than imagining what an emergency would be like, and then doing things now that will make life easier then. A well-maintained short-term emergency kit will enable you to be self-reliant in the case of an emergency.

## What Should You Put in a Short-Term Emergency Kit?

The table at the end of the chapter contains a tailorable list of all the items you should consider putting in your short-term emergency kit to survive three to four days on your own. The table is organized into four columns: the bare minimum required for survival; other essential additions; items to improve your convenience level, and "luxury" items. You can tailor your own kit to your own family and your own situation and your own limits of time, space, and money. Start by gathering the items listed in the "survival" column as a minimum. Then add the items listed in the "essential" column. It is highly recommended that your emergency kits also include all or most of the "convenience" column items. Quantities will depend on the size of your family. If you have time, room, and money, you may want to add some of the items in the "luxury" column, although this can make the kit larger and less portable. Here are some additional tips to improve your emergency kits:

### Overall Tips

- Keep a copy of the list you used to assemble your kit as an inventory.
- If you use the following table, mark items that you don't want to keep with the kit but may want to grab in a real emergency if time and space allow.
- Review and update the contents of your kit every six months, when you set the clocks back or forward for daylight savings time.

### Food and Water Tips

- Include familiar foods that are tasty.
- Stress changes eating habits; try smaller servings of a variety of foods, rather than a large helping of a single dish.
- Select low-preparation foods; you won't want to cook much in an emergency.
- Babies have special needs depending on whether they are nursing, or on formula, or eating solid foods. Store pouches, not glassware, and include extra bottles, nipples, and cleaning supplies.
- Store food in unbreakable, rodent-proof containers.

- Don't forget food and food/water dishes for pets.
- Store at least one gallon of water per person per day.
- For emergency water storage, two-liter soda bottles work best; milk jugs degrade, glass breaks. Single-use water bottles are useful for personal use, but you may wish to have bulk storage to minimize the number of containers. It is also helpful to store a larger collapsible container in case you need to obtain water at a public site.
- Include water purification tablets and instructions.
- Don't store heavy items on top of water; containers could crack.

## Shelter and Bedding Tips

- "Space" blankets don't take up much space. If you can afford them, buy "bivy bags" instead of blankets since they give better protection.
- Wool blankets, polypropylene, and synthetic fleeces insulate even when wet. Cotton and down do not.
- Sleeping bags are ideal for emergency kits but more expensive and bulky.
- Store foam earplugs for everyone; they may make it easier to sleep in noisy public shelters.

## Clothing Tips

- Make sure clothing is sturdy, warm, large, and layerable.
- Make sure you keep up with children's growth; check every six months.
- Store shoes that have sturdy soles: disasters often leave debris and foot hazards.
- Include knit caps and knit gloves or mittens.
- In cold or even cool weather, getting wet can lead to hypothermia. Rain gear could be lifesaving: large garbage bags work as ponchos in a pinch.
- Include a small sewing kit with safety pins in case you have to repair or adapt clothes.

## Light/Heat Tips

- A flashlight with fresh batteries and an extra bulb is essential. LED flashlights are inexpensive, powerful, and stingy with batteries. When in doubt, get extra ones.
- A strap-on headlamp will give you the ability to do tasks that require two hands. A battery lantern will light a space best (LED models are widely available).
- Flashlights that take standard batteries are the simplest.
- Candles or flame lanterns do not store well (especially in warm garages or trunks) or transport well and can create additional fire hazards.
- Charcoal (takes up lots of room), solid-fuel emergency stove, or backpacker's stove (may require special canisters or liquid fuel) can be used for cooking. Don't forget matches.

***Safety note:*** *Do not use open flames until you are sure there are no gas leaks. Ventilate adequately. Never leave an open flame unattended, and keep children away. NEVER cook indoors with charcoal; carbon monoxide is deadly.*

## First-Aid Tips

- A good first-aid manual is a must.
- The major objective of an emergency first aid kit is to treat minor injuries and prevent infections: include antiseptic pads, antibacterial ointment, adhesive bandages. More serious injuries will require professional care.
- Match the contents of your first-aid kit with your knowledge level.
- Include aspirin, acetaminophen, or ibuprofen for pain relief. Be sure to have child-sized doses if you are caring for children.
- Add antihistamines for allergic reactions, stuffy noses, and nausea.
- Don't forget personal medications (ask pharmacist about storability). Depending on your medication, you might need to rotate a fresh supply every month.
- Large sterile dressings, gauze rolls (get plenty), tape, and elastic bandages can be used for larger, more serious injuries.

- A bandanna has many uses in first aid and in general. See chapter 35
- Don't forget scissors, tweezers, and a needle.
- Disposable nitrile gloves can help prevent the spread of contamination and body fluids.
- Periodically check the expiration of medications and the condition of alcohol pads, and the like. Replace as necessary.

## Sanitation Tips

- Hand sanitizer is quick and convenient, but it has a limited shelf life. Double-bag it to minimize leaking. Moist towelettes are convenient and versatile. If they dry out, add a little bit of water to rehydrate. Include some hand soap as well; double-bag it.
- Paper towels come in handy.
- A five-gallon bucket with plastic sacks/ties and some disinfectant can make an improvised toilet.
- Don't forget toilet paper.
- Each person will want a personal comfort kit: toothbrush/paste, hand towel, soap, comb, and so on.
- Remember diapers and feminine hygiene products.
- Extra zipper plastic sacks and garbage bags have a variety of uses.

## Communication Tips

- Store an extra phone charger cable and a variety of adapters.
- A battery-powered radio (with extra batteries) is essential for keeping current on the situation. There are reliable models that include solar and crank-powered options. Some will even recharge a cell phone by crank power. Make sure it has an earphone jack and store some earphones so others don't have to listen if they don't want to.
- Include a paper list of key contacts and phone numbers. The electronic directories we have on our phones are useless when the battery dies.
- Include a pencil (pens can dry out) and some paper in case you want to leave messages for someone or keep notes of things you learn.

- Recent photos of family members can be a morale booster and can help officials locate missing persons more quickly.

## Personal/Valuables Tips

- Many emergencies will render ATMs and credit cards inoperative. Cash will be needed if any purchases can be made: store small bills and coins.
- Include copies of important papers. The originals should be kept in a secure place.
- Include extra glasses, denture supplies, elderly or infant needs, extra pacifiers, and so on.

## Utensils/Tools Tips

- A sharp pocket knife is vital.
- Disposable dishes can conserve water as well as make clean-up easy.
- Include a cooking pan, pot holders, and cooking/serving utensils if you plan on cooking.
- Don't forget a can opener if you've stored canned goods. Army surplus stores sell small can openers that will store anywhere. Get a couple of them and tie them on lanyards; they are easily lost.
- Leather gloves protect hands while working or cooking.
- Versatile additions: nylon rope, duct tape, aluminum foil.

## Morale Tips

- Hard candy stores well.
- Toys, games, and puzzles will keep kids busy. Pack a game kit and include instructions.
- Don't pack a high-density book; pack magazines, word/number games, short story collections, and easy reads.

Emergency preparedness:
Do one thing today.

How to use these tables: Put together an emergency kit to meet your own needs and fit your own time/space/money limits. Start by gathering the items listed in the "survival" column as a minimum. Then add the items listed in the "essential" column. It is recommended that your emergency kits also include all or most of the "convenience" column items. Quantities depend on family size. If you have time, money, and room, you may want to add some of the items in the "luxury" column, although this makes the kit quite a bit larger and much less portable.

| Category | Survival Minimum | Essential Additions |
|---|---|---|
| 1. Food/Water | Food, none (adult)<br>Water: 2 c/day: 2 qt/person<br>Water purification & instructions | Food, any (unbreakable packages)<br>Water: 1 gal/person per day<br>Refillable container<br>Expedient can opener |
| 2. Shelter/Bedding | Space blanket | Space bag or bivy bag<br>Umbrella |
| 3. Clothing | 30-gal garbage sacks<br>gal & quart plastic bags (plain not zip) | Warm, layers (fleece/wool)<br>Wool cap, hat w/ brim<br>Warm, dry, sturdy footwear |
| 4. Heat/Light | Matches (waterproof) | Flashlight w/batteries<br>Cooking heat (Sterno or solid fuel) |
| 5. First Aid | Basic kit<br>First-aid manual<br>Bandanna | |
| 6. Sanitation | Hand sanitizer (double bagged) | Toilet paper<br>Trowel<br>Plastic bags, ties<br>Soap (hand/dish)<br>Feminine hygiene<br>Diapers (if needed)<br>Moist towelettes, wet wipes<br>Nitrile gloves, var sizes |
| 7. Communication | Cards w/phone numbers | Contact plan<br>Family pictures w/names<br>Extra phone charger cable |
| 8. Personal/Valuable | Personal medication (rotate) | Cash: small bills and coins |
| 9. Tools/Utensils | Sharp pocketknife<br>Sturdy container or pack for kit | Plastic forks, spoons<br>Aluminum foil<br>Paper towels<br>Rope/cord/string<br>Plastic bags, zip type, var sizes |
| 10. Morale | | Radio w/batteries<br>N95 masks<br>Dust masks |

| Category | Convenience Additions | Luxury Additions |
|---|---|---|
| 1. Food/Water | Food ready-to-eat<br>Water: 5–10 gal/person<br>Pet food<br>Special diet foods | Luxury foods<br>50-100 gal/family<br>Salt, sugar, spices<br>Multiple purification methods |
| 2. Shelter/Bedding | Ground cloth or tarp, stakes, cord<br>Sheet plastic<br>Blankets (wool or fleece)<br>Foam earplugs (for public shelter) | Tent, trailer<br>Sleeping bags<br>Closed cell foam pads<br>Pillow cases |
| 3. Clothing | Rain jacket/pants/poncho<br>Extra socks, underwear<br>Warm gloves or mittens | Change of clothes<br>Sewing kit, shoelaces, safety pins<br>Laundry soap |
| 4. Heat/Light | LED headlamp w/batteries<br>Flint and steel<br>Hiker's stove/fuel<br>Hand warmers | Multiple fuel sources<br>Emergency generator<br>Battery lantern<br>Camp stove w/fuel<br>Space heater w/fuel |
| 5. First Aid | Expanded kit | EMT kit<br>Fire extinguisher (A-B-C)<br>Insect repellent, sunscreen |
| 6. Sanitation | Plastic bucket w/tight lid<br>Large plastic bags<br>Toilet seat<br>Disinfectant, bleach<br>Hand towel, cloth<br>Toothbrush, paste, floss<br>Lip balm<br>Paper towels | Port-a-potty<br>Deodorant<br>Shampoo<br>Shaving kit<br>Nail clippers<br>Comb, brush |
| 7. Communication | Whistles<br>Paper and pencil (not pen) | Flares, light sticks<br>Map, compass |
| 8. Personal/Valuable | Copies of important papers<br>Valuables<br>Watch/clock | Mirror (metal)<br>Infant/elderly special needs<br>Sunglasses, extra glasses |
| 9. Tools/Utensils | Manual can opener<br>Skillet, lid<br>Cook pot, lid<br>Gloves, leather<br>Steel wool, pot scrubber<br>Hot pads<br>Extra plastic sacks (small) | Crescent wrench<br>Screwdrivers<br>Pliers, scissors<br>Baling wire, duct tape<br>Solar still<br>Shovel<br>Axe, saw, whetstone<br>Crowbar, hammer |
| 10. Morale | Hard candy<br>Toys, games, puzzles<br>Paper, crayons<br>Emergency survival book | Journal, pencil (not pen)<br>Hobbies, crafts<br>Magazines, books<br>Scriptures |

# Evacuation Planning

## What Do You Take? Where Do You Go?

The key lesson from Hurricane Katrina was the same key lesson from the East Palestine hazmat spill, which was also the same key lesson from the Tohoku Earthquake, which was also the same key message from . . . well, you get the picture: get out when authorities (or your own good sense) tell you to get out (see chapter 11). Maybe even before they tell you. This lesson is the one that will preserve your lives. Throughout the year we hear of events and calamities requiring people—sometimes few, sometimes many—to leave their homes. Evacuations can be forced by rising waters and flooding; they can be caused by chemical spills or releases; they can be caused by wildfire. Nearly every year Gulf and Atlantic Coast residents are forced to leave their homes as hurricanes threaten to come ashore, with associated storm surge. Some parts of the world are threatened by volcanic activity, lava flows, mudslides and ash fall. Even a house fire causes an evacuation of one family.

Evacuations can last hours or, less frequently, days. After Katrina, they lasted for months, and some of the residents just plain relocated. Most of us have never been required to evacuate. In the case of disaster or emergency, when should you evacuate? Where would you go? What should you take? What should you expect?

### When to Evacuate

Leave when you are in danger. Thousands of lives were saved on 9/11 because people evacuated when they were told to, or when they saw the danger. In many cases, you won't be able to make that determination by yourself because you don't have access to all of the critical information. You may not be aware of the chemical spill. You won't be able to predict a river's peak or a storm's path. In these situations, you should leave when authorities tell you to. Authorities will use public communications (TV, radio) when they have enough time. In short notice situations, they may use vehicle-mounted public broadcast systems and even door-to-door notification if necessary. In the case of storms and hurricanes, forecasters can give a day or two of notice. Sometimes potential evacuees are given hours of notice, but in other cases some are given no notice. In Ohio in 2023, a freight train derailed, spilled hazardous chemicals and caught fire. The closest neighbors had no warning and were out of their houses for days. In cases like this, evacuees will only have a minute or two to grab family members—and maybe a well-placed emergency kit—and go.

The most important thing is to get your family to safety, but if you have time, here are some additional actions you might take:

- Don’t panic.
- Gather essential items. A possible list is described later in this chapter.
- Secure your house. In hurricanes that means boarding up windows. In floods it means putting furniture and valuables on upper floors. In a chemical spill it might mean closing the windows, vents, and air intakes. Disconnect utilities if told to. Take actions to prevent freezing pipes if weather is a problem.
- Put on sturdy and practical clothes, especially shoes.
- Let others know where you are going. Call your out-of-state contact.
- Make provisions for your pets if you plan on going to a public shelter—many shelters do not accept pets for health and control reasons.

## Where to Go

When authorities direct an evacuation, they may also determine a safe evacuation route for you to follow. Traffic is likely to be heavy and slow. Be extra patient and extra courteous: all those around you will be just as disoriented as you, maybe more. Don't take shortcuts.

Stay on recommended routes to avoid being trapped by unexpected road closures or running into a drifting chemical cloud. Follow all traffic regulations: an accident in an emergency situation is doubly dangerous, and emergency services may be tied up elsewhere.

You may already have determined in your family emergency plan where you will go and how you will contact each other in an evacuation emergency. Each family should have at least three evacuation locations determined in advance:

1. A safe place outside of the home where you can gather if you need to escape a burning house. When you have fire and exit drills, be sure to practice going to this spot.
2. A friend or family member's house outside of the immediate neighborhood but close enough to walk to, where you could go in a localized evacuation.
3. A friend or family member's house outside of the community for larger evacuations, like hurricanes. Also, check the school emergency plan to make sure that you know where your schoolchildren will be sent if they are required to evacuate their schools.

If you cannot get to one of these family plan locations, then public shelters—set up and run by the Red Cross or other community service organizations—are a possible solution. You may be able to find a shelter by texting SHELTER and then your zip code (e.g., SHELTER 12345) to 4FEMA (43362) to find the nearest shelter. If authorities don't direct you to a public shelter, the radio may broadcast shelter locations you can go to. In the absence of other information, check public buildings—schools, municipal buildings, and churches—since these are the most likely places for shelters to be established.

Once you get to your temporary location—wherever it is—check in with your out-of-state contact. Having someone outside of the area or state gives you a single checkpoint for all your family to report their status. This will help you exchange information to reunite in the event that everyone did not make it immediately to the planned gathering spot. Designate your out-of-state contact, make it part of your family plan, and make sure that everyone in the family memorizes the number and carries a copy of it with them.

## What to Take

Short-term emergency kits. One of the reasons emergency kits must be pre-gathered—and not just a list of stuff you have somewhere in your house—is that you may need to grab them at a moment's notice and evacuate with them. Shelters may not have everything you need or want. They provide protection from the elements and may supply food and water. Here are some other things you may want to bring for your own comfort:

- First-aid supplies for minor injuries
- Personal medications, including prescriptions
- Extra clothes
- A child's favorite toy
- A battery-powered radio (with jack for earphones)
- Quiet entertainment, books or games, paper and pencil
- A recent picture of each member of your family, to help locate them
- List of phone numbers: family, neighbors, places where family members might go
- Earplugs: it may be difficult to sleep in a shelter without them
- Cash in small denominations
- Important papers: financial and investment, insurance, household inventory, deeds, wills (originals stored safely in another location)
- Your own personal hygiene items
- Car resources. Since you will likely evacuate in your car, don't forget all of the resources you may have available in your car too. It's a good idea to keep your car on the full side of the gas tank.
- Some things not to take: panic, alcoholic beverages, firearms

## What to Expect

Each shelter situation will be different, but in general you might expect the following:

- Expect to sign in and to receive instructions from shelter managers. Following directions will reduce the confusion level.
- Don't expect all of the conveniences of home.

- Don't expect all of the privacy or quiet or order of home. Be patient.
- Expect information from time to time about what's going on and when you can expect to go home.
- Expect to be responsible for your own hygiene. Be as sanitary as you can—wash your hands often. Be especially careful with food storage and preparations.
- Expect food and water, but don't expect a huge variety of gourmet selections. Eat as balanced a diet as you can. Drink lots of water—at least a quart a day or more, if available.
- Expect to do your part to keep improvised toilets clean and sanitary.
- Do not expect smoking to be allowed in shelters. Be considerate if you must smoke.
- Expect to be responsible for your own children. Keep them under control—improvise games to keep them occupied.
- Expect to be responsible for shelter safety and security.
- Expect to be patient. Shelter volunteers do the best they can under difficult circumstances. Give them a break and let the little things go.

## Returning Home

When returning home, remember: safety first. Do not enter a damaged structure until authorities determine it's safe. Take pictures and keep careful records of any damage and/or repair costs for your insurance agent. Document damage and loss as thoroughly and as soon as possible.

Wear appropriate safety gear: heavy shoes, gloves, and safety glasses. Follow instructions from authorities. Be meticulous and thorough if decontamination procedures are recommended.

Check for gas leaks. Have the gas company restore gas service if shut off or damaged. Restore utilities carefully only after checking for broken pipes, exposed wires, or other damage. Clean up hazardous chemicals or medicines that may have spilled, as well as broken glass and other hazards. Beware of exhaustion. Pace yourself and get plenty of rest. Wash your hands often. Don't drink the water until authorities declare it safe. Throw out spoiled or suspect food.

Use the guidelines here to get ready for an evacuation. Then, if evacuation is ever required, don't panic. Roll with the punches, be resourceful, be patient. Your preparation now will make it easier for you to protect your family by getting out of harm's way at a moment's notice.

Emergency preparedness:
Do one thing today.

# First Aid

## Learn First-Aid Skills and Make a Kit

Injuries are a potential component of any emergency situation. The more widespread the emergency, the greater the chances that you may have to deal with injuries to yourself or your family before help can arrive. Certainly, if you have life-threatening or serious medical emergencies, you should try to get help or get to a facility, but in many cases, the emergency medical system may be too overwhelmed to get to the less-serious injuries quickly. Although no one expects you to be an ER physician, learning several things and having the right supplies on hand will improve your effectiveness in a medical emergency.

### Learn First Aid

Take a course. If you've never had a first aid class, now is the time to find one and sign up. The Red Cross teaches first aid, as do some community education programs, fire or police stations, community colleges, and workplaces. You will learn how to assess a victim for life-threatening conditions; clear airways, check for breathing and circulation, and administer cardiopulmonary resuscitation (CPR); recognize and treat shock; treat internal and external bleeding; treat burns; treat broken bones, sprains and dislocations; treat injuries from extreme heat and cold; treat bites, stings and poisonings. Even if you have had first aid training in the past, it pays to update your knowledge on this ever-expanding topic.

Get a good first aid reference book that tells you how to recognize and treat various medical emergencies. Some hospitals or urgent care centers distribute emergency handbooks for glove compartments or households. Most commercially prepared first aid kits will also have a handbook. Although your first response to an emergency usually won't give you time to consult a handbook, there is usually some point where you will be able to review the proper section of the handbook to make sure you've done all you can. The handbook is also a good review resource when you want to brush up your skills.

## Prepare a First-Aid Kit

What goes into your first aid kit depends on what emergencies you expect and what first aid skills you have. For example, someone with medical training might include a suture kit for sewing up wounds. Some lesser-trained people might be uncomfortable with the idea of sutures or IVs.

Your home kit (wide range and smaller injuries) will be different than a commuter's (auto accident trauma) or a backpacker's (personal injuries far from help). Although some good pre-packaged first aid kits are available, you will be better off if you create your own kit. Then you won't pay for items that you will never use, and you can add items that you know you frequently use. Best of all, if you build the kit, you know what is in it. Whether you buy it or build it, keep a list of the items you have in the kit to make updating and replenishing easier. Most kits will include the following (see the table of first aid kit supplies at the end of the chapter):

- First-aid manual
- Over-the-counter pain medication, like aspirin, acetaminophen, or ibuprofen (often the most used items of any kit)
- Antihistamine tablets to reduce the allergic reaction to stings and bites (if you have severe allergic reactions, see a doctor about portable epinephrine injection devices)
- Nitrile disposable gloves to wear when giving first aid
- Rescue breather for giving CPR
- Hand sanitizer, antiseptic wipes; alcohol or iodine, for cleaning your hands as well as wounds

- Small plastic syringe for irrigating cuts and scrapes
- Antibiotic gel or cream to put on cuts and scrapes
- Assorted adhesive bandages—medium, large, and butterfly type
- Assorted gauze dressings (2″ × 2″, 3″ × 3″, 4″ × 4″)
- Assorted width gauze roller bandages (2″ and 3″)
- Ace elastic bandage
- Bandage tape
- Pressure bandages (diapers, nursing pads, & feminine hygiene pads all could be used here)
- Bandannas have many uses, from pressure dressings to splint ties and slings
- Cold packs are useful for reducing swelling or treating painful burns
- Safety scissors are useful for cutting bandages and removing clothing
- Needle and tweezers are handy for removing splinters and stingers
- Sterile eyewash
- Safety pins have uses in securing wraps and slings
- Some people also store splints, but usually you can find all sorts of things to improvise with. In many cases, you don't need to splint at all—you only need to immobilize until help comes.

## Practice First-Aid Principles in Emergencies

- Don't panic. Take a deep breath and remind yourself that you know some things that might help. Your confidence will be contagious.
- Make sure the scene is safe, and avoid becoming another victim.
- Always summon help first in a medical emergency. When in doubt, call. If the emergency turns out to be less serious than you thought, you can send them home. If it is serious, they will arrive that much faster.
- Treat the victim where you find them; don't move them unless the scene is not safe.

- The first priorities are usually to assure the victim has a clear airway, is breathing, and has circulation. If the victim is conscious, these things are present. If these things are not present, apply the techniques you've learned in your CPR course.
- Bleeding from even minor injuries can look worse than it is, so don't panic: stop bleeding with direct pressure over the wound. First-aid courses will teach you the tools and the techniques.
- In all emergency situations, even small ones, assume the victim is in shock or will go into shock, and treat them as you were taught in your first-aid course: keep them comfortable and warm.

• • •

A well-rounded emergency preparedness plan includes training and equipment for first aid. Like all emergency preparedness, you may never have to use it. But then again, someone you love may need you to know it.

## Emotional First Aid

In any emergency, physical safety and first aid are immediate and pressing concerns. But emergencies are also stressful and psychologically traumatic; first aid for the emotions may be required. Children often have unique emotional needs in an emergency.

### Preparation Minimizes Emotional Trauma

Preparation is the first step in reducing the psychological impact of a disaster. Children can and should be involved in emergency preparedness. A key consideration is that emergency preparedness should be an on-going activity. If you only occasionally discuss preparedness by emphasizing all the things that can go wrong, and then don't take any steps to prepare, you may scare children into being afraid of everything. With emergency preparedness as an on-going activity, however, children see that there are some dangers, and they also participate in mitigation efforts and see that the risks become less.

### Some Ways to Involve Children

- Teach children common danger signals: the sound of the smoke alarm, the smell of smoke, the smell of natural gas.

- Even young children can be taught to use 911. All children should be taught their name, age, address, and parents' full names as early as possible.
- Children should be taught how to call the out-of-state contact.
- Children can understand basic principles such as staying calm, assessing the situation, escaping if required, and reporting emergencies. All children should know safe places to go (neighbors' houses and so on) if they must leave the home.
- Children should know basic street safety principles such as staying in groups, not talking to or taking anything from strangers, noticing suspicious cars, writing down license plate numbers, how to react if threatened, safe places to run, and so on.
- Teach fire safety and fire response. Practice fire escapes.
- Involve them in home hazard hunts. Make it a game to see who can spot the most hazards and then involve children in fixing them.
- Children can learn safe locations to go in case of earthquakes or tornadoes.
- Involve children in emergency practices as well as routine maintenance.

## Short-Term Emotional Response—Stay Calm and Listen

If you stay calm, those around you will stay calmer. No situation gets better with panic. Your calm influence will go a long way towards reassuring children (and other adults). Be honest. Only say what you know about the emergency. Do not speculate. Do not lie. Don't make promises you can't keep.

Listen to the upset individual. Realize their feelings are real feelings. Do not dismiss or make light of them. Discuss them one at a time. Listen. Really listen—don't interrupt. Give them your attention; give them eye contact. Do not argue or use force.

Provide warm, nourishing food and encourage rest when possible. Most obstacles look smaller when your stomach is full, and you are rested. Do not administer drugs unless under a doctor's supervision.

Typical fears of children after a disaster include fear of recurrence, fear of separation from family, and fear of being left alone. Reunite children with their families as soon as possible. If the family is already together, keep it together as much as possible. Try not to leave children in a "safe place" while you go off to survey the damage.

Listen to children express their fears, even if they aren't rational. Listen to their version of the event. Encourage children to talk. Reassure them with words as well as actions—let them know that you will take care of them. Let them know it's okay to be afraid. Gently help them to realize many of their fears are unlikely. Speak to children at their level, both physically and mentally. Don't speak down to them, but put the situation in words they can understand. If appropriate, use reassuring physical contact.

## Long-Term Emotional Response—Be Patient and Listen

Keep listening with patience. You may have to listen to the same stories and the same fears and give the same reassurances over and over again. Also, resume normal routines as soon as possible. Routines are comforting and reassuring. Include children in age-appropriate cleanup actions. Be understanding but be firm in retaining control over family activities. Avoid being overly permissive about getting back to normal routines. If there is difficulty at bedtime, parents and children should agree on the day for the child to return to his own bed and then stick with it. Be firm, but avoid spanking or shouting to enforce your expectations.

Some effects may last for a while. There may be depression, insomnia, nightmares, anger or incorrigibility. Many of these effects will dissipate with time and care, but some may need professional help. Realize your role—you cannot be all things to all people. You may not have proper training. You may not have unlimited time or energy to devote. You may need to seek professional assistance on behalf of the victim. Realize that this is not a sign of failure, but a mature and loving response to speed the recovery of the victim. Don't be afraid to seek professional help for emotional problems when you don't know what to do. Professionals are trained to identify specific emotional conditions and are experienced in providing appropriate responses that lead the victim to resolution. You should call professionals:

- any time you don't feel capable of responding to the victim's needs
- when your patience wears out

- when aggressive behavior or regressive behavior persists beyond a few days
- when fears and irrational anxiety increase rather than diminish

Start with a call to your pediatrician or family physician. In many cases, advice can be given over the phone. In some cases, an interview will be requested. Some regressive behavior like bed-wetting, thumb-sucking, or clinging can be normal, but should only last a few days. Focus on reassurance and positive reinforcement to overcome the behavior.

All emergencies, whether specific to your family or widespread, will produce a range of normal emotional reactions. Preparation can reduce the extent of negative reactions; calmness and patience are the best tools for responding to them.

Emergency preparedness:
Do one thing today.

# First-Aid Kit Supplies

| Item | Use | Include in these kits: Home Kit | Car Kit | Pocket Kit |
|---|---|---|---|---|
| First-Aid Manual | Remind yourself of what you learned in class | Yes | Yes | Optional |
| ***Bandages*** | | | | |
| Adhesive strips, various sizes | Dress small injuries, cuts, scrapes, bites; prevent infection. This is the most-used part of most kits. | 100 total | 20 total | 10 total |
| Butterfly, adhesive | Close larger cuts | 8-10 | 4-6 | 2-3 |
| Sterile dressings: | | | | |
| 2x2, 3x3, 4x4 | Dress larger wounds, scrapes, burns, etc. | 4–6 total | 10 total | 2 total |
| 5x9, 8x10 | Dress very large wounds, scrapes, burns, etc. | 10 each | 4 each | |
| Gauze rolls: | | | | |
| 2″, 4″ | Hold dressings in place | 3 each | 3 each | |
| Tape, 1″, 2″ | Hold dressings in place, temporarily close wounds | 1 each | 1-2″ | 1-1″ |
| Pressure pads | Apply pressure to bleeding wound | 4–6 | 10 | |
| Elastic roller wrap, 3″ | Hold dressings in place, provide support to joints | 2–3 | 2–3 | 1 |
| Coban/Coflex | Self-adhesive wrap to keep dressings in place | 1-2 | 1-2 | |
| Bandanna | Dressing, sling, pressure, washcloth, towel, etc. | 1–2 | 2–3 | 1 |
| ***Medicines*** | | | | |
| Acetaminophen, ibuprophen, aspirin | Pain relief, inflammation reduction: include children's doses—follow instructions | 100 ct | 10 ct | 4 ct |
| Antihistamines | Allergic reaction treatment | 4–8 ct | 4–8 ct | 4–8 ct |
| Antidiarrheal | Loperamide for diarrhea | 4-8 ct | 4-8 ct | 4-8 ct |
| Cough drops | Also, hard candy, for minor throat irritation | 10-20 | 5-10 | |
| Antiseptic wipes | Cleanse small wounds (incl alcohol wipes) | 10 pks | 10 pks | 5 pks |
| Hand sanitizer | Clean provider hands (60% isopropyl min) | 1 med | 1 med | 1 sm |
| Antibiotic gel | Protect small injuries from infection | 1 tube | 1 tube | 1 tube |
| Sterile eyewash | Cleanse foreign material or chemicals from eye | 1 bottle | 1 bottle | |
| Burn gel | Treat small burns | 10 sm pk | | |
| Hydrocortisone | Treat stings, bites, skin irritation | 1 tube | 1 tube | 1 tube |

## First-Aid Kit Supplies (continued)

| Item | Use | Include in these kits: Home Kit | Car Kit | Pocket Kit |
|---|---|---|---|---|
| Calamine lotion | Treat bites, poison ivy, nettles, etc. | 1 tube | | |
| Oral glucose, tabl/gel | Treat hypoglycemia | 2-3 doses | 1 dose | |
| ***Tools, etc.*** | | | | |
| Rubber gloves | Minimize risk from infection, blood-borne pathogens | 10 pair | 5 pair | 1 pair |
| Rescue breather | Minimize risk from infection | 1 | 1 | 1 |
| EMT shears | Remove obstructing clothing, seat belts, etc. | 1 | 1 | 1 |
| Tourniquet, windlass | Stop life-threatening bleeding on limbs, extremities | 1 | 1 | |
| Irrigation syringe | Irrigate wounds to remove foreign materials | 1 | | |
| Splints, small to large | Immobilize broken bones, injured joints | various | various | |
| Cold packs | Reduce swelling, reduce burn pain | 2–3 | 1–2 | |
| Needle/tweezers | Remove splinters, quills, etc.; treat blisters | 1 each | 1 each | 1 each |
| Flashlight | Provide aid in dark; look in throats, ears | 1 w/batt | 1 w/batt | |
| Thermometer | Measure temperature | 1 | | |
| Sunscreen, lip balm | Minimize sunburns | 1 tube | 1 tube | sm tube |
| ***Other*** | | | | |
| Water bottle, sterile | Wash wounds | 1 bott | 1–2 bott | |
| Cotton swabs | Apply medications | 20–50 | | 2–5 |
| Safety pins | Hold bandages/slings in place, repair clothing | 5–10 | 5–10 | 2–3 |
| Moleskin | Prevent/cushion blisters on feet while hiking | 1 sheet | | ½ sheet |
| Nail clippers | Trim hiker's toenails; treat hangnails, etc. | 1 | | 1 |
| Space blanket or bag | Provide warmth, treat shock | 2 | 2 | 1 |
| Matches, waterproof | Sterilize needles, tweezers; start fire | 25–50 | 25–50 | 25–50 |
| Plastic bags | Various | 5 various | 10 various | 1–3 |
| Paper and pencil | Send information, instructions; make notes | 1 each | 1 each | 1 each |

# Water Storage & Purification

## Emergency Water Storage Q&A

### Q: How much water should I store?

A: Although basic survival is possible on less, store about one gallon per person per day. Additional water could be used for things like sponge baths, flushing the toilet, and "survival laundry." Most authorities agree that you shouldn't try to store more than a two-week supply.

| Family of | Minimum Supply | "Luxury" Supply |
|---|---|---|
| 1 | 14 gallons | 28 gallons |
| 2 | 28 gallons | 56 gallons |
| 3 | 42 gallons | 84 gallons |
| 4 | 56 gallons | 112 gallons |
| 5 | 70 gallons | 140 gallons |
| 6 | 84 gallons | 168 gallons |
| 7 | 98 gallons | 196 gallons |

### Q: What types of containers should I use?

A: You have several choices, each with advantages and disadvantages.

- **Glass**: If you use containers smaller than one gallon, you will have too many to worry about. No glass containers larger than a gallon are likely to be available. Glass can be sterilized, but it breaks easily (like in earthquakes).

- **Metal**: must be of a suitable alloy (stainless steel) or appropriately lined (polyethylene) and will be expensive.
- **Plastic**: The best solution for bulk storage is the HDPE barrel. They come in fifteen-gallon, thirty-gallon, and fifty-five-gallon sizes and can be purchased new or used as soft drink syrup barrels. If you go with used, be sure that only food products have been stored. They must be thoroughly washed and repeatedly rinsed (the local car wash has high pressure water), but they make an efficient way to store large quantities of water. Avoid milk jugs. Two-liter soda containers are made of less porous PET plastic and will clean better and last longer than milk jugs. Two-liter bottles are light and portable but are also flimsy and awkward to carry. Another kind of storage container is the mylar bladder in a cardboard box. These are more expensive, but they are square and store more easily than other containers. Be careful not to stack too high or the lower boxes could be crushed and collapse.

*Never store drinking water in containers that have been used for petroleum products or other chemicals*; they are impossible to clean and will certainly leach contaminants into the water.

Keeping some five-gallon containers handy is useful; in a long-term disruption of water service, relief agencies will likely bring water trucks to a central neighborhood location, and the smaller containers are more portable than the barrels.

### Q: How can I get water out of a large drum?

A: Hand pumps made especially for large drums are available at emergency preparedness stores. You can also use a simple siphon made from a clean rubber tube or garden hose. Instead of sucking on the hose, fill it with water to get it started. If you store the drum slightly above the ground (on pallets or two-by-fours), you can even siphon the last bit without wrestling the container.

### Q: Why shouldn't I use plastic milk jugs to store water?

A: The plastic is not formulated for long-term use and will degrade over several months' time. Also, high porosity makes it impossible to clean and allows odor/taste pickup from the storage area.

### Q: Where should I keep my stored water?

A: Water weighs about eight pounds per gallon; a fifty-five-gallon barrel will weigh over four hundred pounds. The larger the container, the less mobile it will be. If you choose a large capacity container, you may still want to have a few smaller, lighter bottles around in case you need to evacuate. Always store heavy items like water bottles on lower shelves. If you have glass containers, cushion between the bottles with cardboard: glass rattling against glass in an earthquake could create quite a mess. Store water out of sunlight, which can stimulate bacterial growth and affect plastic. Store it at a cool temperature, which will also retard bacterial growth. Some recommend keeping part of your water in the basement and part in the garage in case quake damage makes it difficult to get to one or the other. Do not store plastic containers near fuels, pesticides, herbicides, and so on because all plastics are porous to some degree, and contamination could be a problem. If you will store the water where it might freeze, leave several inches of headspace in the container to allow for expansion.

### Q: Do I need to purify water when I put it in containers?

A: Your own culinary water is usually clean, and chlorinated tap water should not need additional treatment, but sometimes the container can have residual bugs. The Centers for Disease Control and Prevention (CDC) recommend purifying water with eight drops (1/8 teaspoon) of fresh (less than one year old), unscented liquid bleach (four to six percent sodium hypochlorite) per gallon. A quarter teaspoon or sixteen drops should be used if the water is cloudy.

### Q: How often should I replace my stored water?

A: Experts differ on how often—if ever—to replace your water. You can check it frequently for smell and taste and replace it as needed. For peace of mind try to empty and refill your containers about twice a year.

### Q: Do I need to purify the water again when I take it from the container?

A: Only you can tell when you inspect the water. Clean water should be clear without any odor, unless there is a leftover chlorine smell from the purification. If you smell any questionable odors or see any growth in the containers, purify the water. In fact, if you have any question at all, purify.

## Emergency Water Purification

There are many sources of water in an emergency, but most require purification before use.

### Water Sources

- **Stored Water**: The most reliable source of water will be whatever you store. Experts recommend storing about one gallon per person per day for up to two weeks.
- **House system**: Water heaters and supply pipes contain from thirty to sixty gallons of water. To protect this water from being contaminated or siphoned out of your system, shut the main water valve into your house immediately after an emergency. If there is a reasonable chance that the water main has become contaminated, then the water heater and house pipes will also be affected if that water flows through them after the emergency. If there is any doubt about safety, treat the water. Also, turn off the gas to the water heater if you are going to empty the water without refilling it.
- **Toilets**: Toilet tanks (*not* the bowls) can be sources of drinking water *only* if they do not contain a colored disinfectant. Always purify.
- **Water Beds**: *Not* safe for drinking. The plastic used for the mattress was probably treated with fungicides or bactericides and may leach toxins into the water. Most of us have also added chemical treatments to the water, which makes it unsuitable for human consumption. Do not count on this water for any purpose except non-drinkable sanitation uses, flushing toilets, and so on.
- **Swimming Pools/Spas**: *Not* safe for drinking. Because of the chemicals used to purify and balance the pH, swimming pools and hot tubs build up salts that can damage the kidneys if the water is used for drinking. Do not count on this water for any purpose except non-drinkable sanitation uses.
- **Surface water**: This source includes rivers, canals, lakes, ponds, and other standing water. Surface water should always be purified.
- **Ground water**: Access to this water requires a well. If there is any doubt about its safety, treat the water.

## Water Purification Methods

A number of elements can make water unsafe:

- Parasites, the most infamous of which are giardia and cryptosporidium
- Bacteria including strep, staph, salmonella, E. coli, and pneumonia
- Viruses (rare)
- Pollutants including fertilizers, pesticides, and petroleum products

If the water looks, smells, or tastes odd, or comes from a questionable source, purify it. Any time your water source is open or outdoors—no matter how clean the water "looks"—you need to purify. There are three main methods of purification: boiling, chemical treatment, and filtering.

### Boiling

Water can be disinfected by bringing to a rolling boil. The CDC recommends boiling the water for one minute at sea level or three minutes over an altitude of six thousand five hundred feet.

### Chemical Treatment

- **Chlorine**: Household bleach that contains four to six percent sodium hypochlorite (check the label) can be added to clear water at the rate of two drops per quart (eight drops or one-eighth teaspoon per gallon) for clear water and four drops per quart (sixteen drops or one-quarter teaspoon per gallon) for cloudy, and allowing to stand for thirty minutes. Use newer bleach, since the strength of bleach weakens with time. Double the treatment for bleach that is over a year old; do not use bleach that is over two years old. A slight chlorine odor should be detectable after treatment. If not, repeat the treatment. Liquid bleach treatment may not be fully effective against cryptosporidium (add boiling, as described above). Halazone tablets are a solid form of the same treatment and should be used according to manufacturer's instructions. Halazone, however, does not store for long periods, and loses most of its strength in days after the package is opened. If you buy extra bleach to have on hand for purification, be sure to store it out of reach of children, and make sure it cannot fall and split open in an earthquake.

- **Iodine**: This comes in commercial tablet form (Potable Aqua and so on). Pay close attention to the expiration date, older tablets lose their strength. Buy small quantities (store out of reach of children) more frequently and keep your supply fresh. Follow manufacturer's instructions for storage, dosage and contact time, the time you let the water sit before drinking. Also, treated water takes on a taste that some find objectionable. Ascorbic acid (vitamin C) helps, and powdered drink flavorings may make the water more palatable.

  ***Safety note**: Pregnant women and people with thyroid problems should not ingest iodine.*

## Filtering

Here, we're talking about filters specifically designed to purify water. Your water softener, for example, can remove minerals and suspended solids so the water tastes better, but it cannot make water safer to drink. The same thing is true for many under-the-sink or faucet-end filters. Water-purifying filters work on the principle that if you pump the water through holes smaller than the microorganisms, the bugs will stay behind. Some filters additionally flow the water through a bed of iodide compound or silver nanoparticles to kill biological agents. Most models also come with carbon filters that remove organic chemicals and tastes. These filters are remarkably effective, although the output is usually measured in pints per minute.

The main drawback to portable filters is cost. Although you can find cheap copies of the reputable devices, this is not a piece of equipment you want to scrimp on; buy the best you can afford. You can purchase reverse osmosis filters or micro-straining filters that rely on pore size to remove germs and cysts like cryptosporidium and giardia. Look for a certification that the filter has been tested and certified by NSF Standard 53 or NSF Standard 58 for cyst removal.

Magazines with an outdoor theme such as "Backpacker" or "Outside" frequently review and evaluate equipment like this. Look for these filters at outdoor equipment or emergency preparedness stores.

• • •

Any of these methods is adequate to produce safe drinking water, but if you have no way to purify water, you should carefully weigh the possible hazards of drinking untreated water against the obvious need to sustain life. Antibiotics are available to combat giardia, for example, if you need to drink untreated water to stay alive. Remember, the purpose of preparedness is to give you and your family the greatest odds of getting out of an emergency situation with the least harm.

Emergency preparedness:
Do one thing today.

# Long-Term Food Storage

## Food Storage Key Principles

For many, "emergency preparedness" is synonymous with "food storage." In addition to emergency preparedness, though, there are many practical reasons to store food:

- Buying in bulk can be cheaper than day-to-day shopping.
- Fewer trips to the store means less impulse buying.
- Food on hand gives you options for those "what should we have for dinner?" nights.
- By preserving your own produce, you control the quality and content.
- Stored food provides a cushion, allowing your family to weather financial crises like unemployment or unexpected financial burden.

Food storage, however, is more than buying wheat in nitrogen-packed buckets and putting it in the basement. Here are four key principles of food storage.

### 1. Store What You Eat

If you don't store what you regularly use, you will throw it away in a few years. If you don't store what you use, you will unnecessarily increase the stress of an emergency by having to fix and eat completely different foods. If you don't store what you will use, your body may not adapt well to food (like whole wheat . . .) that you have to eat in an emergency.

Here is a simple process for deciding what to store if you want to have a year's worth of food. Families eat the same ten to twenty meals about 80-90 percent of the time. These are the meals we fix so often that we almost don't need to look at recipes to whip them up. You probably could list them right now, with a little thought. Or you could post a piece of paper on the refrigerator and keep track for about a month. Write down main dishes and add side dishes to make a nutritionally balanced diet.

Once you have a list of meals, write down next to each meal the required ingredients. You'll find that you use similar ingredients—tomato sauce, for instance—for different meals. Also note what items you use regularly, like spices, because you'll need a supply of staples on hand, too. Compile this information on a single table by listing meals down the left side and ingredients across the top. When you have filled ingredient quantities for all the meals in the table, sum each ingredient at the bottom. For example, in the twenty meals you have identified, if four of them require two cans each of tomato sauce, then the sum for tomato sauce would be eight cans. Do the same for each ingredient.

Now count the number of meals you have identified and divide into 365 to calculate how many times you would have to eat each meal to cover a whole year. For example, if you identified fifteen meals, you would have to eat each one twenty-five times (round any fraction up) in a year. If you have identified twenty meals, you would eat each one nineteen times, and so on. Multiply this number by each of your ingredients to calculate how much of each you would need to prepare your meal list for an entire year. For example, say you came up with fifteen meals and the sum for tomato sauce to fix all those meals once is eight cans. Since you'll need to fix each meal twenty-five times in a year, multiply eight cans by twenty-five and you'll find that you need two-hundred cans of tomato sauce for a year's meals. Do this for each ingredient, and do the same for breakfast and lunch menus. Voila! There are your family's requirements for a year's food storage. Use this list as a shopping planner (watch for sales) and an inventory checklist. Also note that you don't have to have ambitions for a year's storage. You could start with a month's storage, or three, and tailor the math to your needs.

Finally, don't forget non-foods like soap, shampoo, toilet paper, pet supplies, and so on.

## 2. Use It or Lose It

No food has an infinite shelf life. In fact, most foods begin to lose nutrition and palatability almost immediately. Over time, some foods even become unsafe. County extension services in all parts of the country have compiled lists of recommended storage durations for foods stored at room temperature, refrigerator temperature, and freezer temperature. Flour, for example, is only recommended for six to eight month's storage at room temperature. Many unopened foods last several months, but even the longest storing foods are recommended for only about two years.

If food only lasts several months in prime condition, then it is clear that we must rotate food supplies to avoid throwing them away. And tossing food that is spoiled before you eat it is no different from tossing food that no one ate. If you follow the "store what you eat" approach, then rotating food is easy because you can use it up in your everyday cooking.

Rotation doesn't happen automatically. You must make it happen: if they do not already have manufacturing dates on the label, date the foods as you buy/store them (use a crayon, wax pencil, or magic marker—put month and year on label); put newer foods behind the older; conscientiously use the older foods.

## 3. Store It Cool

Temperature, more than almost any other factor, determines the storage life of your food as well as its condition. For prepared foods and leftovers, for example, getting them into the refrigerator immediately can be a matter of safety.

Cooler storage temperatures slow the deterioration of food and the loss of nutrition and taste. Cooler is always better. Build shelves in the basement or a part of the house where the temperature is cool year-round. If you have the space and budget, consider buying an extra freezer for your storage area.

## 4. Be Safe

If there is any question about the safety of the food you have stored—in smell, taste, texture, appearance—throw it out. If a can is bulging, is leaking, or spurts when you open it, throw it out.

When canning, handle food in a clean area with clean hands. Don't change canning recipes or take shortcuts on processing. Recipes are carefully formulated and tested to assure your food will be safe. If you change anything, the acidity may be altered or the processing time and temperature may no longer be valid. Use only calibrated pressure canners (county extension services test pressure canners) for foods that require pressure processing.

For storage, remember that cooler is always better.

- **Refrigerator**: Keep it at 34–40°F
- **Freezer**: Keep it below 0°F, colder is better.
- **Always**: If you have any question about the safety of the food, throw it out.

• • •

Many of the ideas in this chapter are taken from county extension service pamphlets. The extension service is an excellent source of reliable information about food production and storage. Check online, or printed information can be purchased for about the cost of reproduction, and knowledgeable staff are ready to answer your questions.

Emergency preparedness
Do one thing today.

# Preparedness Skills You Ought to Have

Part 1 of this book has compiled a series of basic skills and principles that will serve you well in every emergency from the smallest daily crises to the largest area disasters. Knowledge and skills are the most valuable and versatile commodities you can store. They are infinitely updatable and never out of style. Furthermore, you always have them with you. To underscore these valuable skills, let's review.

## Staying Calm

If you panic, you lose access to all of the other information in your head. Cultivate calm by planning, by being aware of the situation, and by practice, practice, practice.

- Create a family plan. A plan gives you focus in the first unsettled minutes of an emergency and changes your attitude from "victim" to "survivor."
- Situational awareness—paying attention to what's going on and what you might do if there is an emergency—cultivates calmness by reducing the surprise factor. Play the "what if?" mental game. What if there is an earthquake while I'm at the mall? What if there is a power outage tonight? What if the water is unsafe? Review and refresh your plan of action. If you don't know an answer, find out: read a book, ask a friend, or go online.
- Calmness can be practiced. Notice how you react to life's unexpected situations. The more you are aware of your reactions, the earlier you can catch and modify them. Then practice maintaining a cool exterior; a cooler interior will result.

## Knowing CPR/First Aid

These skills are best learned from experts, and they need to be kept current. Techniques and tools are always improving, so if you learned these skills long ago, go back and refresh. The best source of training is an organization like the Red Cross, a local fire department, or a hospital. Expect to pay a modest fee for each of these classes and to commit several evenings to the training. Then build first-aid kits containing materials you are prepared to use. Assemble kits for home, car, and your pocket, if you spend time outdoors. Each will contain different items depending on the type of injuries that you might encounter (see chapter 5).

## Turning Off Utilities

Teach everyone in your family how and when to turn off the utilities. This includes knowing where the main shutoffs are and how to activate them. Include electricity, water, and gas.

## Purifying Water

In many emergencies, there will still be water, but it may not be safe to drink. Learn to purify water by boiling, chemical treatment, and filtration (see chapter 6). The most reliable sources of information include county and state health departments, FEMA (ready.gov), and the Centers for Disease Control and Prevention.

## Cooking without a Stove

Even minor emergencies can leave you without conveniences. Learn to create healthy and tasty meals without your oven and range. Practice with the barbecue or a Dutch oven. Go camping and practice over an open fire—a tough skill to master. Camp gear makes a great emergency kitchen. Collect recipes and store emergency food supplies geared to non-stove cooking methods.

## Finding Shelter and Warmth

Where would you stay if your house was uninhabitable in bad weather? Learn how and where to evacuate, and keep a grab-and-go kit available in case you don't get much warning. Camp trailers and tents are good emergency shelters. Learn to find or make shelter in the outdoors from survival handbooks (see Additional Resources).

## Sanitation Skills

Teach good hygiene to all family members. Learn how to wash hands with limited water. Practice good food preparation techniques. Store trash bags to manage food wastes and keep pests at bay. Learn about expedient containment (and disposal) of human wastes if the toilets stop working for some time. Check with the county or state health department.

## Cooperating

In an emergency, we all need each other, but that is when our nerves will be most frayed. Learn to work and play well with others (see chapter 29). Emergencies are inconvenient, so practice patience. Meet your neighbors now, under less stress. Store comfort items, like teddy bears or toys, for small children, and entertainment items or treats for older children and adults. Pack earplugs in your evacuation kit to ease sleeping in a crowded shelter: everyone is more cheery with more sleep.

## Improvising, Adapting

Nothing will go exactly as planned, so learn to adapt. Pack duct tape and baling wire. Pack multiple solutions for light, heat, cooking, and repairs. The skill of improvising can be cultivated. Practice while camping: resist the urge to go buy every little thing you forget. You can also practice having emergencies. Try living on your short-term emergency kit, even for a day: turn off the power, avoid using the stove, ration water. See how creative you become.

## Making Your Own Fun

What would life be without electronic entertainment? Maybe pretty fun. Learn to play simple games with few pieces or parts. Collect instructions for card games and parlor games. Store playing cards, dice, pencil and paper, and other items that support a variety of different games. Every now and then get out your emergency lights, make snacks from your emergency supplies, and play an old-fashioned board game.

Emergency preparedness:
Learn one skill today.

# Preparedness for People with Strength, Mobility, or Disability Concerns

Disasters are especially hard on the elderly and people with disabilities. People with special medical or physical conditions should prepare for emergencies; who knows your abilities and limitations better than you? As you plan, consider these adaptations to your situation:

## Preparedness Plan

In addition to all of the plan elements in chapter 2, people with special needs also need to have a get-the-word-out plan. A person with special needs has already learned one of the key principles of preparedness: create a network and work together. Start your planning with a written list of all of the people in your life who help you meet your specific needs. This can include your medical team: doctors, pharmacists, therapists, in-home care, personal assistant, and so on. It may also include family members, neighbors, church members, care or agency personnel, co-workers. You might also list your landlord and the handyman crowd: your plumber, fix-it guy, car mechanic, and yard-care service worker. From this network, identify those who are closest and most able to check in with you in case of an emergency, and arrange for them to do so. Designate several checkers, in case conditions make it hard for the primary contact to get there. You may be able to register with a local hospital or fire or police departments to assure you are near the top of their response lists, as well. In addition to people checking on you, you also need to have a way to tell others when you are in distress. A debris-scattering earthquake that might be minor for others can be a big deal for someone in a wheelchair. Keeping a fully charged cell phone on your person at all times is a must, and you might consider other options like medical alert systems, pagers, signs in the window, or just a good old-fashioned whistle.

All of the elements of a reunion plan and a communications plan, including an out-of-state contact still apply here, but your get-ready plan may take some additional effort. For example, you may wish to train members of your network how to operate critical medical equipment, how to change batteries, and how to do basic maintenance. Keep copies of operating manuals close at hand. You may wish to put spare parts for your critical equipment in your emergency kit. If your equipment depends on electricity, contact the provider to find out about emergency backup power and other options for when the power goes out. If you use a powered scooter, you should have a manual wheelchair on hand for emergencies.

## Short-Term Emergency Kit

The same principles and the same categories of supplies listed in chapter 3 still apply if you have special needs, but consider:

- Store food and water in packages that you can open with your strength and dexterity. If you use adaptive devices, consider getting extras to put with your kit. Store no-cook foods to reduce the obstacles to keeping up your energy and morale. Store smaller containers of water that are easier to lift, and make sure you have tools to help you get them open if your grip strength is low. Store your kit in a rolling container so you don't have to lift to move it, and make sure it is in an accessible place.
- If you are vision or hearing impaired, you will also need to consider how you will obtain critical information in an emergency, whether by an assistive device or by having someone help you. If you are hearing impaired, you may still want a battery-powered radio so an aide can listen and help you get the information.
- Include items for personal hygiene needs.
- Your first aid kit should have extra supplies for dealing with the urgencies and emergencies that are unique to your own situation.
- Make sure you have extra medications on hand at all times. Check

with your doctor about getting a prescription for a few extra days or weeks of medications. Keep a complete and up-to-date list of all medications you take, including the dosage and frequency.

## Evacuation

Your home is your best refuge and the location of all of your resources, but there are times when you must leave it, sometimes immediately. Make sure you have two planned exits from each room and an outside meeting place to get back with your family or members of your team. If you have special medical needs, you may be able to prearrange with a hospital or other care facility for you to stay with them in case of a local or smaller-scale evacuation. Identify family or friends that might host you in case you need to get farther away. If you go to a public shelter, be sure your supplies and equipment are marked with your name to avoid confusion and loss in a busy place.

• • •

While it might seem that your special needs cause you to be vulnerable in an emergency, there are some silver linings: you already know that you need a network of people, you know who they are, and you know how to articulate your needs. You have experience being resourceful and determined, and overcoming obstacles. And if you do some planning and a little preparing, you can measurably boost your odds of getting safely through an emergency.

Emergency preparedness:
Do one thing today.

# PART 2
# RESPONDING TO EMERGENCIES

# The Potential Emergencies around Us

Early in your family's preparation planning, you should assess which disasters are most likely in your area and your life and then focus your planning on those likely events. It would not be the best use of your time to prepare for a tsunami, for example, if you don't live on the coast. Even among those emergencies that are possible in your area, some are definitely more probable than others, so your first efforts should focus on the most probable risks. Also, you'll find that as you prepare for the likely events, you'll be more prepared for the less likely events, since many preparation principles are the same.

The following table lists some potential emergencies that you can sort through to determine your most likely risks. The first two columns list the emergencies and summarize who might be at an increased risk. This is just a starting point; you and your family should review each of the emergencies yourselves and decide on your level of risk.

In addition to listing the potential risks, the table shows the most likely scale of each risk. This information might be best used to determine how much help you might have and how extensively you must prepare to be on your own. For example, in a household accident, you can and should call immediately for public services like paramedics and ambulances. In a serious earthquake, however, public services may be so overtaxed that you will need to fend for yourself for some time.

First, read through the list of potential disasters and mark the ones that seem possible for your family or in your area. You may need additional research to uncover other risks that are specific to your area, like potential hazardous materials storage areas and transport routes. Don't forget to include a risk assessment for other locations at which you spend time: work, school, shopping centers, and so on. If your list of possible emergencies is long, pick a couple to get started, perhaps house fires and power outages, for example.

Part 2 explicitly addresses many of these emergencies. Because this book is intended as a basic guide, and since some of the potential disasters are rare or require advanced preparation, some of them are not specifically treated in this book, but if you prepare for the most likely events, you'll be in pretty good shape for everything else.

The task of risk assessment and prioritization is easy to do, but don't let the magnitude of the preparation tasks discourage you. Remember some of the basic principles in this book: any preparation is better than no preparation; it doesn't have to be perfect; the best preparedness commodity to store is knowledge; and do a little bit every day. In fact, the most potent advice is to remember the theme of this book:

Emergency preparedness:
Do one thing today.

## Disaster Risk Assessment

| Disaster | Who is at Risk? | What's the Scale? | | | | |
|---|---|---|---|---|---|---|
| | | Personal | Neigh-borhood | City | Region | Nation |
| Accident, medical emergency | Everyone | × | | | | |
| Avalanche | Residents of or travelers through mountainous areas | × | × | | | |
| Cold, extreme | The entire US, but especially those areas where winter storms would be unexpected. Ice storms pose special risks | | | | × | |
| Dam failure | Residents near a waterway with any man-made water storage. Includes dams, ponds, and large tanks | | × | | | |
| Drought | Everyone | | | | | × |
| Earthquake | Almost entire US, especially California, Alaska, Mountain States, New Madrid fault zone, and upper New England | | | | × | |
| Epidemic/pandemic | Everyone | | | × | × | × |
| Financial panic | Everyone | | | | | × |
| Fire, house | Everyone | × | | | | |
| Fire, wildfire | Residents within one mile of wildlands or heavily wooded areas | | × | × | | |
| Floods, flash | Residents in drainages, like canyons, narrow valleys, or riverbeds | × | × | | | |
| Floods, river | Residents in a river floodplain | | × | × | | |
| Hazardous materials spill | Everyone, especially within a mile of highways, railways, waterways, pipelines, or storage depots | | × | | | |

| Disaster | Who is at Risk? | What's the Scale? Personal | Neigh-borhood | City | Region | Nation |
|---|---|---|---|---|---|---|
| Heat, extreme | Everyone | | | | × | |
| Hurricane | Residents near oceans, especially Gulf Coast and Atlantic | | | | × | |
| Landslide/ mudslide | Residents near steep slopes, whether developed or not | | × | | | |
| Radiological accident | Residents within 25 miles of nuclear power plant, nuclear military facility, or spent fuel storage | | | × | × | |
| Riot | Residents in urban area, or attendees of large events, games, concerts, and so on | | × | × | | |
| Storm surge | Residents near oceans, especially Gulf Coast and Atlantic | | | × | × | |
| Stranded car | Residents of or travelers through remote areas, or severe weather | × | | | | |
| Terrorism | Everyone: low chance of being in an incident; high chance of being impacted by the reactions | | × | × | × | × |
| Tornado | Everyone; highest risk in central plains and southern states | | × | × | | |
| Tsunami | Residents of coastal areas, especially West Coast | | | | × | |
| Unemployment | Everyone | × | | | | |
| Utility failure | Everyone. Includes power, gas, water, and sewer | × | × | × | | |
| Volcano | Residents near an active volcano (Western US) | | × | × | | |
| Volcano ashfall | Anyone downwind of a volcano | | | | × | |
| Winds, high | Everyone | | × | | | |

# Case Studies

Disasters and emergencies seem remote, improbable, and far away from us—until they are not. They occur in every locale, and some crisis is happening somewhere in the world literally all the time. Each event, whether a neighborhood crisis or a national disaster, could (and probably should) be studied for important lessons to be learned and applied. Though every emergency has its own characteristics and nuances, the following case studies were selected from a variety of periods, and were included because of the complexity, scale, or universality of the lessons to be learned. While each disaster is unique, some common themes run through these stories.

- The priority in any disaster is to preserve life—yours and others. This is a good criterion for decision-making in the moment of crisis. Property protection and convenience are second-order considerations.
- Frequently there is public warning, such as in storms, extreme weather, and wildfires. Even in disasters that occur without warning, there is typically early response and advice from officials. In many of the following cases, it will be obvious that heeding instructions from authorities either before or during the crisis would have saved the lives of many.
- Because sometimes there is no warning, it is important to have emergency items already collected—a kit—to provide resources (medications, first aid, water, food) for the first critical and chaotic hours. Evacuation, if required, means that you must grab and go, without time to gather anything else.

- Disasters are frequently complex, multi-faceted, and cascades of events that require preparation for a multitude of challenges that may spread out over days. An earthquake triggered a tsunami, which triggered a nuclear emergency and so on.
- It takes time for government assistance to reach individuals and families. This highlights a real need to make plans to care for yourselves and help your neighbors for the first critical three to four days.
- Any situation that takes out power takes out cell phone towers and, hence, communications and connectivity. Information stored online or on a battery-powered phone may not be available mere hours later when recharging options are limited.
- Disasters are community events where we can help and be helped. Groups do better both physically and emotionally than individuals. Neighbors and networks are critical, and there are many stories where elderly or mobility-challenged people are literally saved by their caring and aware neighbors.

Additionally, some common themes and lessons are not emphasized by the format chosen for these case studies, but they deserve a mention here:

- Initial media reports are always incorrect, either in scale or in facts. Initial inaccuracy is to be expected. Professional journalists and media outlets must rush reports to meet close deadlines. Compounding the confusion is the fact that nearly everyone carries a camera and a portable broadcast studio in our pockets but are untrained in journalism and unable to see more than just a narrow view around us, so we, too, are likely to get and give wrong information. Inaccuracies get straightened out over time, of course, but we humans sometimes remember only the first things we heard, which adds to the inherent chaos of a disaster.
- Beyond well-meaning but harried reporters, there are those who intentionally twist facts and provide misinformation and disinformation that adds to the fog. Some get a thrill of being the focus of attention for a second, or being an "expert" for a minute. Videos from other disasters are recycled as if they are current, and with the advent of generative artificial intelligence (AI), some information

and some images are just invented out of thin air. Rumors have always been a part of disasters and emergencies, but with the technology developed in the past twenty years, rumors have increased in numbers, speed, and believability by orders of magnitude.

- Chaos provides a target-rich environment for scammers. Post-disaster fraud, scams, and confidence schemes are a reality, preying upon our fears and incomplete understanding of the situation. Schemes range from bogus repair services and advance payments, to charity fraud, to identity theft, to financial theft.

Regardless of the scale, complexity, or specific conditions of any given disaster, a key lesson from these case studies is that any preparedness is better than no preparedness. There are physical things we can do, and gear to acquire to give us options, but the mental preparedness goes with us no matter what—our calm, our awareness, our knowledge, our patience and perseverance, our creativity in adapting, and our survivor attitude. It pays to learn what you can, and to try to do one thing today.

## 9/11 Terrorist Attack

### Summary

On September 11, 2001, a group of terrorists hijacked four airplanes. Two were intentionally flown into the towers of the World Trade Center in Lower Manhattan, one was flown into the Pentagon, and one crashed into a field in Pennsylvania after passengers fought to regain control. Because of the damage inflicted by the intense jet fuel fires, both World Trade towers collapsed, destroying or damaging a number of nearby structures. In addition to death, injuries, and destruction, there were nationwide interruptions to communications and transportation systems.

### Results/Effects

- **Casualties**: 2,996 people died; over 6,000 were injured. An estimated 18,000 additional people developed health effects from dust and hazardous materials dispersed by the collapsing towers.
- **Economic effects**: The towers were destroyed, and a number of nearby buildings were severely damaged, many of which required demolition. The stock market tumbled when it reopened several

days later; the stocks lost 1.4 trillion dollars over the next week. The New York economy lost about 2.8 billion dollars in work/wages over the next several months, and thousands of small businesses were destroyed.

- **Communications/transportation**: All commercial flights were immediately grounded, which lasted three days. Flights already airborne were diverted to the closest airports. The transportation upset stranded tens of thousands of people in unexpected locations. Communications equipment mounted on the North Tower and lines that routed through the World Trade Center were destroyed. Because of the highly localized nature of the attacks, communications were quickly rerouted through other hubs. Most of Manhattan's and Brooklyn's transportation—roads, ferries, subways, buses—was snarled for days.
- **Other**: Some looting was reported.

## Preparedness Lessons Learned

1. The North Tower was struck first, and the damage destroyed stairwells so that no one above the point of impact had any escape route. Some tried to go to the roof, but access doors were locked, no rescue plan was in place, and the raging inferno made helicopter operations impossible. Many people in the South Tower evacuated when they saw the North Tower attacked, which saved thousands of lives. The South Tower impact left one staircase intact, allowing several dozen people above the point of impact to escape. It was reported that some dispatchers instructed people not to evacuate on their own but to wait for responders.

   **Lessons**: Usually it is best to follow the instructions of authorities, but in this case, those who correctly assessed the situation and made their own decision to evacuate early saved their lives. In an emergency, it is best to err on the side of conservatism. Whether you work in a high-rise or just visit occasionally, be sure you know multiple evacuation routes. This goes for hotels as well as office buildings.

2. There were alarms and warnings to evacuate the building. Although tower collapse was not immediately predicted, survival depended upon getting out of the buildings and away from the complex. It is

estimated that over seventeen thousand people were in the World Trade Center complex when the attack began. The ones who survived are the ones who heeded the alarms and the warnings and got out of the building.

**Lessons:** Get out when told to get out. Don't delay, don't seek a second opinion, don't justify staying longer. Maybe even get out before being told.

3. The attacks on a few blocks comprising the WTC affected the whole Lower Manhattan area and hundreds of thousands of inhabitants, workers, and commuters. Tunnels and bridges were closed due to fears of subsequent attacks. The subway system was stopped. Bus routes were interrupted. Evacuation generally proceeded on foot, as taxis and cars were unable to access the larger affected area.

   **Lessons:** Prepare for a walking evacuation. People who had to walk long distances quickly found out if their shoes were good for walking. The attacks occurred on the morning of a mild autumn day; if they had occurred at night or on a winter's day, flashlights and/or coats would have been in demand. It is important to have an evacuation kit and plan. Because of the chaos, there were many families that had to wait for hours to find out if their loved ones were safe; a contact plan is an important part of your family plan. It may also be helpful to identify some nearby safe places to evacuate to that don't require you to walk for miles from work.

4. Travelers were stranded in all kinds of unexpected places. Planes already in the air were diverted to the nearest airport and grounded for days, heedless of inconvenience. Flights not yet started were canceled. Rental cars quickly became scarce, even in cities hundreds of miles away from the disaster.

   **Lessons:** When traveling, keep a small emergency kit with some extra personal medications and supplies to tide you over during small delays and inconveniences. Some extra emergency cash could be helpful. Travel with a full water bottle (bring empty through security and refill at the gate) and a couple of energy bars.

## Conclusion

Terrorism attempts to affect many people by a public attack on a smaller number. Our systems are still vulnerable to terrorism in ways we have not yet imagined: transportation, communications, food supply, medicine, water; and because of our media saturation, we are vulnerable to panic-inducing images and reports. The odds of being directly involved in such an attack are very low, but the consequences can affect anyone, nationwide or even worldwide. Because attacks can take a variety of forms, it is not possible to prepare for each permutation. But the core principles of preparedness—a communications plan, an evacuation plan, and a few emergency supplies at your place of work, in your luggage, or in your car—will give you options to respond if anything happens. And your ability to keep your cool and stay aware of the situation will enable you to reach out and pull someone along with you. The stories of survivors from 9/11 are full of gratitude and awe at the way people helped each other, in many cases saving lives.

## Camp Fire

### Summary

In November 2018, a wildfire was ignited by electrical transmission equipment along the Camp Creek Road (hence the name: "Camp Fire") in Butte County, in northern California. Unusually dry conditions and high winds exacerbated the fire spread and slowed the response, and within just a few hours the communities of Concow and Paradise were nearly totally destroyed, while significant damage was inflicted on Magalia and Butte Creek Canyon. The fire raged for seventeen days, its smoke plume blanketing the Bay Area and Central Valley (and identifiable as far away as New York) as it consumed 150,000 acres of wildland and structures until the first winter rain helped firefighters contain the blaze. It was the deadliest wildfire in the United States in a hundred years, and the most expensive natural disaster globally in 2018.

### Results/Effects

- **Casualties:** Eighty-five deaths were confirmed, with one missing and seventeen injured.
- **Economic Effects:** Nearly 19,000 structures were destroyed, most of them within the first six hours. The total losses have been estimated at approximately seventeen billion dollars. In response to its liabilities, PG&E (Pacific Gas and Electric) filed

for bankruptcy, and later pled guilty to eighty-four counts of involuntary manslaughter. PG&E emerged from bankruptcy several years later and proposed to settle victim claims up to a total of 13.5 billion dollars.

- **Communications/transportation:** About 52,000 people were evacuated over two and a half weeks. The evacuation was complicated by a glitchy opt-in alert system, and damage to cellphone towers. Narrow roads were clogged by evacuation traffic.

## Preparedness Lessons Learned

**1.** The fire started as early as 6:15 AM and, fanned by forecast high winds, entered Concow about 7:00 AM. Amidst a steady stream of 911 calls, the evacuation was ordered about 8:00 AM. Many residents of Concow (population less than 800) and Paradise (population about 26,000) did not have a chance to evacuate before the fire reached them. The phone alert system was a patchwork of equipment, and only notified opt-in subscribers. The 911 system was overwhelmed by calls. Evacuation orders were slow and partly ineffective, leaving out some areas of the communities and incompletely notifying even subscribers. Communications were significantly impacted by the loss of a large number of cell towers. The early response of fire fighters properly focused on getting residents out alive, not protecting structures. Many residents evacuated the city, though some gathered at different community locations and sheltered together in place. Analysis of fatalities indicated that many more deaths were due to failure to evacuate than occurred during evacuation. Evacuees found shelters in nearby Chico, though an outbreak of norovirus from poor hygiene sickened more than 100 of the sheltered.

**Lessons:** The main objective in any emergency is to stay alive. In the Camp Fire, this was achieved by either getting out of the area or sheltering in community locations. The lesson here is a familiar theme: get out when authorities say to get out, and maybe even sooner, if your personal radar indicates. Do not stay so you can protect your property investment. The Camp Fire scaled up to a firestorm (fire so intense that it creates its own wind system, sucking up available oxygen and whipping up erratic and violent winds that increase the intensity and temperature of the fire in an unpredictable positive feedback loop) in Paradise, easily overwhelming anything any individual might do. Sign up for any alert system that is on an opt-in basis, as was Paradise's. Residents might have watched weather reports of high wind and low humidity, which caused PG&E to notify customers about a possible pre-emptive power shut-off two days earlier. Because of the speed of the wind fanning the fire (55 mph), even stopping for a few treasured possessions dramatically increased survivability risk. If an emergency might involve evacuation, you must have your grab-and-go kits be truly ready to grab and go. Kits must be complete, and immediately accessible. You will not have time to stop for fuel, so it might be helpful to keep your vehicle tanks over half full. Any resources already in vehicles also went with evacuees. At shelters, it is critical that you continue good hygiene practices, such as washing hands, using sanitizer, and being rigorously safe when handling food and/or wastes.

**2.** With increased building at wildland-urban interfaces—where natural environments meet the built environment, like towns in forested areas—states and local communities bear some responsibility to establish protective codes and zoning, and to promulgate best practices with regards to design, building materials, landscaping, fuel reduction and alert systems. They also provide first responders. Most of the structures lost in the Camp Fire were built before code updates; buildings less than twenty years old fared substantially better than older structures. While there were some unexpected conditions in the fire in Butte County in 2018, wildfires were certainly not unexpected; the area had a dozen large wildfires in the previous twenty years. Since the Camp Fire, policies and preparedness have improved in Butte County, but there are many more communities that think it won't happen to them and are not moving with urgency.

**Lessons:** If you have a house, business, or even a cabin in the wildland-urban interface, make sure you know whether it complies with current fire-resistant codes. If it was built before more recent code updates, consider modifications to bring it up to current code. If you haven't bought yet, place extra emphasis on finding options built to code and at some distance from the next house: one of the biggest factors for Paradise houses catching fire was whether there was a neighboring structure on fire. Implement best practices for landscaping and proximal and neighborhood fuel reduction (see chapter 20); go beyond recommendations if possible. Identify and familiarize yourself with ALL evacuation routes; while there may be a preferred road, it may be blocked or congested, and you may need to adapt on the fly. Investigate if fire insurance is available—it may not be, depending on the fire risk designation of your location—and make sure that the replacement value of the structure is covered.

**3.** In the Camp Fire, drought and wind conditions created tinder-like conditions that enabled the rapid spread of the fire. Drought is not uncommon and climate scientists predict that it will get worse, though it is not yet possible to pinpoint affected spots. But that is not the only way a variable climate and extreme weather can contribute to risk; a wetter-than-normal spring contributed to an excess of grass and other annual fuels in the Butte County wildland. A higher-than-normal wind attacked from a previously unexperienced direction. The fact is that people who live at wildland-urban interfaces are at risk despite mitigations, planning, and preparation. And while Paradise has implemented improvements in alert systems and evacuation planning, and the entire town is being rebuilt to newer fire-resistance codes, most experts agree that the lessons learned from the Camp Fire will dilute over time and distance, and many other vulnerable communities will not pursue improvements as urgently.

**Lessons:** At best, local government measures cannot prevent fires, but can only mitigate loss. When it comes to siting your home in areas prone to natural disasters—and all areas are prone to some type of natural disaster or another—the rule is "caveat emptor." Learn all you can about the history of the area, what alert systems are in place, where evacuation routes go, where evacuation shelters will be set up, and other details of your community's response plan. One possible way to tell what you are up against is to consult with an insurance agent to find out what events and emergencies can be insured against. Homeowners in flood-prone areas as designated by FEMA maps, and homeowners in fire-prone areas as designated by states (or individual insurance companies) have similar difficulties obtaining disaster-specific insurance coverage. Will your coverage include structures, personal property, business impacts, loss of income, health/mental health, and any other potential impacts?

**4.** In all disasters, the creation and release of hazardous materials creates another risk for those affected. These are not merely nuisances, but real immediate and long-term health risks. Fires create hazardous vapor plumes, such as benzene and other organic compounds from burning plastic. Fire concentrates metals, which collect in the ash. Fires also release household hazardous materials that may have previously been controlled in garages, sheds, and cabinets. The end of the Camp Fire was marked by heavy winter rains, which transported contaminants into surface runoff and groundwater. In Paradise, water systems were initially cleared for use, and then restricted as testing showed contamination. Ash and solid debris had to be cleared before rebuilding could begin, and a large cleanup effort costing about three billion dollars was implemented to remove over five million tons of potentially hazardous waste to properly permitted landfills.

**Lessons:** After the fire is gone or the disaster has passed, residents naturally wish to recover what can be recovered and start rebuilding but they may encounter hazardous materials. Officials should test potable water systems, but you will have to be aware of other types of hazards from paints, solvents, fuels, pesticides, sewage, and commercial and industrial chemicals. You may be exposed through breathing them as vapors or as fly ash, ingestion, absorption through the skin, or injection through a puncture injury or open wound. The lesson here is to go slow, heed authorities' warnings, and to anticipate and protect against hazardous materials. For site work, use PPE (personal protective equipment) that includes heavy-soled boots, sturdy, skin-covering work clothing, nitrile (chemical protective) gloves; heavy leather gloves; and possibly filtration masks—not light dust masks, but industrial-quality, face-sealing masks with engineered filtration canisters. A discussion of the selection, fitting, and testing of competent and effective masks is beyond the scope of this book. Local authorities, including hazmat-trained fire responders may be able to provide additional guidance and advice. And, as in any disaster, pace yourself, be sure to hydrate and rest regularly, and be aware of physical hazards as well as chemical and biological ones.

### Conclusion

The first objective of preparedness is to survive a disaster. Local authorities at the epicenter of the fire were as overwhelmed as residents, and well-intentioned watch and alert systems were not fully effective. But though there were a number who did not receive much, if any, warning, there were thousands more who had warning and time to get out. All preparations besides what could be grabbed in a moment for evacuation were consumed by a violent and unpredictable fire. Many disasters involve evacuation, so plan for it. As part of your planning, you may identify family or friends outside of your immediate area and agree that in a disaster in your area, you have a place to go, and vice versa in case of a disaster in their area.

## Hurricane Katrina

### Summary

On Monday, August 29, 2005, at about 6:00 AM, a Category 3 hurricane in the Gulf of Mexico with winds of about 125 miles per hour crossed the Louisiana coastline and headed toward New Orleans. A large storm surge breached the aging levee system and seawater flooded over 80 percent of the city. Damage was extreme, and casualties were worsened by a late and incomplete evacuation. The region was in chaos for days, with no utilities, little effective police presence, and lack of transportation and supplies.

### Results/Effects

- **Casualties**: At least 1,833 people died in the hurricane and subsequent floods and chaos.
- **Economic effects**: Total property damage was estimated at 108 billion dollars.
- **Communications/transportation**: The majority of the roads into and out of the city were damaged, and the I-10 Twin Span Bridge collapsed. The airport closed and did not resume commercial flights for over a month. Cellular phone networks were destroyed, three million people in various states were left without power, and communications were completely disrupted in some areas, with HAM

radio operators the only means of communications for days. A single AM radio station remained on the air for the first several weeks.

- **Other**: Reports of crime, looting, and violence were widespread, and the governor mobilized National Guardsmen to assist local law enforcement to restore order, which reportedly took about a week.

## Preparedness Lessons Learned

1. The storm was tracked by the National Hurricane Center starting on August 23, nearly six days before it hit New Orleans. The possible impact on New Orleans was forecast as early as August 26, with watches turning to warnings as the day went on. By Sunday August 28, it was clear that it was a large storm and that New Orleans and all of the areas lower than sea level were vulnerable to the huge storm surge. Evacuation orders, both voluntary and mandatory, began to be issued as early as August 27. A mandatory evacuation order for New Orleans was issued about twenty hours before Katrina made land, but by then, it was too late for many. A large segment of the local population depended on public transit, which was idled by a lack of bus drivers. Although some 80 percent of the population evacuated, over a quarter million people were unable or unwilling to leave.

   **Lessons**: Get out when you are told to get out. Katrina's size and pathway were well known with sufficient time to evacuate, but officials started with "voluntary" evacuation orders, which were widely ignored. Maybe even get out before you are told to get out. Be aware of neighbors or friends that may not have resources or pathways to evacuate and assist them, as you are able.

2. The Louisiana Superdome was designated a "refuge of last resort" by the city, and preparations were made to feed fifteen thousand refugees; nearly thirty thousand showed up. About twenty-five thousand sheltered at the Civic Center, which had no preparations. In both locations, supplies were insufficient for the demand, sanitary conditions deteriorated rapidly, and relief did not arrive for days. Refugees were told there would be no supplies and to bring their own. There were few cots, no sick bay, and no medical responders on site. Reports of crime and violence were not officially confirmed, but safety was a continual concern.

**Lessons**: The government cannot save you. Not the city, county, state, or federal governments. You must take responsibility for your own safety and your own response. Your preparations should include evacuation plans and contingencies so you can avoid the public shelters that may not be as well supplied or tightly controlled as you hope. Your short-term emergency kit should be portable so you can take it with you, because there may not be other supplies for you. If you must go to a shelter or "refuge of last resort," you may need to take measures to improve your security by banding together with other trustworthy refugees, staggering your sleeping schedules, and keeping your own watch over those for whom you are responsible. And when your gut tells you that it is time to get out, get out.

3. The city of New Orleans has vast tracts of land that are below sea level. There are levees and dikes to protect the city, but it was apparently known before Katrina that a large storm surge could overtop and destroy the levees.

   **Lessons**: While it is impossible to find a location that does not have some kind of natural hazard associated with it, most of the information you need to make a decision on where to buy or build a house is readily available. For example, FEMA manages a program to continually update floodplain mapping, and a quick reference to the proper map (at msc.fema.gov) will tell you your flood risk, and, as important, whether you'll be able to obtain flood insurance. There are similar maps for faults and earthquake risks, landslide risks, and even wildfire risks. It just makes sense to check things out.

4. After Superstorm Sandy pushed another unprecedented storm surge ashore in New York and New Jersey, residents of New Orleans sent messages to victims summarizing things they had learned. A large number of the messages advocated patience and persistence in rebuilding and extolled the benefits of doing it together as a community. They talked of personal and community strength born of facing adversity with their neighbors.

   **Lessons**: In an emergency, your neighbors are going through the same things, and maybe worse. Knowing that the government is likely to be unable to help enough people, how will those with special needs get through it? By the care and concern of neighbors. Get to know your neighborhood and your neighbors before an emergency makes it necessary. Hold a summer barbecue, give them holiday wishes on special days, learn names, and understand special needs. Agree to check on each other in extreme circumstances, and when the need comes, you'll be better prepared to help others through it.

### Conclusion

Wherever you live, there are hazards both natural and man-made. You can spend a little time learning of the hazards particular to your area. By knowing more about the vulnerabilities, you will better know what to do when extreme conditions are predicted. If you knew that you lived below sea level and the National Hurricane Center predicted a direct hit of a record storm, you would be able to decide how serious to consider the warning and how early to evacuate. Yes, your house might get flooded, but your staying wouldn't prevent that anyway. This kind of knowledge and preparation might spare you the experience of going to a public shelter and hoping someone will be able to take care of you. But if you've read this far, it is unlikely that you would expect someone else to take care of you anyway.

## Ohio Hazardous Material Spill

### Summary

On February 3, 2023, at about 9:00 PM, part of a Norfolk Southern train derailed near the little town of East Palestine, Ohio, near the Pennsylvania border. Fifty-one of the one hundred and fifty cars derailed; eleven of them tankers that carried hazardous materials including vinyl chloride, isobutylene, benzene, and others. About one-hundred-thousand gallons spilled onto the ground. Most of the derailed cars ended in a pile, which caught fire and burned for several days, forcing the evacuation of about fifteen hundred residents within a mile of the fire. Other nearby counties advised residents to shelter in place, that is, stay indoors to lessen exposure. On the third day of burning, officials worried that the fire might cause some of the vinyl chloride tankers to explode, spraying shrapnel and chemicals over a wider area. They decided to breach the tankers and burn the chemicals in a more controlled way. Responders emptied the vinyl chloride tankers into a trench and lit the liquid on fire. Black smoke poured into the sky, and the burning created hydrogen chloride and phosgene gases. Environmental officials acted to contain the spilled liquid, and monitored air quality for the duration of the response. Although they did not detect residual hazardous contaminants in the air, the pervasive chemical smell still worried residents. The evacuation order was lifted on February 9, as officials determined that air quality was back to normal, and the fire and liquid spill had been contained.

## Results/Effects

- **Casualties:** No deaths were reported. About half of the respondents to a CDC Assessment of Chemical Exposure survey conducted about a month later reported symptoms of exposure, including headaches, anxiety, coughing, fatigue, skin irritation, and so on. Some members of the team conducting the survey also reported symptoms and stood down for a day until they dissipated. Some stories of pets and other land animal deaths were reported, and some loss of aquatic life was documented.
- **Economic Effects:** Fifteen hundred to two thousand people mandatorily evacuated; others in the wider area of effect voluntarily left. Impacts included lost wages and direct costs for housing and expenses. No structures or infrastructure were lost in the accident. Costs to Norfolk Southern have reached approximately one billion dollars in recovery, investigation, and compensation costs.
- **Communication/Transportation:** When the derailment and spill were known, a state of emergency was declared. The National Guard was mobilized to help establish an evacuation zone, notify residents of evacuation orders, and assist in environmental monitoring. Officials went door-to-door notifying residents of the evacuation order. The track on which the derailment occurred was closed to train traffic for five days.
- **Other:** The public was skeptical of EPA, CDC, and Norfolk Southern information. Residents who were affected by the chemical smell and experienced symptoms were frustrated with official reports that contaminants did not exceed recommended limits, and that all was back to normal. Additionally, some conspiracists proposed

theories ranging from the accident being intentionally caused, to the accident being purposefully covered up by reports of a foreign spy balloon, concurrently in the news at the time of the accident.

## Preparedness Lessons Learned

1. First responders were caught off guard by the contents of the train. The train cars carried the required placards identifying the chemicals, but the resulting fires destroyed them quickly. Further, responders did not have full confidence in the currency of their training or their outdated personal protective equipment.

   **Lessons:** Know the risks. In rural areas and small towns (New Palestine, Ohio, population approximately five thousand), first responders can include volunteers, professionals, or a mix. Personnel may be local residents or may be shared from nearby jurisdictions. Hazardous materials incidents require a high degree of training and current equipment. Since each of us certainly lives or works close to storage areas and transportation corridors for hazardous materials, it may be useful to request information from local government officials and responders as to threats and plans for response.

2. East Palestine, OH, officials reacted quickly and issued evacuation orders for residents in a one-mile radius. National Guard units were deployed to help with the notification and evacuation.

   **Lessons:** Get out when you are told to get out, and maybe even before. There were no human fatalities in this disaster, at least partly because residents left when ordered to leave. Other residents not in the mandatory evacuation zone still chose to leave. In any evacuation, the evacuation route and final destination matter. The reason for evacuation was to avoid exposure to toxic fumes. The size and direction of a vapor plume can change minute by minute, depending upon the breeze direction and atmospheric conditions. It is critical to follow official instructions to get crosswind or upwind from an airborne plume as quickly as possible. Many residents who did not have to evacuate were advised to shelter in place. This is essentially a recommendation to stay indoors, where exposure to the hazard is likely reduced long enough for the plume to pass over. And like all evacuation emergencies, you must have your short-term emergency kit up-to-date and ready to go with no warning.

3. Misinformation abounds in any disaster. Partly this occurs because news media outlets report what they can find out immediately and then update as more accurate information about the scale and impacts becomes known. This understandably takes time, though it can be frustrating. Increasingly, bad actors intentionally inject disinformation for their own agendas into official and unofficial media reports. Some have ideological narratives they want to support.

   **Lessons:** In any disaster, accurate and timely information is important to the decisions we must make to reduce our risks. A few guidelines might help weed out the spurious information:

   - Give most weight to credible news outlets. Although none is perfect, professional journalists will cite their sources of information and will flag information that is mere hearsay.
   - Be skeptical of anonymous sources, or vague "experts say" reports.
   - Be wary of all early news reports.
   - Constantly ask yourself about sources and credentials. A named source with credentials relevant to the disaster might be a more dependable source than an anonymous social media post. Listen for or ask about evidence.
   - Pay attention to the tone of the report: is it hysterical or sensational?

## Conclusion

Hazardous materials and wastes are shipped in increasing quantities across our roads, rails, and pipelines. Accidents and incidents are inevitable: over a thousand train derailments occur each year in the US, with about twenty of those involving hazardous materials. There are additional potential risks hauling hazardous materials over the road or flowing through pipelines. There will always be some level of risk. For hazardous materials incidents, the best preparation is being ready to evacuate without much notice, and to follow official instructions when you do.

# COVID-19 Pandemic

## Summary

Sometime in the last quarter of 2019, a novel strain of virus (SARS CoV-2 [Severe, Acute Respiratory Syndrome-Coronavirus 2]) in the reasonably well-understood coronavirus family began to spread in a city of eleven million inhabitants: Wuhan, China. The disease it caused was dubbed COVID-19, and its flu-like symptoms focused on the respiratory system. Like many of the 1.6 million viruses in the wild, SARS CoV2 is classified as zoonotic, meaning it can jump from an animal host to humans. Because it was novel, there was no immunity in the population, and it spread quickly. China responded with a hard quarantine but partly based on the delay in identifying the virus, and partly based on the fact that asymptomatic people could spread the virus without knowing, SARS CoV2 had already escaped containment and soon spread around the world, striking Italy, Iran, and Spain particularly early and hard. The United States declared a public health emergency on January 31, 2020. The virus struck hard in New York City and nearby New Jersey, and raged across the nation. It was quickly discovered that elderly people in close communities such as nursing homes were particularly vulnerable, as were many others with underlying conditions of heart or lung disease or diabetes. Public information systems took weeks to upgrade to the need, and epidemiological indicators such as cases spread by an individual (R0 or "R-naught"), hospitalization rates, and case fatality rates were elusive early on. Public health messaging was uneven and sometimes contradictory in the early phases. Initially, cases were confirmed with doctor-administered tests; the mid-pandemic advent of self-administered tests made tracking of case numbers impossible from that point, though hospitalizations and excess deaths were still tracked. Public health officials and political leaders were hampered by incomplete and ambiguous data.

The early response was to institute a society-wide quarantine. Public activities and events were suspended—stay-home orders became enforceable laws in forty states—and "non-essential" businesses were shuttered. This, combined with panic-buying, created shortages of many consumer goods; toilet paper was in such short supply that it became emblematic of the first chaotic months of the pandemic. Social distancing of six feet was established in all public spaces, and handwashing, surface decontamination, and family/individual isolation were implemented in a bid to "flatten the curve" of infections and relieve the demand on hospitals. At the multiple pandemic peaks, infections and hospitalizations overwhelmed some health facilities. Nonessential medical treatments were postponed to free trained staff and bed space.

A novel vaccine based on messenger RNA was quickly developed, rushed through trials and approvals, and was rolled out to the public in December 2020. Clinical treatments were developed for the most critical cases, but the virus was not eradicated.

The pandemic raged on with surges and relief through the next three years, when key indicators signaled it was safe for the United States to suspend its emergency declaration in May 2023. The virus still circulates in mutations and variants, and is considered now to be endemic, that is, a normal part of the seasonal illness complex. Public health monitoring now also includes sampling of human waste systems for virus load trends.

## Results/Effects

- **Casualties:**
  - » **Deaths:** Worldwide, nearly seven million people have died from COVID-19; in the United States, about 1.15 million are estimated to have died.
  - » **Cases:** As noted earlier, the advent of self-testing rendered case-count data incomplete. It is estimated that about eighty percent of the United States adult population has contracted COVID-19 at least once. Over ninety-six percent of the United States population have COVID-19 antibodies in their blood, either from infection or vaccination. Worldwide data are likely similar. In a significant fraction of cases (twenty-eight percent in early 2023), symptoms have been abnormally slow to clear, resulting in so-called "long-COVID." About a third of those cases linger even longer.
- Economic Effects: No buildings or infrastructure were damaged. High-level economic impact is measured by global GDP (economic output), which fell in 2020 at the beginning of the pandemic, but has rebounded since. In the United States (and other places) government-funded stimulus payments were sent to individuals, while

businesses received partially forgivable loans. The five-trillion-dollar stimulus added to the national debt, and the impact of this cash infusion is still being studied, along with its potential contribution to a recession.

A number of industries were harmed by the extensive lockdowns/quarantines, including entertainment and hospitality businesses such as travel, tourism, sports, restaurants and hotels. Other industries—especially manufacturing businesses—were affected by both intermittent and long-term supply chain interruptions as lower-tier suppliers curtailed production or suffered materiel supply issues themselves. Small businesses of every type were negatively impacted by lower traffic or supply-chain issues. In 2022, one in five small businesses reported serious negative effects from the pandemic and its responses. Many permanently closed. A small number of industries thrived, notably door-to-door delivery businesses, on-line businesses, and Internet-based video conferencing and on-line productivity applications sources.

- **Communications/transportation:** Throughout the pandemic, the utilities infrastructure—water, sewer, electricity, gas, Internet, communications, gasoline—largely stayed functional. The Internet became a critical source of information from both official sources and social and family contacts. As the lockdowns grew and schools were shuttered, many students were provided with portable and tablet computers and instructed to join classwork on-line. On-line schooling required much support—both technical and emotional—from parents, and was difficult for families without robust Internet access, or where parents had to continue to work outside the home. A large number of students ceased to participate, and many others struggled to stay engaged. National and local metrics of learning fell during remote schooling and are estimated to take years to recover.

  Many workplaces also implemented remote and remote/hybrid work options. This affected transportation systems as many fewer commuters used public roads and transit options. Connectivity equipment and software went from a lightly used option to critical for many workers. Video meeting options increased, and connection quality and reliability improved. A large segment of the workforce learned how to participate remotely, which has markedly changed how businesses operate post-pandemic. On-line shopping and doorstep delivery expanded exponentially.

- **Other:** The SARS-CoV2 virus mutates continuously as it infects more people. This makes a targeted vaccine difficult to formulate. Each mutation can vary in how fast it spreads and how serious the infection is. The continuous march of variants means that the SARS CoV-2 will now be part of the pool of pathogens. Annual vaccine updates and vaccination campaigns are expected.

The isolation and constant stress of the lockdown approach resulted in increased anxiety, depression, suicidal ideation, and substance abuse.

## Preparedness Lessons Learned

**1.** While the initial purpose of the lockdown was to slow the rapid transmittal of disease so hospitals would not be overwhelmed, it also had effects on the availability of food and nonfood supplies. Panic-buying initially stripped grocery store shelves, and manufacturers struggled to keep up with demand. The first lockdown was only expected to last for a few days, but many people did not have the resources to care for their families without going out for days at a time.

**Lessons:** Each family should keep on hand enough food and supplies to be able to avoid trips into public spaces for a time. Some commenters suggest three days, some suggest four, and some as much as a week. The obvious starting point is to begin to collect nonperishable food supplies that enable you to prepare your regular meals one or two extra times before resupplying. A switch to a completely unfamiliar menu during a high-stress quarantine is not recommended. Other critical supplies, such as toilet paper, can be stored well in advance of an emergency.

Additionally, the lockdown required families to care for and entertain themselves. While utilities remained operational—and, thus, our TVs, streaming movies, electronic games, and Internet—it would be prudent to also store some entertainment options that do and don't require power. Board and card games, crafts and hobbies, musical instruments and creative pursuits are all good.

2. In Salt Lake City during the first week of the lockdown, a magnitude 5.7 earthquake shook the area and damaged roads and buildings. Between June 1 and November 30, 2020, the Atlantic hurricane season produced a record number of storm systems, a record number of which made landfall. Tornadoes still rampaged across the United States. Volcanoes still erupted; fires still raged. Civil unrest following the death of George Floyd in Minneapolis involved some fifteen to twenty million people in protests across the nation. Houses still caught on fire, illnesses were still diagnosed, transportation accidents still happened. In the middle of a pandemic, this just seems like insult added to injury, but the fact is—pandemic or not—other emergencies still happen.

   **Lessons:** We still need to remain prepared for all of the many other possible disasters. Each locale will have its own list of possible emergencies, and preparation for one type of crisis usually has significant overlap with other crises. The chapters that follow provide ideas and advice for the various risks of your locale.

3. A pandemic is not a short duration event. The influenza pandemic of 1918 lasted well into 1920, and outbreaks were noted years later. Despite expectations that only a few days were needed to flatten the curve, the emergency declared in 2020 was not rescinded until 2023. The early stages were characterized by acute shortages, unclear information, but also community spirit. The late stages were characterized by more reliable supplies, but also crisis fatigue and divisiveness.

   **Lesson:** In general, emergencies are a team sport; we usually don't have to face disasters by ourselves. Family, neighbors, neighborhoods, communities, and networks all support us, and we support them. For many people, though, these interlocking systems broke down during the pandemic. Families were split, communities polarized. Much of this was related to the information fog, some of which was natural and some of which was fabricated, politicized, and conspiratorial.

   The first line of defense is on-going situational awareness: staying aware through credible news outlets of global, national, and local news and events. This does not mean "doom-scrolling," the practice of surfing through social media to hear the latest horrifying tale or rumor. The next defense is a healthy approach to vetting information sources and thinking critically about what we hear or see. It can be helpful to use a series of red flags when we encounter uncertain information: what is the source, what are their credentials? What evidence have they cited? Can news be verified through multiple sources? Are we being encouraged to act within a limited time window? Is news reported in a hysterical or sensational tone (think tabloid headline)? Who benefits? Are they asking for money? Does it feel right? Is it too good to be true? What are the risks and the trade-offs?

### Conclusion

There have been many pandemics throughout history. Our next pandemic is a matter of "when," not "if." While each pandemic will have its own character, the main commonalities are that each household will need to be on its own for an extended period, and accurate information will be precious. In making action decisions, the priority in pandemics, as in every disaster, is to preserve life, to survive. Comfort and convenience should come in a distant second place.

## Tohoku Earthquake and Tsunami

### Summary

On March 11, 2011, a magnitude 9.0 earthquake lasting six minutes struck off the coast of Tohoku, Japan. It was one of the five largest earthquakes recorded in the world since record keeping began and the most powerful to ever hit Japan. The earthquake triggered a 133-foot-high tsunami, which traveled inland up to six miles in some places. The tsunami was much more deadly and damaging than the earthquake itself. The earthquake and tsunami also led to cooling system failures at three nuclear reactors near the coast, which, in turn, led to fuel rod meltdowns, hydrogen gas explosions, and radiation leaks. Residents in a twelve-mile radius were evacuated; a fifty-mile radius was recommended.

### Results/Effects

- **Casualties**: 15,881 people died, with 6,142 injured and 2,668 missing.

- **Economic effects:** 129,225 buildings were totally collapsed, with another nearly one million buildings sustaining damage. The earthquake resulted in about 30 billion dollars in insurance claims, while the World Bank estimated total economic impact at 235 billion dollars. The Tohoku earthquake/tsunami was therefore the most expensive natural disaster ever.
- **Communications/transportation**: Roads and railways were severely damaged by both the earthquake and the tsunami flooding. Airports, railways, and roads were all closed for some period. One and a half million households in northeastern Japan were left without water. And 4.4 million households were left without electricity.
- **Other**: The earthquake triggered at least one dam collapse, some liquefaction, and many fires.

## Preparedness Lessons Learned

**1.** An analysis of the fatalities recovered in the first month revealed that about 93 percent of victims died by drowning. The non-drowning victims either died from internal injuries, were crushed, or died from burns. Only 58 percent of people in possibly dangerous coastal areas listened to tsunami warnings after the earthquake and headed for higher ground—only 5 percent of these people were caught in the tsunami. Almost half of the people who didn't heed warnings were hit. (Note that there was a warning system that gave Tokyo about a minute of warning before the ground waves reached the city, giving them time to duck and cover.)

**Lessons**: The tsunami was the most deadly element of the disaster, and warnings based on the earthquake were provided to encourage evacuation. Even though the reach of the tsunami was unprecedented, the vast majority of those who tried to evacuate were spared the danger of the water. Those who didn't evacuate were much less fortunate. This might feel like a familiar phrase by now, but get out when you are told to get out. Maybe even get out before you are told, if you can figure it out for yourself.

**2.** Over 65 percent of all victims were sixty years old or older; 24 percent were in their seventies. After a year, it was reported that 70 percent of missing victims were sixty or older. This may be due to the demographics of those who were at home when the disaster struck.

**Lessons:** While sixty and seventy years old is not particularly elderly, and while it is not clear that the elderly were victims because of their age or associated infirmities, in general the elderly and those with strength or mobility issues are more vulnerable in disasters. Those with strength or mobility concerns can prepare for emergencies and should plan to have additional family and neighbor connections to help them out in times of need. See chapters 2 and 9.

3. There was at least one derailed train in the region; passengers were not rescued until the next morning. Because it was early March, the nights were chilly.

   **Lessons:** When traveling by any mode, keep a small emergency kit with some extra personal medications and supplies to tide you over during small inconveniences. Dress for travel with the idea that you may have to leave the vehicle in an emergency, and take seasonal and weather conditions into account. Some extra emergency cash could be helpful. Travel with a full water bottle and a couple of energy bars.

4. The earthquake and tsunami caused failure of some critical cooling systems at coastal nuclear facilities. There were explosions from hydrogen gas buildup, and radiation leaks resulted in the evacuation of surrounding communities to a radius of twelve miles, though fifty was recommended.

   **Lessons:** There are power plants, factories, chemical processing plants, and all kinds of man-made risks all around us. You need to know about the risks in order to plan for them. The good news is that your community may have already catalogued these potential hazards and developed response plans for similar emergencies. Call your city hall and see if a local emergency planning council has been created and if a city emergency plan exists. The bad news is that it may not exist or may be badly outdated. If you know what the risks are and how close to them you are (there are a number of easy-to-use map applications on the Internet), you can plan evacuation routes and destinations and be ready to go when alerted.

5. Supplies of water, food, and medicine were delayed in the first week after the earthquake. Many shelters were undersupplied with food, water, and medical equipment, and poor sanitary conditions developed. Early spring temperatures and electrical and gas outages exacerbated difficulties.

**Lessons:** Even in civic-minded, authority-respecting Japan, the government was unable to care for all who needed it. Each family must develop evacuation and communication plans and prepare to be on its own for three to seven days.

### Conclusion

The 2011 Tohoku earthquake/tsunami has many relevant lessons for us because it has so many different elements, each with its own character. This disaster was unique because of its intensity and size; it was completely unprecedented. Because of this, it is tempting to say, "There will always be an emergency bigger and badder than we expect, so we cannot plan for it." While it is true that there will always be record-setting disasters, it does not follow that planning and preparing are futile. The nature and idiosyncrasies of any disaster will undoubtedly disrupt the smooth flow of your plans, but having them as a starting point and having the attitude that you must take care of yourself puts you in a stronger position to weather the crisis. And any preparation is better than no preparation.

## Superstorm Sandy

### Summary

On October 29, 2012, Sandy—a post-tropical cyclone with a circulation spanning over one thousand miles—pushed a record storm surge ashore in New Jersey and New York, flooding tunnels and subways and coastline communities. Sandy was called a superstorm, not only because of its size but also due to the influence of two other storm systems—one that deflected it back to the west toward land and one that brought additional moisture and colder temperatures. Accurate strength and trajectory predictions from the National Hurricane Center enabled states to issue evacuation orders and to implement other measures such as school and business closures to reduce the impact and hasten the recovery. Coastal flooding damaged many shore properties. The high winds and the extensive coastal flooding knocked out power to over 5 million people in the New York/New Jersey area alone; power outage and transportation restart were inconveniences to many millions of people in the area for days and sometimes weeks.

## Results/Effects

- **Casualties**: An estimated 285 people died in multiple countries, from the Caribbean to Canada.
- **Economic effects**: The economic impact was variously estimated at between sixty and eighty billion dollars in damage in just the United States.
- **Communications/transportation**: Thousands of flights were cancelled, and subway, rail, and bus services were suspended as Sandy approached. Subway tunnels were flooded, and bridges and roads were either damaged or covered by debris. The restart of public transit took days, and it was weeks before it ran smoothly again for the millions who depend on it. Power outages made fuel dispensing difficult, and damaged pipelines or closed roads and bridges made resupply impossible for days, necessitating rationing.
- **Other**: Coastal flooding did the most visible damage and was reported widely in the press. Inland, downed trees were responsible for extended power outages. Where flooding occurred, the water was often polluted with raw sewage after pumps lost power. In other cases, hazardous chemicals and wastes were washed into flood waters, creating further hazard.

## Preparedness Lessons Learned

1. An analysis of over one hundred fatalities in the northeast United States reveals some patterns: over a third died from drowning, either in their homes or in their cars. The second highest cause of death was falling trees, and the third highest cause of death was slips and falls, particularly among the elderly. In fact, about half of the victims were people over age sixty-five. A cause of death in a significant number of victims was carbon monoxide poisoning from portable generator fumes.

   **Lessons**: The landfall of Sandy was accurately predicted days prior to its actually happening. Every single person in Sandy's path had warning and time enough to evacuate. Just as in 9/11, Katrina, or Tohoku, the same lesson is repeated here: if you want to save your life, get out when you are told to get out. Maybe get out *before* you are told to get out. If your home is going to be flooded by the storm surge, you can do nothing by being there, and your presence means nothing but danger to you and perhaps to the brave responders who may be called out to rescue you.

In any emergency, the elderly are disproportionately affected, whether by health or mobility issues, or by location, or by lack of resources. If you aren't as spry as you used to be, or if you have health or mobility issues, you need to develop a network of people you can call on for help. It may be family if you are fortunate enough to have some in the area; it may be kind neighbors who can look in on you; it may be social agencies that serve you; or it may be a church "family" that can help you out. Many people are happy to help and simply need to be alerted to your need.

Also, in emergencies, common sense often takes a holiday. People try to do things they would not ordinarily think of doing and get into situations where accidents can happen more readily. In Sandy, several people were injured by chain saws. There were electrocutions, car accidents, heart attacks, and the aforementioned falls and asphyxiations. The best thing to do in an emergency is stop, take a deep breath, and approach every task with sense and caution. All of the circumstances and urgencies of an emergency will quickly pass, even if you don't climb on your roof with a chain saw in the middle of a storm.

2. Falling trees took out thousands of power lines. Even though utility companies pre-positioned response crews and brought in outside help, many people were without power for days and weeks. Sandy highlighted the fact that our national power grid is fragile and vulnerable to just about any emergency.

   **Lessons**: We depend upon electricity for so much, and we take our mobile phones, which didn't do much a decade ago, for granted. Our phones have become our lifelines to so many things we do, including work, family, and even social connections. We use them to get news and information about the weather. They store our reference information, our contact list, our address collection, maps, and even account numbers and passwords. But the batteries only last a day or two, and then they need to be recharged. A number of products on the market right now, with more emerging all the time, will recharge your phone by deep-cycle batteries, solar cells, or temporary generation. Make sure you have several backup plans for keeping this important tool alive in the most critical of times, and make sure you have several recharge cords available.

3. For the largest majority of those affected, Sandy boiled down to a long power outage and transportation/commuting difficulties. For a few days, fuel shortages led to rationing, long lines, and short tempers. With no power to traffic signals, each intersection became a four-way stop, except when it became a no-way stop. Stores were picked bare, and resupply was slow in reestablishing.

   **Lessons:** Really, no one is prepared for a weeks-long power outage. Veterans of Sandy learned valuable lessons that can serve us:

   - You need water storage. A case or two of bottled water doesn't go very far.
   - You need fuel. If you have a fireplace to heat your home, you should try to calculate how much wood it takes to heat the house all day and into a cold night.
   - The smallest things become big things. Patience is in short supply too.
   - Cash is crucial. Without power, you can't use your credit card, no matter how much money is in the bank.
   - Food storage is worthless if you can't or don't know how to prepare it or the kids won't eat it. And you need a lot more food when everyone is home all day.
   - It is well and good to feed your own kids, but what will you do when the neighbor's kids come around? Sandy brought us many heartwarming stories of people helping each other through it all. It also brought us stories of frayed nerves, looting, and shootings.
   - Plan some comfort items as well. After a few days, you'll need a cup of cocoa or a bite of chocolate. Have some board or card games to play and have a guitar around.
   - When the trucks stopped rolling, the first things to become scarce during Sandy were fuel, matches/lighters, toilet paper (think about that one for a minute), paper plates and cups, milk, bread, aspirin and cold medicines, and anything to do with a portable generator.

## Conclusion

Superstorm Sandy brought disaster home to the nation's most populous urban center. Millions of people were affected by power outages and shortages of food, fuel, and just about everything else. For a minority of people, the emergency was about high winds and storm surges that brought water and sand into their yards and houses. In many of those cases, the homeowners were uninsured for that kind of flooding. For millions more, it was simply dark and cold and really hard to get supplies for days. Can it happen to you? And will you be prepared to weather it? Heroic action isn't needed, just a survivor's attitude and the willingness to do one thing today.

# European Heat Waves

## Summary

The summer of 2022 was unusually hot in Europe with a series of devastating heatwaves that caused an  estimated 61,672 excess deaths from May 30 to September 4. Although the heat was forecast, extreme temperatures lasted for days, with more severe impacts in urban areas, exacerbated by the heat island effect. Extreme heat can affect humans in several ways. As temperatures rise, dehydration can set in; muscle cramps, while not fatal themselves, can indicate dangerous conditions. Prolonged exposure to extreme heat can result in heat exhaustion, frequently indicated by excess sweating, clammy skin, and nausea. At extreme temperatures, heat stroke can occur, where the body loses its ability to regulate cooling, and the body temperature rises uncontrollably; death can occur. Additionally, excess heat can cause injury or death for those with existing health conditions.

Although previous heatwaves gave officials a preview of possible problems, and despite municipal prevention and response plans in place, the summer of 2022 was particularly deadly, partly because most European households are not air-conditioned. Italy, Spain, and Germany had the most fatalities of the 35 countries studied.

## Results/Effects

- **Casualties:** 61,672 deaths were attributed to heat effects. This number was calculated by comparing normal death rates with death rates during a heatwave. Because the effects of extreme heat might manifest as other illnesses and conditions, such as high blood pressure, cardiac or respiratory illness, and other serious conditions, a calculation of injuries was not possible. Heat-related death occurred most frequently in the very young—infants and young children—and the very old: eighty-years-old and older. People with existing health conditions were at higher risk. Women represented about 57 percent of deaths compared to men's 43 percent.

- **Economic Effects:** Direct costs of heatwaves include cooling centers, outreach activities, and increased emergency response and health care costs. Indirect costs accrue through reduced economic activity when workers cannot get to work or are unable to work due to heat or illness. Outdoor and construction work slows down as workers are affected. In 2022, direct and indirect losses were estimated at 40 billion euros.
- **Communications/Transportation:** Heat waves put increasing load on power grids, sometime resulting in complete blackouts, rolling blackouts, or brownouts. Prolonged extreme heat can also melt blacktop-paved surfaces, and buckle concrete roads. In a multicultural society like Europe, people who do not speak the local language may not receive warnings or instructions. Other marginalized groups, such as migrant and homeless populations are disproportionately affected by heatwaves.
- **Other:** Heat, solar radiation, and air pollution can combine to worsen air quality during heatwaves.

## Preparedness Lessons Learned

1. Heat waves, as meteorological phenomena, are somewhat predictable, typically with several days' notice. Urban officials in Europe had some experience with prior-year heatwaves, and implemented response plans in 2022 but with mixed results.

   **Lessons:** Like many other emergencies, if you are faced with a heatwave, you should take responsibility for your own safety and health. Pay attention to weather forecasts. When a heatwave is projected, make sure you have some emergency supplies on hand, and have plans to move to a cooler location, or take advantage of public cooling centers when the heat is extreme. Arrange your days to avoid outdoors errands or travel in the sun and heat of the day.

2. Heatwaves take the highest toll on women, the old, the very young, and the ill.

   **Lessons:** Long before a heatwave occurs, get to know your nearest neighbors, and arrange to check on each other, especially the vulnerable. Remind yourself and others of the symptoms of heat-related illness. In a heatwave, frequently check on your neighbors, and assist those who need medical care to get appropriate help. Remind your neighbors to hydrate continuously and to avoid alcohol and caffeinated drinks. Help those with mobility or strength challenges to manage the heat in their residences (such as closing shades on the sunny side of the house, moving to a cooler room or basement if possible), and to get to a public cooling center when needed. In extreme cases, a cool bath, or a spray water bottle and an electric fan can provide temporary relief. Increase the frequency of your neighborly check-ins if the power goes out.

3. The official designation of a heatwave varies from jurisdiction to jurisdiction. Declaration can be as simple as exceeding a single temperature threshold, or it can involve other variables such as humidity, overnight high temperatures, and heat duration.

   **Lessons:** Contact local officials to understand how they define and designate a heatwave, how they will notify the local population and what, if any, measures they will take during a heatwave.

• • •

Disasters and emergencies always present the same challenges to all of us: what you can get done before, especially if there is some warning; how you can best ride it out and stay alive; and how soon you can get back to normal after. In each of these large disasters and in countless smaller ones, there are similarities that can motivate us to do something today.

- What can you do before? Get some stuff together that will not be available in an emergency.
- What can you do during? Get out when you are told. Otherwise, keep your calm, use common sense, and stay alive.

- What can you do after? Be resourceful, be helpful to your neighbors, and be patient and optimistic: it will pass.

And do one thing today—every day.

# House Fires

## A Too-Common Emergency

When we think of emergency preparedness, we often think of hurricanes, tornadoes, and earthquakes. But consider this: in the United States from 2016 to 2020 there were an average of over 350,000 residential fires, killing over 2,700 people, injuring over 11,000 more, not counting firefighters. While earthquakes are difficult to predict, and impossible to prevent, many house fires can be prevented or mitigated. Here are some fire safety tips.

### Prepare to Prevent Fires

- Practice safety in the kitchen; cooking equipment is the leading cause of all house fires. Clean up and remove combustible materials from around the stove. Don't let grease build up. Keep your attention on the stove; never leave it unattended. Especially don't leave children unattended in the cooking area. Don't use cloth dish towels as hot pot holders, especially if you have a gas stove with an open flame. Long sleeves with loose-fitting cuffs can be a fire hazard in the kitchen. Keep a fire extinguisher in plain sight.
- Most house fires occur from December through March. Space heaters can be dangerous. Keep them at least three feet from combustible materials like bedspreads, curtains, and clothing. Never drape wet clothes over them to dry. Never leave space heaters operating while sleeping. Never leave them unattended. Frequently check wires for fraying or overheating.

- Be smoker wary. Provide smokers with deep, stable ashtrays. Empty ashtrays daily; make sure that all butts are out cold. Make it an ironclad rule that no one smokes in bed.
- Treat electricity with respect. Buy only lab-tested (such as UL) electrical devices. Do not overload sockets or extension cords. Make sure all outlets have cover plates. If there are small children in your home, invest in socket covers too. Do not run wires under rugs, or puncture the cords with nails or staples. Replace worn wires on appliances and lights—this is easier and cheaper than replacing all of your belongings after a house fire. If you live in a house with a fuse box, be sure that the proper-sized fuses are installed. If a fuse keeps blowing, check the circuit for overload; don't just install a larger fuse.
- Teach fire safety to your children. Teach the smallest to tell an adult about any matches or lighters they find. Store matches and lighters out of children's reach.
- Clean up your storage and work areas. If you need an excuse to throw out piles of papers, magazines, and other junk, do it for fire safety. Throw out the old half-cans of paint and solvents. (Be sure to dispose of them properly. Many communities and waste management companies have annual hazardous waste collections for materials like these.) Store the flammable materials you need to keep in original, marked, metal containers out of reach of children and outside the house in a shed. Never store flammables near heat and flame sources like the furnace and water heater.
- Protect your house from fireplace sparks by putting up a metal or tempered glass screen. Have the flue checked regularly to see that it is in good working order and that creosote, a tar-like byproduct of burning firewood, is not building up. Make sure that the chimney has a spark arrestor screen on the outlet. Don't burn paper in your fireplace.
- Minimize open flames. Use candles only under adult supervision, and never leave a candle or other open flame unattended.
- Clean dryers, inside and out to remove any lint build-up. Clean out the dryer vent regularly.
- Strictly enforce fireworks safety rules. Adults should supervise all fireworks. Light only one item at a time and keep all spectators

at a safe distance. Douse used fireworks in a bucket of water and keep a hose ready. Only use fireworks on clean, flat surfaces. Follow all directions and keep away from homes, trees, and dry grass or weeds. Never point or throw fireworks at others.

## Prepare to Minimize Damage and Injury

- Install and maintain smoke detectors. Install one on each level of your home and near each sleeping area. Check detector function once a month and replace batteries every nine to twelve months. Have children help you check the smoke detectors so they will hear and recognize the warning signal. Replace smoke detectors over ten years old. Install carbon monoxide (or CO) detectors. They can alert you to a buildup of carbon monoxide, a poisonous gas created by incomplete combustion, caused by malfunctioning furnaces and other flame appliances.
- Sleep with your bedroom doors closed. This slows the spread of smoke and fire.
- Make plans to escape a burning house. Identify at least two exits from every room. Make sure everyone knows how to open windows. If you have second floor bedrooms, have a fire ladder in each bedroom. Designate a safe spot outside of your home where everyone will gather after evacuation. Practice emergency escaping and reassembling at the designated spot twice a year. Caution: If your small children must exit a second floor bedroom, you can practice all but the dangerous descent procedure.
- Train the children, even the smallest, when and how to use 911. Teach them what to say when they call in an emergency. Help them understand the seriousness of using 911.
- Keep multipurpose (ABC) fire extinguishers handy in several places in your home: kitchen, basement, shop, garage, and car. Learn how to use them. Learn when to fight a fire and when it would not be safe. Watch the dial to know when to recharge or replace them.

## Prepare to React Safely If a Fire Strikes

- Get out and stay out. Call for help on a neighbor's phone. Meet the rest of your family at the gathering spot so you'll know when everyone is out. Reentering a burning building without proper training and equipment could result in you becoming another victim.

- If trapped in a burning building, stay low and crawl under smoke and heat. If trapped in an upper story with no escape route, hang a sheet out of a window so rescuers know you need assistance.
- Test doors with the back of your hand before opening. If they are hot, don't open the door; use your second exit.
- If your clothes catch on fire, stop, drop, and roll to smother the flames.

• • •

A house fire is more likely than many of the disasters we usually worry about. It is also more preventable than many other emergencies. Fire safety is often about good housekeeping, paying attention, and using common sense, but like all other emergency preparedness, it requires that you take time—with your family—to learn and implement these suggestions.

Emergency preparedness:
Do one thing today.

# Earthquakes

## Find and Fix Hazards before a Quake Shakes Up Your Life

Almost all of the United States has some risk of earthquake, although risks are highest along the Pacific Coast, Alaska, the Mountain States, the New Madrid region of Missouri, and the upper New England region. For example, experts tell us there is about a 43 percent chance of a magnitude 6.75 earthquake along Utah's populous Wasatch Front region in the next fifty years. Experts also tell us, though we don't always listen to this part, that the chances of smaller quakes are much higher. Although a magnitude 4.75 quake is one hundred times smaller than a 6.75, it can still topple furniture, break glass, and rearrange your interior decorating. Find and fix home hazards now, so your house will be a safer place in a quake, big or small.

Go through each room imagining what would happen if the house began to shake side-to-side. Did you know that over half of the injuries from an earthquake are caused by falling objects and not collapsing buildings? Make a list of things to fix as you go through each area. Pay special attention to places where you spend a lot of time sitting or sleeping.

- Rearrange furniture so pieces that could topple or "walk" won't block exits.
- Secure tall furniture, like bookshelves and china hutches, to wall studs with straps or earthquake safety hardware from the hardware store. Be sure the hardware attaches to studs and not just into the drywall.

- Install lips or restraining wires on shelves to keep items from vibrating off. Look into earthquake putty or museum wax to secure items on open shelves
- Move the heaviest objects to the lowest shelves.
- Put hanging light fixtures on closed hooks or carabiners. It's best not to hang plants, but if you must, use plastic pots, assure they are solidly secured into ceiling joists (not just into drywall), and make sure they can't swing into windows.
- Aquariums are top heavy; attach them securely to stable stands or attach to a wall.
- Televisions, printers, microwave ovens, and other heavy items can slide off flat surfaces. Install restraining straps or mount with hook and loop (Velcro-type) fasteners. Note that sticky-backed fasteners can mar furniture when removed.
- Hang heavy pictures from sturdy, closed hooks or wrap the wire around the hanger.
- Make sure no heavy or glass items—mirrors, heavy frame pictures—can fall onto beds. Move beds away from windows. Insist that kids straighten up rooms—exit pathways must be kept clear.
- Sliding doors should be of tempered glass.
- There are extra hazards in the kitchen. Wedge refrigerator rollers so it won't move. Consider child latches on cabinets so dishes don't become missiles. Make sure gas appliances have flexible couplings.
- Cleaning supplies, yard chemicals, paints, solvents, and even medicines can become hazards if they fall and spill. The first storage priority is to keep chemicals out of children's reach, but, where possible, store heavy containers low in locked cabinets. Avoid glass containers. Build restraining bars across open shelving or secure containers to walls with wires or elastic cords.
- One of the most important things you can do is secure your water heater to a brace (check with your gas company for details; see pages 113) or a wall. Replace "hard" gas couplings with flexible connectors.
- Locate main utility shutoffs and make certain they are accessible now and won't be buried by your belongings in a quake.

- Outside, check your AC or evaporative cooler; it might need additional bracing. Brace a masonry chimney and determine where pieces might fall. If you don't have solid sheathing on your roof, you can protect occupants by making a protective apron around the chimney. Screw plywood to the ceiling joists in the attic.

Now that you are hazard-conscious, repeat your hunt at work or school. Then take your list and begin to work through it. Do the easy things first but persevere until you finish the tough ones too.

## Misconceptions About When "The Big One" Hits

What can you expect when "the big one" hits? Some people focus too closely on the first, confusing, media-saturated hours after a quake and end up drawing inaccurate conclusions that could result more in hysteria than useful preparation. Here are some misconceptions people may have about what life will be like after a large earthquake.

### Misconception: Expect no support from your community after an earthquake.

There is some truth in this statement: one lesson of the Tohoku earthquake (Japan 2011) is that the government cannot be expected to meet every citizen's every need in an emergency. But on the other hand, our entire society will not collapse with the overpasses. First, not every area of an earthquake zone will be hit equally hard. The location of the earthquake, its magnitude, soil structure, type and age of construction, and other factors combine to determine the severity of damage in a specific location. Neighborhoods right next to each other can experience dramatically different results. Nearby communities will have the ability to help the more severely impacted, especially after the first hours when the situation becomes clear.

Yes, emergency crews will be overwhelmed after an earthquake. But not too many on-duty, off-duty, or volunteer responders will abandon their posts. Medical and emergency responders are professionals who have worked years to develop their skills; to suggest they will bolt from their stations at the first sign of trouble would be simply unfair. They are guided not only by their employers but also by their ethics and integrity. In other quakes, emergency personnel have performed heroically.

## Misconception: There will be no utilities or services for weeks. Stores will be picked clean.

Water, sewer, electricity, gas, and phone services are all likely to be interrupted, and maybe over a wide area. Go ahead and kiss them goodbye, but don't be teary—they'll be back. They'll be back in hours for many, days for most others, and weeks only in isolated instances. Stores are more likely to be closed immediately following a quake than to be picked clean. Aisles will be clogged with fallen merchandise; electric registers won't work without power; and store employees that remain will have a huge mess to clean up before they can serve customers. After they open, resupply will be determined by the condition of the roads, and it may take some days to reestablish supplies to each store. This probably means that you'll have to range a little farther for a while. Fuel rationing is possible, but if necessary will only last a few days. In Superstorm Sandy (2012), rationing lasted about two weeks, mostly due to the inability of tanker trucks to get to individual stations. Pumps will likely shut down from lack of electricity but will work again when power is restored.

## Misconception: Rampaging fires will destroy everything.

We can expect some fires. Gas lines may be ruptured by ground movement and ignited by electrical sparks in isolated incidents. Other earthquakes have shown that unsecured water heaters tip over and rupture gas lines, which can then be ignited in a number of ways. In the Tohoku earthquake, wooden and paper structures collapsed onto cooking fires and stoves and some neighborhoods were burned. Lack of water will complicate firefighting. Fire risk will be highest where buildings are close together. In the suburbs, well-spaced houses and open expanses should mean that the inevitable fires will be mostly isolated and contained.

## Misconception: All buildings will collapse. All roads will be impassable.

In recent earthquakes in Turkey, Haiti, and Iran, large temblors destroyed wide swaths of unreinforced masonry buildings. But in the United States, unless you live in an unreinforced masonry home (wood frame with brick facade doesn't count), it is likely that your house will remain habitable even if damaged. Single-family, wood-frame homes built in compliance with building codes can be expected to sustain little structural damage. This is especially true of one- or two-story structures on soft soils like clay, where earthquake waves are larger but farther apart. Higher frequency waves that might damage smaller buildings may occur in rocky areas. Although cracks may appear in roads and slabs, stretches of most roads will likely be passable or easily cleared, and any ground rupture will be limited and close to the fault. Long-span and older overpasses are at risk, but the freeway reconstruction constantly upgrades bridges and spans to more stringent earthquake standards, which will increase the probability of continued passability.

### Misconception: Injuries will be untreated; bodies will lie unrecovered in the rubble; disease will be rampant.

A large earthquake will cause injuries, perhaps even fatalities. In recent earthquakes, responders have prioritized rescue of injured people, and recovery of fatalities. Life-threatening injuries will still receive care by medical professionals, although triage is likely and conditions may not be optimal. The injured may have to be transported to hospitals by friends, and medical facilities may sustain their own damages, but health-care professionals will still provide the best possible services. Minor injuries will probably have to wait longer for care, but that is expected in a large-scale disaster. Recovery of bodies will be swift. Disposal of human waste could be a problem, and unsanitary conditions could contribute to spread of disease. But most people do not stay long at shelters; if there are outbreaks, they will likely stay localized.

### Misconception: There is nothing you can do.

Each earthquake has its own character, its own surprises. Things could be locally much worse or much better than described here. But don't panic; effective preparation requires calm thinking and deliberate action. First, although "the big one" is possible, smaller quakes are certain. Realize that even a modest quake can displace your belongings and disrupt your life. True, you cannot prevent or even predict earthquakes, but you do have some control over how much it affects you. Gather your family and make some plans. Identify the safest spots in each room to "duck, cover, and hold." Secure furniture that might fall; move heavy items from top shelves or above beds. Strap down your water heater and connect the gas with a flexible coupling. Secure hazardous materials to avoid spills. Designate an out-of-state friend for everyone in the family to contact; long distance may be easier than local calls, and you can leave messages. Gather some emergency supplies for a short-term emergency kit and take a first-aid course from the Red Cross or a comparable organization. Practice locating your utility shutoffs; practice stepping to your safe spots; practice having the lights off for a few hours one night. Talk with your neighbors about how to check on and help each other in a crisis. Do they have special needs? Where are their utility shutoffs?

Finally, many counties sponsor community emergency response team (CERT) training, and most communities have volunteer emergency preparedness committees. Invest some time and effort to assure that people get help from their communities, which include neighbors as well as governments. Things will be a mess for a while after an earthquake, but the situation is far from hopeless; your own preparedness will serve your family, and your communities and neighborhoods will come together to help each other.

## How to Secure Your Water Heater

One of the most important things you can do to prepare for an earthquake is to secure your water heater. This action will prevent your water heater from toppling in an earthquake. Not only will you reduce the risk of broken gas lines and fire or explosion, but you will also preserve thirty to fifty gallons of drinking water.

Securing your water heater consists of two things: (1) immobilizing the water heater so it will not fall over, and (2) installing flexible couplings so any slight movements the water heater may make won't rupture the gas line.

### Immobilize the Water Heater

There are many sound methods for preventing your water heater from toppling. Follow these guidelines for maximum safety:

- If you have a thirty- to fifty-gallon water heater within twelve inches of a stud wall, follow the directions on the diagram on page 113. This is not the only approach; another method, for example, uses L-shaped shelf braces to immobilize the water heater from each side.

- If your water heater is within twelve inches of a concrete wall, the same method will work, but you'll need to use ¼-inch expansion bolts to attach to the wall.
- If your water heater is more than twelve inches from a stud wall, there are commercial earthquake braces available. A licensed engineer or plumber will be able to recommend a sound method, or check with the gas company for recommendations.
- Make sure all of the connections to the wall attach to studs. Attachments to sheetrock alone will not be strong enough to hold a bucking water heater.
- Only nonflammable materials like metal straps and spacers should contact the water heater. Take special care to not create any fire hazards.
- If you have any questions, consult a licensed plumber or engineer.

## Install Flexible Couplings

Although many newer houses already have flexible couplings on the water heater, many older houses have rigid gas connections. If you are not certain which type of connection you have, contact a plumber. If you have rigid connections, have a licensed plumber install a flexible, corrugated metal hose where the gas line connects to the water heater.

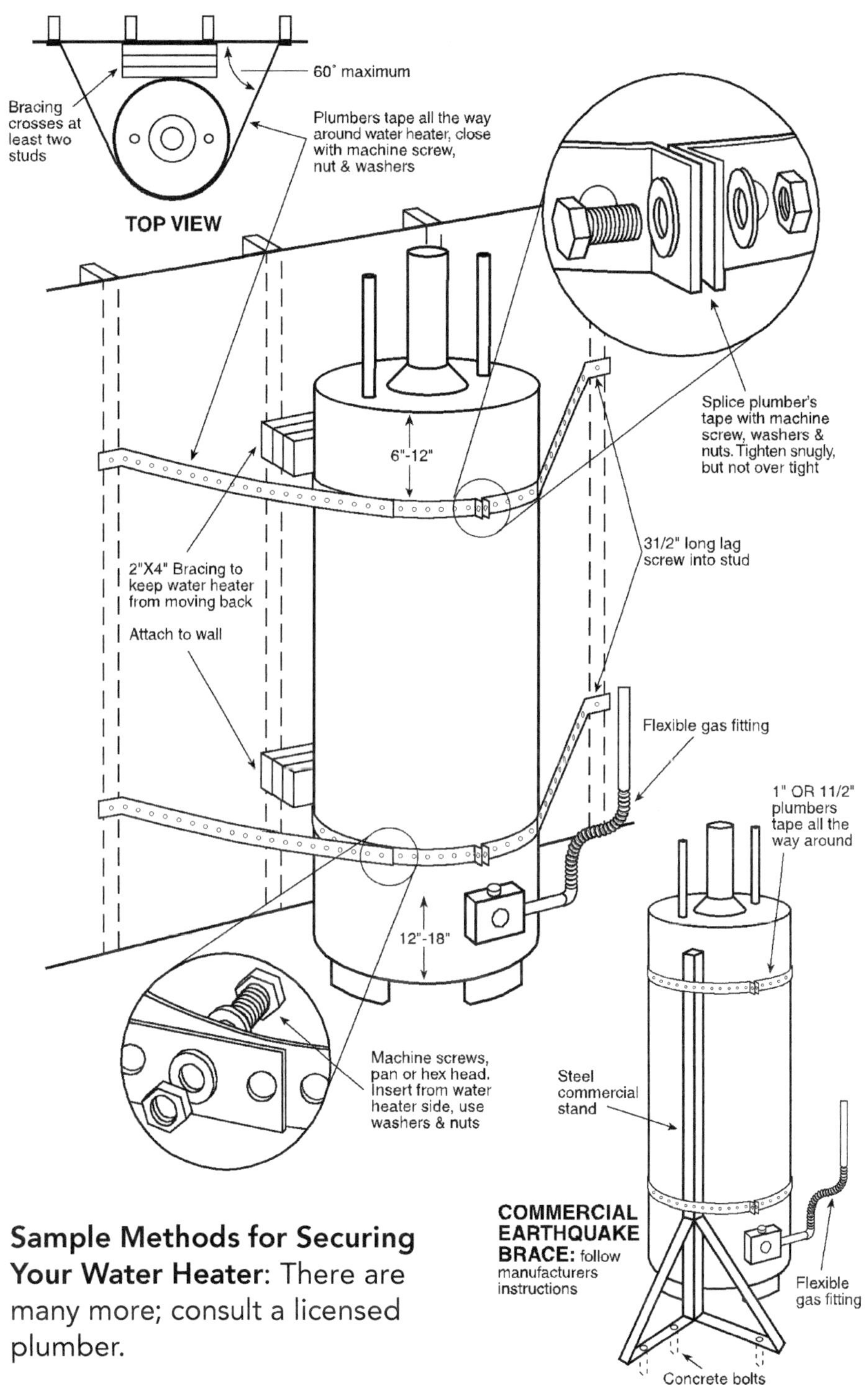


**Sample Methods for Securing Your Water Heater**: There are many more; consult a licensed plumber.

## What Do You Do after an Earthquake?

So, you've done a home hazard hunt and fixed things in your house that could be hazardous in a quake. You've secured your water heater so it won't topple, and you've installed flexible couplings so the gas line won't rupture. You've worked out a family emergency plan and put together a short-term emergency kit, so you have some ready resources in case of emergency. Just a few more quake-related items to discuss and you'll be in pretty good shape.

Decide in advance where you want to ride out a quake. Identify a safe spot or two in every room. Remember that the ground motion will make it hard to move more than a step or two. Safe places include doorways, hallways, and wall corners where the building structure is strongest. Underneath sturdy tables and counters can be safe, although, in general, kitchens are full of hazards. Stay away from fireplaces (falling bricks, stones, or flues), windows and mirrors, bookcases, and tall furniture. Also try to stay aware of safe/hazardous spots in stores, malls, schools, and other public places. In a pinch, drop to the floor, scoot over to a wall, and cover your head.

When an earthquake hits, you'll have little warning, and it may take a second or two to realize what's happening, but there may be many more seconds of shaking ahead. In the Tohoku earthquake, shaking lasted for about six minutes. What should you do?

- Stay calm. Your best emergency tool is between your ears; don't lose it.
- Stay put. If inside, stay inside. If outside, stay outside. People are injured by falling debris at building entrances. The possible exception to this is in a downtown area with tall glass buildings. If there are no open spaces to get to, you may be better off getting in a nearby building. If you are in a car, stop as quickly as safety will allow. Pull off to the side if you can. Never stop on a bridge or under an overpass. Stay in the car until the quake is over. After, proceed cautiously, watching for road damage and debris.
- Take cover. If the stove is on, turn it off first. Move quickly to your safe place and stay alert. You may as well enjoy the ride; there's nothing you can do to stop it.

- As soon as the quake is over, make sure everyone is all right. Don't move any seriously injured people unless they are still in danger. Administer first aid. Get help.
- Minimize travel immediately after a quake. If you are not at home, reuniting with your family is a priority, but listen to the radio to determine if you can travel safely. If not, stay put. The situation will stabilize in a few hours; take enough care and time to get home safely.
- Put on sturdy shoes. Broken glass and tripping hazards may abound.
- Check for damage to electricity, water, and gas lines. Turn off the power and do not use matches or open flames until you are sure there is no fire hazard. Do not use the fireplace until you are certain the chimney is not damaged. Turn off your water where it enters your home. Even if your house pipes are fine, a broken main could siphon water from the pipes and water heater. There are many gallons of usable water in the pipes, and shutting the valve protects them.
- *Do not* turn off the gas immediately, unless you smell gas, see broken pipes, hear gas hissing, or are instructed to by authorities. If you do turn it off, you must call the gas company to check your appliances, restart your gas, and relight your pilot lights. It could take days for the gas company to get to you.
- Check for other hazards in your home. Sweep up glass, clean up spilled cleaners, chemicals, and medicines. Use caution.
- Comfort each other. Stay with children and reassure them.
- Check your home for structural damage. If uncertain, leave the home; you may have to wait for an engineer's inspection to be sure your home is safe.
- Check household sewer lines for damage before using the toilet.
- Call the out-of-town contact you identified in your family plan. Otherwise, stay off the phone unless you have a serious injury/rescue situation.
- Check on your neighbors and others as you have arranged.
- Listen to your radio for updates and instructions.

- Do not go sightseeing.
- Be aware of the possibility of aftershocks.
- Don't forget to eat and drink something on a regular schedule. You'll feel much better. Remember to only use charcoal broilers outdoors.
- Practice good sanitation. Wash your hands frequently—this would not be a good time to get sick.
- Where possible, document the damage for future insurance claims.
- Be wise and go slow in clean-up and recovery. There may be lots of physical and even chemical/sewage hazards. Wear sturdy clothes, especially shoes, and beware of over exertion: a heart attack can kill you just as surely as falling bricks.
- In some cases, people are reluctant to go back into their homes to sleep. If this is the case, go to a nearby shelter, or even camp out in your yard.
- Be patient and flexible

One final note: the first few hours after a quake may be confusing and stressful, but no matter how bad things seem to be, they will get better, and help will come.

Emergency preparedness:
Do one thing today.

# Hazardous Materials

## A Hazardous Materials Accident in Our Town?

On a cold day one December, a tank truck carrying propane rolled over on the main freeway. The next day, a truck carrying sodium azide (airbag propellant) overturned on a nearby road and caught fire, sending a potentially hazardous plume across the local area. The next day, on the emergency detour route, several containers of sulfur dioxide tumbled off a trailer, causing more concern.

Our modern society requires a lot of chemicals, some of them hazardous, to produce the lifestyle we enjoy. During production, storage, transportation, use, and disposal, these chemicals can be accidentally released, creating a potential for harm. Considering the vast quantities of chemicals produced and used, very few hazardous material ("hazmat") accidents actually occur.

Could a hazmat accident happen in your town? There are many potential sources of hazardous materials. Our communities encompass freeways, highways, waterways, and rail corridors. These arteries transport many things, including some hazardous materials. Local chemical plants and refineries produce chemicals. Local industries also store and use materials that can be hazardous. Farmers and ranchers use fertilizers and pesticides that can be hazardous in large quantities. The chlorine used to treat drinking water or sanitize swimming pool water can be a hazard if released in quantity. Even gasoline stations and the natural gas lines that serve our homes and churches could be sources of hazardous materials.

Our communities regularly have minor hazmat accidents that are handled quickly and efficiently by highly trained fire and hazmat response crews. But occasionally, an incident escalates and grabs headlines for days. Recently in Ohio, fifty-one train cars derailed, piled up and caught fire. About 100,000 gallons of hazardous materials were spilled on the ground and into drainages. Nearby residents were immediately evacuated, while crews preventatively burned off the contents of several cars. Residents were out of their homes for days. Although most hazmat incidents are minor, there are several things we can do to be more prepared in case a major event does occur.

## Before a Hazmat Accident

- Be aware of the hazards around you. Federal laws enable communities and interested citizens to learn about the types of materials stored and used in the community. This process starts with a phone call to local authorities who may have established a local emergency planning council ("LEPC" in government parlance) to identify and monitor hazardous materials. The laws are clear: communities and residents have a right to know what chemical hazards are in their midst.
- Support zoning decisions that group industrial activities together and adequately protect high population and residential areas from accidents. Support tough penalties for those who break the law in using or disposing hazardous materials.
- Prepare to evacuate at a moment's notice. Store your short-term emergency kits in a container that you can grab on the way out—you may not have any time to pack anything else. Keep a list of other items you would like to take if you have time.
- Discuss with your family where you can go and who you should contact if you have to leave your neighborhood or if you are not allowed into it due to a hazmat incident. Establish an out-of-state contact that everyone in the family can call or text to relay information between separated family members. (This is the same person you should call in an earthquake if local phone service is disrupted.) Keep this phone number in your wallet, purse, or backpack.

## During a Hazmat Accident

- In a hazmat accident, authorities may evacuate residents miles downwind from the spill. Their first job is to protect human life. If you are directed to evacuate, gather your family and go. Grab your kit if it's handy, but do not stop to pack or prepare your house unless authorities allow it, which is unlikely. Make your way to your pre-arranged family contact point or a designated public shelter using an approved route. Do not take shortcuts or cross barriers; you could end up in a contaminated area. Report to your out-of-state contact.
- In some cases, authorities may direct residents in a wider area to "shelter in place." This is essentially direction to stay inside and stay isolated from the outside air. The presumption is that any vapor plume will quickly pass over the residence and then be gone. If directed to shelter in place, follow instructions. Bring family and pets inside. Close doors, windows, vents, and fireplace dampers, and turn off ventilation systems. Take your emergency kit and radio, move into a ground floor room with the fewest openings to the outside, and close all interior doors. Authorities should give an alert or signal that your area is safe again and may give additional instruction for decontamination.
- If you are the first on the scene of a highway or rail accident that may involve hazardous material, remember: responding to hazmat incidents requires training (hundreds of hours of class and field work for experts) and specialized clothing, gear, and even breathing apparatus. If you don't have these things, do not approach the site, even if there may be injuries. There may be hazards that you cannot smell or see, and shifting winds can trap you in hazardous plumes. Well-meaning but untrained people can become additional victims in a hazmat situation. If you suspect hazardous materials are involved, notify authorities and secure the site until trained responders can arrive. If there is threat of a fire or explosion, move back one-half mile. Some toxic chemicals require an even greater distance. Stay uphill, upwind, and upstream. Avoid contact with spills, fumes, vapors, and smoke. Even odorless fumes could be dangerous. If you become contaminated, notify authorities immediately, and they will assist in decontamination.

## After Evacuation from a Hazmat Accident

- Do not return home until authorities say its safe.
- Open up windows and ventilate the house.
- If your house and yard are contaminated by contaminated dew or ash, be rigorous in following authorities' decontamination procedures. Keep work clothes and inside clothes separate: contaminated shoes could bring residue into your house; contaminated clothes could contaminate your living spaces. Wash hands frequently. Residue on the hands could be transferred to food or drink or other people.

Hazardous material accidents in our communities are possible but usually small and isolated. Our local fire departments have extensive training and quick access to specialists if required. Be sure your family knows that individuals without training and equipment should not attempt to help with hazmat accidents. Families should be prepared to evacuate if authorities require.

Emergency preparedness:
Do one thing today.

# Winter

## A Little Winter Weather Preparation Can Save You Grief

Every year, there are needless injuries and damage due to winter weather. With a little preparation, you can avoid many of the seasonal hazards.

### Prepare Your House

- Inspect your furnace annually.
- Have a professional inspect the fuel system, fireboxes, and flues of older furnaces.
- Examine motors and belts for wear.
- Examine wiring for signs of overheating: cracking, discoloration.
- Clean or replace filters.
- Clear trash and combustible materials away from furnace and flue.
- Cover your evaporative cooler if you have one; stuff insulation into the cooler duct to reduce drafts. Make sure the water to the evaporative cooler is off and the supply line completely drained. Swamp cooler water lines can freeze in unheated attics and split, flooding insulation and ceilings.
- Replace door seals if ineffective. Install weather stripping. Install storm windows if you have them.
- Clean leaves off of roofs and out of gutters so melting roof snow can flow freely to the ground.

- Winterize your water pipes: caulk or stuff external wall penetrations. Insulate or heat trace exposed pipes and pipes in overhangs and unheated spaces. In extreme cold, let faucets drip to prevent freezing. If pipes freeze, do not use open flames to thaw. Wrap frozen area in rags and pour hot water over the rags.
- Make sure the main water shutoff is accessible.
- Routinely check all electrical cords for wear, and don't overload electrical circuits.
- Keep a fire extinguisher (or three) on hand. Check all smoke alarms (every level should have one or more) and all carbon dioxide detectors.
- Keep fire hydrants clear of snow buildup.

## Keep an Up-to-Date Short-Term Emergency Kit (see ch.3)

- Include: Water, food, extra blankets or sleeping bags, warm clothing, flashlight/batteries, candles/matches (observe fire safety), radio/batteries, first-aid kit, personal toiletries, medications.
- Plan to have an emergency heating source:
  - » Fireplace or wood stove and fuel. (Never use charcoal as an indoor heat source. It generates poisonous carbon monoxide.)
  - » Space heater and fuel. Always ensure adequate ventilation when operating a combustion heater.

## Watch the Weather

- Be aware of approaching storms and plan your travel accordingly. Don't travel if you can avoid it. Allow extra time if you must travel.
- Make sure someone knows what route you are traveling and when you will arrive. Make sure your car is in good repair, fully fueled, and has tires with adequate tread. Pack an emergency kit.
- Listen to weather updates on your radio during a storm.

## Practice Fire Safety

- Check outside of fireplace or wood stove flues for adequate clearances and good repair.
- Check inside of fireplace or wood stove flues for creosote buildup. You may need to consult a professional.

- Protect fireplaces with screens. Keep young children away from stoves, space heaters, and other hot surfaces.
- Provide adequate clearance between heater and combustible materials (three feet or more is recommended).
- When running combustion heaters, provide adequate fresh air to prevent carbon monoxide buildup and oxygen starvation.
- Check kerosene and other combustion heaters thoroughly each year. Make sure they have emergency shut-off valves in case heater is tipped over.
- Use only the specified fuel in space heaters, and follow all manufacturers' instructions.
- Store kerosene outside in approved metal containers.
- Never fill kerosene heaters when hot. Always refill outside.
- Clean out fireplace ashes only after they are completely cold. Discard ashes outside immediately in metal container.
- Make sure heaters and fires are out and cold before you go to sleep.

## Dress for the Weather

- Watch the weather and avoid going out in extreme cold or blizzard conditions.
- Remember that wind can provide an extra danger to exposed flesh. Cover all skin in cases of extreme weather, even for short trips.
- Wear layers of loose clothing. The outer layer should be waterproof and windproof. The inner layer should be synthetic (not cotton) to wick moisture away from the body. Layers in between can be almost any insulating material, and many good options exist at outdoor-themed stores.
- Keep dry. Getting wet in the winter can be life threatening. When you are wet, you lose much more body heat, and many materials lose their insulative properties.
- Good mittens will keep fingers warmer than gloves.
- Wear a hat covering the head down to the ears.
- Cover your mouth and nose with a scarf or bandanna in extreme cold.

### Don't Overdo It

- Snow shoveling and car pushing are hard work. Stretch and warm up before any exertion. Rest frequently. Heart attacks injure more people than hypothermia.
- Try not to work up a sweat, especially if you do not have a refuge. When you finally slow down, you'll chill quickly if your clothing layers are soaked.
- Drink plenty of fluids. Winter air is dry, and you can dehydrate quickly.
- Watch slippery sidewalks.
- Don't forget to check regularly on neighbors during winter storms and harsh weather, especially the elderly or those with special needs. Sometimes those with poor circulation are not aware that they are becoming chilled.

As with other extreme situations, don't panic in a winter storm: the best preparedness tool you can have is your brain.

## Tips for Winter Driving

Weather from October to April in snowy areas presents special challenges for drivers. Not only are roads more hazardous, but the consequences of getting stranded are more severe. Prepare your car now and use common sense when planning your travel.

### Prepare Your Car for Winter Travel

- Make sure your car is in good operating condition.
- Check and winterize all systems. Pay special attention to your battery, the antifreeze, and wiper blades.
- Install snow tires or purchase chains.
- Keep a full gas tank, even for short trips. If stranded, you can run the heater longer.

### Keep Up-to-Date Emergency Kits in the Car

- Start with a personal survival kit in the glove box:
    - » One large garbage sack to use as a poncho. Add a space blanket if you have one.

  - Five or six quart-sized plastic sacks to use as expedient socks and gloves
  - A one-gallon plastic sack can be used as a hat. But store a hat too.
  - Hard candy for energy and morale
  - A flashlight
  - Waterproof matches and several candles for light and a little heat. Double-bag candles to prevent a mess if they melt in a too-warm car.
- Put other emergency gear in the back:
  - Ice scraper/brush
  - Blankets or sleeping bag
  - First-aid kit
  - Jumper cables
  - Extra food, high energy
  - Fire extinguisher
  - Tow strap
  - Distress flag
  - Basic tools
  - Hats, gloves, boots, socks
  - Plastic sheeting
  - Flares
  - Pocketknife
  - Shovel
  - Radio, batteries
  - Number 10 can with sealing lid (expedient toilet)
  - Salt/sand/kitty litter
  - Tissues

## Plan Your Trip with the Weather in Mind

- Be aware of the weather on your route.
- Make sure someone knows of your destination, route, and planned arrival time. If conditions force you to change your plans, keep them updated.

- If you encounter weather that seems especially severe, seek shelter immediately. If it's just a brief flurry, you'll be back on your way soon. If it's a monster storm, you won't risk becoming stranded.
- Obey all road closures.

## Use Common Sense When Driving

- Keep windows clear of snow, ice, and interior fogging.
- Allow extra time so you can adjust your speed to conditions.
- Anticipate ice on overpasses.
- Expect slippery conditions and anticipate the decisions of other drivers.
- Anticipate intersections. Brake slowly to avoid locking the wheels and losing control. If you start to skid, steer into the direction you want to go. Brake carefully.

## If You Get Stranded

Every winter, severe storms strand cars on the road. Sometimes it can last a long and scary night. What should you do?

- Stay calm. If you panic, you lose your most important tool—your brain.
- Stay with the car. A car is more likely to be found when the inevitable search crews get out. You are much more likely to get lost, especially in a storm, if you leave the car. The car is shelter from the wind and protection from the snow, and it holds many tools and implements that you couldn't carry with you.
- Avoid overexertion. Avoid exposure. Stay in the car as much as possible. It may be possible to dig your car out of a drift, but it should be obvious after only a few minutes whether or not you might succeed. Avoid working up a sweat that will chill you further when you stop.
- If you try to push the car out, keep away from the wheels. Getting run over will not help your situation.
- Only run the motor for short periods. A good rule of thumb is ten to fifteen minutes per hour. Make absolutely sure that snow has not blocked the exhaust pipe, and crack a downwind window

for ventilation. Remember that car exhaust can be just as fatal as freezing.

- Open doors and windows occasionally to get fresh air and to keep them from freezing shut. Keep a downwind window cracked if you burn a candle.
- Get out and clear off the car once in a while so it looks like a car and not a snow bank and is more visible to rescue crews.
- Exercise and stretch briefly, but vigorously, from time to time. Don't stay in one position too long.
- Don't allow everyone to sleep at once. Someone should keep a watch at all times.
- Use emergency flashers sparingly to conserve the battery, but use them as a signal at night. You may have to get out and clear the snow so they can be seen.
- Your car has many survival resources, so be innovative. The horn can be an effective signal. Use bursts of three, the universal distress signal. Be innovative in the use of car parts: a hubcap makes a crude snow scoop; seat insulation can be stripped out and stuffed into clothes; floor mats can be tied around feet; and so on.

## Be Prepared to Have More Winter Fun

Winter is a great time to enjoy outdoor sports. Skiing, snowmobiling, snowshoeing, and even camping are all great ways to get out of the house, out of the smog, and into the stunning, snow-covered landscape. Because of weather extremes, however, minor mishaps in remote areas could become major disasters. Here are some preparation ideas to give you an extra margin of safety.

### Prepare Yourself for Outdoor Activities

- Wear proper clothing. Wear layers of loose clothing. The outer layer should be waterproof and windproof. The inner layer should be synthetic (not cotton) to wick moisture away from the body. Layers in between can be almost any insulating material.
- Plan thoroughly and ask "what if?" Identify potential risks and then prepare for them. If you are not experienced at your planned activity, consult someone who is.

- Make sure someone knows of your destination, your route, and your time of return. Know the area—the landmarks, the routes to help and safety. Never travel in remote areas alone.
- Pay attention to the weather and plan (or delay) your trip accordingly.
- If you are using a vehicle like a snowmobile, make sure it is in good repair and you are adequately trained to operate it. It is always safer to travel with two vehicles. Use all recommended safety precautions and operate it according to manufacturer's instructions. Many accidents occur when equipment is not used as designed.
- Learn the symptoms and treatment for cold injuries like hypothermia and frostbite. Hypothermia, for example, occurs when the body temperature drops, and it can ultimately be fatal. Hypothermia can occur even in mild weather, especially if rain or wind are involved. The first symptom is uncontrollable shivering, and steps must be taken immediately to get the victim warm.
- Keep an up-to-date emergency kit with you. Include:
  - » High-energy food, candy
  - » Candles/waterproof matches
  - » First-aid kit
  - » Extra socks, extra gloves, hat
  - » Space blanket, garbage sacks (forty-gallon), quart-sized baggies for hand/feet protection
  - » Whistle for signaling

## If You Get Stranded

- Don't panic. Your best survival tool is your brain.
- If you are with a vehicle, like a car or snowmobile, consider staying with it, especially if it is dark or snowing. The vehicle is usually the first thing searchers find, and you can easily get disoriented in blowing snow. Make sure you know where you are going if you decide to travel.
- Keep fuel in your body so it can manufacture more heat. Don't be afraid to eat emergency food right away. Keep drinking; dehydration is a risk. Move vigorously from time to time when stranded, but don't work up a sweat.

## Protect Your Body Heat

The body loses heat in five basic ways:

1. **Radiation**: Heat flows from warmer objects that are exposed to cooler objects. All of the heat of the sun comes to the earth by radiation. In the winter, any exposed area of your body will radiate heat to the snow, the air, or the sky. Those areas where blood vessels are close to the surface, such as heads and hands, are particularly vulnerable.

   The way to beat radiation loss is to "hide the heat." Cover everything up. Layers are especially important in thwarting radiation losses. Aluminized mylar "space blankets" (and bags) are specially designed to shield against radiation loss.

2. **Conduction**: When a warmer object contacts a cooler object, heat is transferred from the warmer. This is the kind of heat transfer that occurs when you are frying a hamburger in a pan.

   The way to beat conduction is to put insulation between the warmer (hopefully you) and cooler objects (like snow). Never sit or lay directly on the snow. If you have to sit, cut some tree branches or pile up some brush or leaves. Try to avoid eating large amounts of snow, since melting snow also takes heat.

3. **Evaporation**: Heat is consumed when moisture is evaporated. This is the principle on which swamp coolers are based. If your body heat is trying to dry out wet clothes, you can consume a lot of energy without getting warmer.

   The way to beat evaporation is to stay dry. Even sweating can be life threatening if you are caught out in the cold. Dress in layers that you can take off or loosen if you have to exert yourself. If you get wet while out, change to dry clothes if you have them. It is better to get out of wet things and into a blanket or sleeping bag than to wait for your clothes to dry. If you can't get out of wet stuff, try to insulate it with a large plastic garbage sack over everything except your face.

4. **Convection**: This is the type of heat loss that occurs when the wind is blowing: the wind chill factor. Air is a pretty good insulator when it is trapped between layers of clothing. But when the wind is blowing, your body will lose heat at a faster rate.

Convection can be beat by getting out of the wind or by covering up. Stay in the car, get behind a tree, get into a ditch (a dry ditch) or a snow cave, or hide behind a snow bank. And cover up all exposed skin. The large garbage sack is especially useful here.

5. **Respiration** (similar to evaporation): When you breathe, you take in cold, dry air and exhale wet, warm air. The whole process costs you heat. (Breathing takes heat, but it's better than the alternative.)

   You can beat respiration loss by reducing the amount of exhaling, reducing your activity level. You can also beat it by breathing through your nose. This pre-warms the air before it comes into your lungs, and it captures a fraction of the heat and moisture that is in your breath when you exhale. Another tip is to breathe through a scarf or bandanna wrapped around your face. Again, this provides a little bit of pre-warming of intake air by capturing exhaled heat and moisture in the scarf. Only use fabric around your mouth and nose. Plastic is hazardous and will not be effective.

There is no need to avoid your favorite winter sports; just use a little common sense and a little preparation to make them more safe.

Emergency preparedness:
Do one thing today.

# Summer

## Surviving Extreme Heat

The United States has many desert regions that possess beauties and wonders all their own. With a flora and fauna specifically adapted to the uniquely harsh conditions, deserts are fascinating and captivating at any season. But whether you are exploring on purpose or just passing through, extreme heat in a summer desert can be dangerous. Even non-desert climates and cities have heat waves that can prove fatal to vulnerable individuals. Here are a few tips to ensure more safety during summer fun or travel.

### Know (and Avoid) the Effects of Heat

- Avoid dehydration. In the heat, your body constantly sweats, even when you don't feel damp. The constant drain of water eventually catches up; your blood gets thicker, and your heart has to work harder against increased pressure. When it has to work too hard, life-threatening complications can arise.
- Heat exhaustion is a form of hyperthermia, or elevated body temperature. The symptoms include cramps, headache, nausea, dizziness, confusion, irritability, excessive sweating, and cold and clammy skin.
- Heatstroke is a more serious injury. The symptoms include hot, dry skin; dry mouth; headache; nausea and vomiting; deep, rapid breathing; muscular twitching; and collapse.

In all cases, the victim should be cooled immediately and should take small amounts of water frequently, if conscious. Seek medical help immediately.

## Protect Yourself When in the Sun, Even on Purpose

- Wear proper clothing: loose-fitting, lightweight, long-sleeved, light colors, cotton. Cotton clothes hold moisture close to you, lowering body temperature by evaporation.
- Avoid getting sunburned. Wear a wide brim hat and good sunglasses with UV protection. Slather on the high-SPF sunscreen and don't forget lip protection. If you are on bright sand or reflecting water, put sunscreen under your chin and nose too.
- Drink a lot of water during summer activities, even before you feel thirsty. If highly active (working, running, biking, hiking), you might need two to four quarts an hour.
- If you plan on desert hiking or biking activities, study up on desert survival techniques and make sure you are equipped and prepared, even for an emergency. Take plenty of extra water and a dish if your dog is going with you, and watch the dog's feet carefully; hot sand and sharp rocks can take their toll.

## Avoid Getting Stranded in Your Car

Follow similar guidelines for traveling in a desert as you do in the winter:

- Make sure your car is in good repair, especially the cooling system.
- Make sure your spare tire is in good shape and full of air.
- Travel on the full half of your gas tank.
- Tell someone your route and your expected arrival time.
- Stay on well-maintained roads; soft sand can strand you as easily as mud or snow.
- Carry an up-to-date emergency kit in your car that includes:
  - » Water for the car
  - » Extra belts
  - » Basic tools
  - » Tow chain

» Jumper cables
» Flares
» Shovel
» Fire extinguisher
» Water to drink
» Water purification tablets
» Plastic for solar still (6′ × 6′)
» High-energy food
» Blanket
» Matches
» Flashlight
» Radio and batteries
» First-aid kit
» Pocketknife

## If Stranded in the Desert

- Stay calm.
- Stay out of the midday sun. Make your own shade if you have to.
- Consider staying with the car; it is more easily found, provides shelter, and contains many resources.
- If in a remote area, make a smoky signal fire. Flashers can be seen a long distance at night.
- Water is the main need if you are stranded in a desert. Make a solar still: dig a hole and place a clean pint- or quart-sized container in the bottom. Fill the hole with leaves and anything else that has moisture in it. Stretch a sheet of plastic over the hole and place a small rock on the sheet so that the low point hangs over the container. Try to keep the bottom side of the plastic clean. Drinking water will condense on it and flow to the cup. Make sure the plastic seals the hole airtight and you could get up to a quart of water in a day. Each time you open and reseal the hole it will take a couple of hours to start producing water again.
- Look for animal tracks or circling birds to guide you to nearby water sources. Follow the instructions on your water purification tablets to make the water safe to drink.

- Don't leave the car if you don't know exactly where you are going. If you have to travel, go in the cool mornings and evenings. Remember that no matter how hot the day, the nights could get chilly.

## Beat the Heat with Common Sense

When we experience a combination of high heat and reduced power in the city, things get miserable quickly. Here are some tips to beat a heat wave in the city:

- Stay out of the heat. Close blinds on the sunny side of the house. Move to your basement if you have one. Run a fan if there is electricity—moving air helps you stay cooler. Use a spray bottle to mist a little water on your exposed skin. The evaporation will give a little cooling.
- Get enough to drink. Drink a little all of the time, even before you are thirsty. If your urine gets darker, drink more. Avoid all alcohol and caffeinated drinks; they flush water from your system.
- Eat smart and have balanced meals. Go for no-cook meals—they don't add heat to your house. Be sure to get enough salt and potassium (bananas or sports drinks—check the label).
- Rest a lot. Don't do any more strenuous activities than required. Hard work costs you two to four quarts of water per hour. Drugs such as antihistamines and thyroid medications can interfere with your body's ability to cool itself—check with your doctor before any strenuous activities.
- Wear loose-fitting clothes and a wide brim hat for all outdoor activities.
- Make sure your pets get plenty of water too.
- Heat waves are especially hard on the elderly. Check frequently on your neighbors during long hot spells. Offer to do some of their outdoor chores. Invite them to your cool house if theirs is hot or they can't afford to keep an air conditioner running. Encourage them to drink plenty.

Emergency preparedness:
Do one thing today.

# Power Outage

## When the Lights Go Out

When the lights go out, every toy on the floor becomes a hazard. Every piece of furniture becomes an obstacle. All activities cease while you try to remember the last place you saw the flashlight. Does it work? Does it have batteries? Are all the pieces even in one place? Once you find the light, everybody wants to use it to search for other lights or to continue whatever activity they were engaged in when the lights went out. A power failure is always inconvenient but rarely life threatening by itself. It can, however, lead to disorientation, injuries, and panic. Here are a few tips for preparing for the lights to go out.

Keep one flashlight in an easy-to-get-to, easy-to-find location. You have to be able to find this flashlight by touch, so know its exact location. Designate this flashlight as the no-kidding emergency light and threaten severe consequences to anyone who even thinks about using it for some other project or game. Buy some inexpensive lights for other uses, so that your emergency light stays put. Make sure your no-kidding emergency light is a good flashlight. It should have a large, bright beam and take standard batteries. If it is a bulb flashlight, as opposed to an LED light, buy an extra bulb or two. Keep a spare set of batteries in a nearby, easy-to-find location. Some people like the rechargeable flashlights that plug into the wall because they are always ready and always in the same place. The hand-generator flashlights will do in a pinch, but all that squeezing gets tiring quickly, so make sure it is not your only option.

The purpose of the no-kidding emergency light is to enable you to find and set up other light sources. It's a good idea to have more than one emergency source of light. You have many options:

- **Flashlights**: just in the past few years, a lot of really good flashlight options have come on the market. We have an array of solid, well-engineered, and energy-miser options. LED lights lead the pack here. Be prepared to spend a little bit extra to get a flashlight that is sturdy and reliable. Look in outdoor stores for options that are hands-free (headlamps), water resistant, or have extra-bright or extra-wide beams. Get flashlights that are only flashlights, and not attached to some other appliance. Get some extras for everyone in the family. Make sure the batteries are a common size and keep enough on hand.
- **Battery-powered lantern**: For area lighting, this is the safest choice, without a doubt. The main drawback is the cost of replacing batteries. If you use a battery-powered lantern often for camping, you might find it less expensive to invest in rechargeable batteries and a charger. LED options have been developed here too, so now might be a good time to upgrade.
- **Propane lantern**: Because there is a flame, these lanterns require considerably more supervision than battery-powered devices. Keep matches and lanterns out of the reach of children, and *never leave any open flame unattended*! Keep a window slightly open for fresh air. Propane lanterns are convenient and have become less expensive in the past few years. The propane bottles are easy to store safely. Also store some extra mantles, and make sure you know where to find the matches. If your family still has an old white gas lantern hanging around, it is time to upgrade to battery power. The white gas lanterns have a liquid fuel that you must also store (in an approved safety container and outside of the house and garage), and refilling can be messy and dangerous.
- **Candles**: Candles are inexpensive, readily available, and easily storable, but should be considered a back-up option. They don't give as much light as other options and are a fire risk. Lit candles should never be left unattended or in the care of children. Tall, thin candles are less stable and require a candleholder. Dripping wax can leave a mess, and if it splashes on your hand, you might be surprised

into dropping the candle, creating a fire hazard. Tub candles and tea candles are more stable and less likely to drip wax, and you can buy candle lanterns to hold them and protect the flame from the draft. Be careful, though, candle lanterns can get hot on top.

- **Kerosene lamp**: Several kerosene lamps are popular, including the hurricane lantern and the "Aladdin" lamp. Observe proper fire safety rules, and you'll need to crack open a window for fresh air. These larger light sources also give off considerable heat but sometimes leave a kerosene smell. It's a good idea to store an extra wick, some extra mantles, and even an extra glass chimney. You'll also need to store kerosene. Use an approved safety container and keep out of reach of children.
- **Chemical sticks**: These don't give much light, but they can be seen from a long distance away and are quite safe. Some commercial vendors tout light sticks as a good light source if you suspect a gas leak, but the best advice if you suspect a gas leak is to leave the house immediately until professionals can fix the problem.

After you have prepared for a power outage, have a lights-out practice or two, either pre-announced or pop quiz style, to make sure everyone knows what to do. Make it fun for the kids by fixing a snack or playing games, and they might even develop a positive attitude about emergency preparedness.

## An Extended Power Outage Can Test Your Preparedness

Think for a minute of all the ways electricity touches your life: the alarm clock to wake you up, the lights that illuminate your predawn house, the refrigerator that keeps your food from spoiling, the range or stove for cooking breakfast, the furnace blower to heat your house, the automatic garage door opener to let the car out, the gas pumps at the filling station, the traffic lights on the road, cash registers at the grocery store, the computer on your desk at work, the TV, the radio, the stereo, the can opener, the water softener, the iron, and on and on. And that doesn't count the zillion devices that we use all day and recharge all night: phones, tablet computers, electronic readers. Our lives are so dependent upon electricity that it's hard to imagine being without it. But there are many scenarios that could deprive us of this convenience for a long time. Superstorm Sandy in 2012 brought high winds that took down trees and power lines with them. It was such a large storm—over a thousand miles across—that the damage covered a large area and repair crews were stretched to find and fix all of the outages. Most of the people affected by Sandy were without power for three to five days. But a significant number were without power for days longer, and in some cases, weeks. Sandy also highlighted the vulnerability of the aging power infrastructure. An accident or terrorist act at a major power plant or two, and large areas would be without electricity for an extended period.

While short-term power outages are frequent enough that we don't worry about getting through them, long-term outages could really test our emergency preparations. Life without electricity is very different from normal—it takes more time, more effort, and all of your patience to do anything. An outage of a few minutes or a few hours can be annoying (you always forget how many clocks have to be reset . . .), but life in an extended power outage is vastly different.

Several years ago, elementary and secondary school children from New England shared their thoughts about the good and bad aspects of their extended power outage. Many of them commented on meeting new people at the shelter, doing things other than watching TV like reading, talking to family, playing games in front of the fireplace, having dinner by candlelight, and partying with neighbors when it was over. But they also noted that there were hard parts, too, like stinky toilets, carrying water for flushing, food spoiling in the refrigerator, damage to houses and cars, soot and smoke in the house from emergency heaters, and boredom.

So, what do you do if there is a power outage? First, check to see if any of your neighbors have lights. If your nearest neighbors have power, then you need to look at your own fuse box or circuit breaker panel. Disconnect or turn off large appliances first. Check the main breaker; if it is tripped, turn it off and then on. Then turn on lights and appliances one at a time and see if the breaker trips again. If it does, it could indicate a faulty appliance or an overloaded circuit. If you are uncertain what to do or can't find the problem, call an electrician. If you have a fuse box with screw-in fuses, a blackened fuse window indicates a blown fuse. If you have cartridge fuses, many of them give no indication when they blow. You'll need to check them with an ohmmeter or call an electrician. If you find a fuse blown because of overload, *do not replace it with a larger fuse!* This is often the cause of electrical fires. Shift some lights or appliances to another circuit.

If the electrical outage is widespread, turn on your battery-powered or hand-cranked radio to find out how widespread and how long it is predicted to last. What you do next depends on what season it is. In the winter you'll need to make a decision about staying in your home or evacuating to a friend's house or a heated shelter. This will likely depend on whether you have a heat source or not. Just because the power goes out does not necessarily mean that the gas goes out. But even if you have gas, the electricity to blowers will be missing. You may need an alternate heat source. A fireplace or wood stove with a good wood supply, or a kerosene heater gives you some options to stay home in extreme weather. In the summer, you may still need to decide if you'll go to a shelter in extreme weather, but exposure is less of an issue.

A word about generators: during Sandy, generators, fuel, and replacement parts were scarce commodities. If you choose to invest in a generator—and they can be pricey—be sure to do your homework. How much power will you need to generate? You will not be able to replace your entire house service, but you might be able to run your furnace fan, or your freezer for a few hours a day. Well before an emergency, have an electrician help you figure out if you can connect your generator into your house panel, and exactly how to do it safely. Practice it often enough that you can do under trying circumstances, like dark or cold. Be sure you properly store fuel and common spare parts. Estimate how much fuel you might need and get a little extra. Remember, you are not trying to maintain your pre-outage lifestyle, you are trying to survive. Also, generators accounted for a significant fraction of deaths and injuries, so follow all safety precautions, especially those about only running it outdoors and managing the exhaust so it doesn't get back into the house.

You'll also have to pay attention to your freezer and refrigerator. A full freezer with good door seals will keep food safely frozen for about two days; less if the door is opened often. Extra space in the freezer or poor seals will reduce the time. If the weather is below freezing, you can put frozen goods in secure containers (animal protection) and place them outside. Note: after a power outage, examine your frozen foods, they may be safely refrozen if they still contain ice crystals or if they remain below 40 degrees. Use refrozen foods as soon as possible. If in doubt, throw it out; risking your health isn't worth a few pennies of food.

## In Winter

- Bundle up in layers that you can add and remove as you warm and chill.
- Stay moderately active to produce body heat. Don't work up a sweat.
- If you have a fireplace or other temporary heat source, open cabinets under sinks to get the warmed air to the water pipes. If your house is unheated and temperatures are significantly below freezing, you may want to drain water pipes or put antifreeze in undrainable traps. Note: Antifreeze is toxic and should not be put into drinking-water pipes.
- Drink lots of water—dehydration is a cold weather risk—and eat hearty meals for energy.

## In Summer

- Your refrigerator and freezer will warm up much more quickly. Eat cool foods as soon as possible. Don't take any chances with spoiled food.
- Drink lots of liquids and eat balanced meals.

## Tips from Sandy Survivors that are Applicable In Any Outage

- Keep your short-term emergency kit up to date. Be sure it contains a manual can opener.
- Keep lanterns and flashlights in working order—it's tougher to service a flashlight after the lights go out, and stores (if they open at all without power . . .) may sell out of lights and batteries first. If you live in a high-rise building, your elevators will not work, and stairwells rarely have windows; you'll need a good flashlight just to get out to the street.
- Store cash. ATMs and credit card machines may not work, even if stores have supplies.

- Don't tough out a power outage alone. Check on neighbors, especially the elderly or the ill.
- You need a lot more food than you think if it is cold, especially if everyone is out of school and home from work all day. But all of the food in the world won't help you if it is inedible. Store what you eat. And store some extra: will you really be able to turn away your children's friends?
- Make sure you have enough toilet paper. Enough said.
- Store some luxury and comfort items too. You'll need that reward after a few days.
- In the winter, it gets dark early. Nights can be really long. Store some cards, store some games, and keep your guitar in tune.
- The power company recommends you turn off appliances and lights and turn them on one at a time when service is restored. This avoids a large load on the system when the power finally comes back on and helps prevent another immediate power failure.
- Don't try to beat it by yourself—go out to dinner if the rest of town has power. Take your friend up on his offer to let you use his shower. And if you are the friend with the shower, offer it to your friends.
- You can still cook outdoors on a gas or charcoal grill, but do not bring the device into an enclosed space to cook; gases from incomplete combustion are deadly.
- Store some paper plates and utensils. They conserve water, and cleanup is easier.
- Pay attention to electrical appliances you use for personal grooming—electric razor, curlers, curling iron, and so on—and make nonelectrical arrangements if these devices are essential to your well-being.
- Get an extra charging cord for your phone. Get two, and keep one handy all of the time; you never know when you will find a socket with power to charge your device for a few critical minutes.
- Although public safety folks tell us that a traffic light outage means a four-way stop, to many it might mean a "no-way stop." Drive defensively.

- Remember: Everyone around you is also at his or her breaking point. After Hurricane Sandy, there were fights over fuel and supplies.
- Be patient. Realize that even simple chores without utilities are harder and more time intensive.

Emergency preparedness:
Do one thing today.

# High Winds, Tornadoes, Hurricanes

## When the Wind Blows

When you think of high winds, you probably think of the extreme winds of hurricanes along the Gulf and Atlantic coasts. Perhaps you think of tornadoes with their short-lived but destructive winds. While these are certainly the storms that get the most attention, virtually all parts of the country are vulnerable to high winds of some kind: hurricanes, tornadoes, thunderstorms/microbursts or other extreme conditions. The result is often the same: houses are damaged, trees are broken and downed, utilities are interrupted for hours or days. Sometimes there are even injuries and deaths. Whatever the cause, here are a few things you can do to minimize the impact of a windstorm.

Before a windstorm you should make sure that your short-term emergency kit is complete, current and available. Every six months or so, you should review the contents of your kit and replace time-sensitive items like medications, water, and some foods. Replace items that were borrowed since the last update. Make sure that batteries are fresh and that clothing fits.

Staying informed of weather conditions is also important. Meteorologists can predict the conditions that lead to wind-producing storm systems and will issue watches and warnings when conditions require. Current weather conditions are broadcast on NOAA weather radios, public radio stations, or TV, so it is important that your emergency kit contain a battery-powered radio and fresh batteries, in case the power goes out.

If you have sufficient warning, prepare your house and yard. Bring in the trash cans, lawn furniture, and other loose items that can become destructive missiles. All throughout the year you should pay attention to your yard, and remove old or unbalanced trees, and trim dead branches and those close to utility lines. In hurricane country, it would be wise to have plywood window covers already cut to install quickly. In tornado country, you will need to find or build a tornado shelter.

During a windstorm, stay indoors if possible. If roof-mounted swamp coolers or antennas become loose during a windstorm, it is safest to let the storm abate before getting on the roof to assess damage and start repairs. If you must go out in the storm, avoid downed power lines. If you see one, always assume that it is live and stay away. If you must drive, watch for debris on the roads. Also remember that intersections with traffic lights become four-way stops if the power is out. When in doubt, yield the right of way. Of course, high-profile vehicles, like campers, RVs and some panel trucks and lightly loaded trailers are at risk in high winds.

## Tornadoes in the South and Midwest

Every year in the US, about 1,250 tornadoes touch down, although in extreme years, it can be closer to 1,800. They leave trails from a hundred feet to hundreds of yards wide, and from a few blocks to miles long. On average, about seventy people die each year in tornadoes. Although tornadoes are reported in all months and all states, most tornadoes occur between the first of March and the end of August. In the United States, most tornadoes occur in Nebraska, Kansas, Missouri, Oklahoma and Texas, although they occur in almost all states. Most tornado damage and destruction comes from high winds and flying debris. Occasionally lightning strikes and locally low atmospheric pressures cause damage.

Preparation consists primarily of staying alert to weather conditions, having a plan for seeking safe shelter, and having a short-term emergency kit current and available. When officials issue a tornado watch, it means that tornadoes are possible. A tornado warning means that a tornado has been sighted. If you see a tornado, or if officials direct you, go to your safe shelter. In a house or small building, go to the basement or storm cellar. If there is no basement, seek an interior room, closet, or hallway—a room without windows—on the lowest level. Get under a sturdy table and protect yourself from flying debris by covering with a quilt or mattress. Stay put until the danger has passed. Mobile homes are not safe in tornadoes, even if anchored. Seek shelter in a permanent structure.

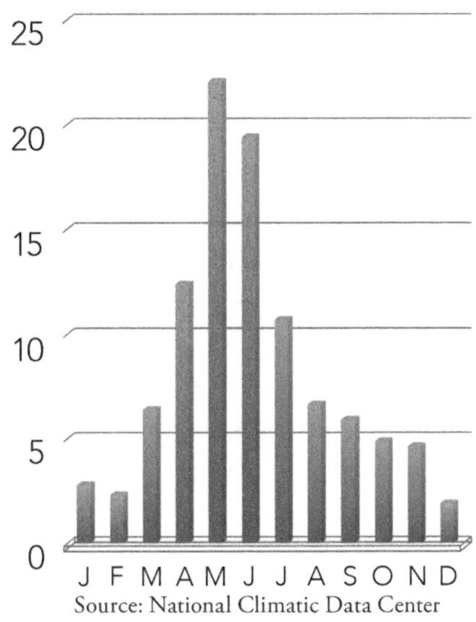


If you are in a car and you see a tornado, stop and seek shelter in a nearby building if there is one. If you are in a car on the road and you get hit by flying debris, pull over, park, and leave your seatbelt on. Try to get your face below the window level and cover yourself with a blanket or coat. If you can clearly see that you can safely get lower than the level of the road, leave the car and seek shelter in a ditch or low spot that doesn't have power lines running over it. Don't go under a bridge or overpass. Lie face down and put your hands over your head. A culvert may not be a safe choice if there is rain since flash flooding is more dangerous and more likely than the tornado itself.

In a public place, go to the designated shelter area. If no area is designated, go to an interior, glassless room on the lowest floor. Stay out of elevators since power outages are common. Avoid buildings with wide-span roofs like auditoriums, theaters, and gyms. A smaller room without windows, like a bathroom, an office, or a maintenance closet would be a safer place to ride out the danger.

After the tornado, use caution getting around. Downed power lines and foot hazards like broken glass and debris may abound. Wear heavy gloves and work boots for cleanup. It is estimated that fifty percent of tornado-related injuries occur after the tornado has passed. Also, keep tuned to the weather news, since tornadoes are often spawned in a weather front that may continue to affect you.

### Hurricanes along the Gulf and Atlantic Coasts

Hurricanes are a real threat, but they are much larger and more predictable storms than tornadoes. Forecasters are now able to give two to five days' notice of an impending hurricane and its predicted path, so pay attention to weather conditions.

Hurricane Katrina, and Superstorm Sandy showed clearly that you should evacuate when authorities say you should leave, and maybe even sooner. Don't stay in harm's way. Board up and move inland as soon as possible. Although the winds and the battering rain are damaging, the storm surge—the huge dome of sea water blown ashore by the storm—is historically far more dangerous and far more damaging than the wind. Moving away from the coast takes you out of the way of the storm surge. Heavy rains also make inland flooding a possibility, so stay away from low-lying or flood-prone areas.

It is important to evacuate to a safe area early to avoid traffic jams and road closures due to storm or debris. Key to a swift evacuation is a streamlined checklist for securing the home or business. Make sure that you know exactly what preparations you want to make, and that you have the materials on hand. For example, permanent storm shutters or pre-cut plywood sheets (5/8-inch marine grade) will greatly speed window protection. Tape will not prevent windows from breaking. Secure outdoor furniture. Fuel your car. If you practice driving the evacuation route occasionally, it will be familiar in the stress of an emergency. When evacuating, take your short-term emergency kits and all of the extra water you can. Make plans about where you will reunite with family members if separated. Use your designated out-of-state contact to facilitate communication with your family.

After a hurricane, stay tuned to TV or radio to find out about special conditions and emergency responses that may apply to your area. Return home only when officials say it is safe. If you cannot return home and need to find a shelter, text SHELTER and then your zip code (e.g., SHELTER 12345) to 4FEMA (43362) to find the nearest shelter.

Realize that flooding may contaminate food and water sources and take proper hygienic precautions. During recovery efforts, pay attention to the warning signs of stress, exhaustion and fatigue and pace yourself accordingly. Heart attacks kill, too.

• • •

High wind emergency preparedness, whether for tornadoes in Kansas, or hurricanes in Florida, consists mainly of paying attention to the weather and keeping a disaster supplies kit current and available for quick evacuation. This is good advice for almost all emergencies, anyway.

Emergency preparedness:
Do one thing today.

# Floods

## Climate Change, Unexpectedly Extreme Weather

Over the past several years, scientists have linked increases in atmospheric greenhouse gases in the atmosphere to an increasing temperature trend: global warming. Scientific studies have proliferated, and the debate has become heated, no pun intended. Without joining the debate on why the climate is warming, let's discuss the implications for your family's preparedness.

No matter the cause, the data indicate that global temperatures are rising. When this effect is added to normal climate and weather variations, such as El Nino/La Nina (seasonally warmer and cooler water off the western coast), and just the random variability in weather patterns, it seems to predict more extreme weather. There are several possible effects:

- Warmer oceans deliver more moisture and energy to the atmosphere, resulting in bigger, more powerful storms, affecting more people, more often.
- Melting polar ice will increase sea levels, thereby increasing flood risks for more people along populous coasts.
- Changes in weather patterns mean that some regions will be surprised by either much hotter or much colder extremes than history has prepared them for.
- Long-term changes in climate patterns can result in flooding in some places and drought in others.

Scientists don't know specifics. Will winter in Des Moines be harsher or milder than usual? Will the spring rains in Texas be heavier or lighter than usual? Will there be more hurricanes and twisters or fewer? The prediction technology is not accurate enough to tell.

But in preparedness terms, this uncertainty is not different from any other season or any other year. In fact, the potential for severe weather is always with us. If the climate wasn't warming and changing, could we let our guard down? Probably not—basic family preparedness principles are the same, with or without climate change. If there are more extreme winter storms, respond as you learned in chapter 15. If there are more power outages because of more high winds, respond as you learned in chapters 17 and 18. Climate change may be happening, but it won't change how your family prepares.

## Seasonal Flooding

In many parts of the world, spring means floods. Although higher elevation areas like the mountain states do not have as much risk of the types of floods that inundate large river valleys, there are still any number of ways individual homes can be flooded, from inside or from out.

### Before a Flood

#### *Know the Risks*

- Drainages, from local rivers to neighborhood ditches, can receive more spring melt and storm runoff than they can handle. FEMA continually updates flood risk maps that cover the entire United States and show where flooding can be expected (https://msc.fema.gov/portal/home).
- A high water table can flood homes from beneath. Water tables rise and fall seasonally.
- Homes in colder climates have some risk of pipes freezing and bursting. A cold spell coupled with a power outage could mean trouble for pipes in outside walls.
- Even a small plumbing leak in any weather can cause problems. One family came back after a week-long summer vacation to find an upstairs leak had flooded all of the levels below. The ceilings collapsed; standing water ruined walls and furniture. The house had to be completely refinished.

- A small amount of soil settling near your foundation can allow thunderstorm runoff from the roof to puddle near the house, or run into window wells, flooding basements.
- City storm drains, if plugged with dirt or debris, can back up and flood nearby property.

*Know Your Insurance Coverage*

- A typical homeowner's policy covers flooding that originates within the home (like broken pipes, overflowing fixtures, and so on) but typically does not cover flooding from outside. External flood insurance usually requires an additional policy or endorsement. When you apply for flood insurance (talk to your agent about options and costs) the company will inspect your property or consult a FEMA map to determine if you are in a high-risk area for flooding, or a"floodplain." If you are, flood coverage could cost more. Assess the risks to your property to determine whether you should spend your money mitigating the flooding risks or investing in insurance.
- Make sure the policy pays replacement value for your possessions; otherwise your reimbursement will be depreciated to current value and may not allow you to replace everything at today's prices. Raising the deductible limit—the amount you pay before the insurance coverage takes over—reduces premium costs.
- Inventory your possessions with lists, photographs, videos, and receipts. Make a copy and put this information, along with insurance policies, in a watertight container in safe place. Store the originals in a safe-deposit box or other off-site location.

*Prepare Now to Minimize Future Damage*

- Make drainage modifications to your property before it rains. Put extensions on downspouts to get roof water away from the house. Use decorative berms and raised gardens to channel water or provide a few extra inches of flood protection.
- Keep roof gutters free of debris, and assure downspouts flow freely.
- Keep storm drains and culverts near your house free of debris.
- Insulate pipes against freezing. Pipes in outside walls are most vulnerable.

- Protect valuable papers, books, photos and heirlooms. Store them in watertight plastic tubs. Store them off the floor on shelves or pallets.
- Everyone in the family should know where all utility shutoffs are. Visibly mark shutoffs so a friend or neighbor can find them easily.
- When you go on a trip, have a trusted neighbor or friend regularly check your house inside and out. Then someone has access to your house if there is an emergency while you are gone.

## During a Flood

- Stay out of floodwater. Water only inches deep can be swift and unbalancing. Floodwater can also be full of sewage, oil, gasoline or other chemicals. Do not drive through flooded areas.
- Be prepared to evacuate. Prepare a short-term emergency kit for quick action, and keep a list of other things you want to grab when the time comes.
- Follow instructions from local authorities. Flood situations can deteriorate rapidly.
- Shut off electricity in a flooded home until you can be sure there is no electrocution hazard.
- Pilot lights in furnaces and water heaters can be extinguished by floodwater, requiring the gas valve be shut off.

## After a Flood

- Make recovery efforts safe. Stay out of germ-laden floodwaters, wear gloves and safety glasses/goggles, and wash hands frequently. Discard food that has come in contact with floodwater. Be aware of electrocution hazards. Wear sturdy boots and gloves.
- Carefully examine your home for damage. Check for structural damage to the foundation and bearing walls. Inspect piping for gas leaks, damage, and unsafe electrical situations.
- Listen for warnings about drinking tap water, which could be temporarily contaminated.
- Damp conditions can cause fungus growth, which aggravates asthma and allergies.

- Inventory your damaged possessions. Take pictures, make notes. Keep detailed records of cleanup costs for insurance claims.
- Professional disaster recovery companies can assist in rapid recovery with manpower and heavy-duty equipment. Insurance companies often accept their damage assessments without question. Make sure you know if your policy covers their services.
- Freeze valuable wet books and papers as cold as possible, as soon as possible. Restoration experts have a better chance of saving them later.
- If water has sat in your home for any length of time, you will likely have to demolish all of the interior finish: carpets, flooring, walls.
- Be aware of stress and exhaustion, and the tendency to try to do everything at once. Realize that recovery may take many days or weeks. Eat well and rest often.

## Hurricane Storm Surge

Another type of flooding associated with always-extreme hurricanes is storm surge. As dramatic and frightening as the wind of a hurricane can be, and as intimidating as the fierce rains can be, the storm surge of a hurricane is by far the most deadly and the most damaging to property. In the northern hemisphere, tropical storms and hurricanes slowly swirl in a counterclockwise direction. Because hurricanes form and strengthen at sea, the high winds push up a dome of seawater ahead of them, on the right-hand side, when seen from a satellite. The sea level can rise up to twenty feet above normal, depending on the location, and can span hundreds of miles of coastline, so it is important to pay attention to the path of the center of the storm, where the winds will be highest, but also pay attention to coastal areas to the east and north of the point of landfall. These are the area vulnerable to storm surge. Storm surges add to the normal tides, so a combination of high tide and storm surge can be quite damaging. Superstorm Sandy came ashore in southern New Jersey, and the accompanying storm surge devastated a long shoreline from New Jersey through New York and even farther north. The high waves eroded beaches and the surge overtopped breakwaters and levees built to withstand smaller storms.

Local and federal governments place beach dunes, soil and rock barriers and levees to protect communities, but they are not foolproof, and each installation has its limits of protection. And as ocean levels rise and storms become larger, what might have been adequate fifty years ago may not protect you today. Engineered shoreline protections can be defeated by a high surge, allowing water to destroy houses, roads, and utilities, and to compromise sewage treatment plants, underground (and above ground) fuel tanks, and hazardous material storage. Much of the densely populated Atlantic and Gulf Coast coastlines have an elevation less than ten feet above mean sea level, so the potential for destruction is high.

You can avoid storm surge by knowing where it is likely to happen (near the coast) and avoiding purchasing property there. FEMA's flood maps assess flooding and storm surge risks, so your realtor and your insurance agent can help you check it out. But there is a great attraction to the seashore, and many houses have been in families for generations. So if you own shore property, just realize that there are times it may not be protected.

The best thing—really, the only thing—to do when you are in the path of a storm surge is to evacuate. In Sandy, some people tried to ride it out to protect their homes, but their homes were still devastated, and they and their rescuers were needlessly endangered. And some died. So when authorities warn you to leave, leave. You should have a couple of days' notice to grab your short-term emergency kits and other supplies and get to that inland location.

Before you leave, move furniture and items you want to save to an upper floor. Turn off the electricity and water. Authorities may also instruct you to turn off the gas. If you do, you will need to get the gas company to come turn it back on after the storm. If the damage has been widespread, that could take days.

After the storm has passed, only go to your home when authorities say the water has receded and it is safe. Your basement may be full of water, mud, and sand, and will likely need to be gutted. Stay out of the water, and wear gloves and glasses or goggles if you have to work near it; as noted above, the water is likely to be full of stuff you don't want on your skin or in your eyes. While putting your life back together, pace yourself, eat right and drink plenty of water, no matter the season. Obey official instructions about what to do with wastes and debris, so you don't create another problem outside of your house.

Climate change and extreme weather may cause flooding problems, but the principles of preparation don't change—do what you can before the storm to minimize damage, get out of the way of the storm and the flooding, and use caution and common sense to recover.

Emergency preparedness:
Do one thing today.

# Wildfires

There have always been wildfires. Nature (and humans) use fires to manage wildlands like forests, grasslands, and prairies. But climate scientists warn that increasing global temperatures can raise the risk of natural fires through vegetation-drying droughts, fire-spreading winds, and unpredictable weather events. And as more humans move into or near natural environments and live, work, and recreate in wildlands, human-caused fires have also increased, and losses of life and property can be devastating. Fire prevention and response professionals lament that there is no longer a fire season, but that fire risks are now year-round. And even though you may not think you live near a wildland boundary, embers from wildfires can travel long distances to threaten structures in seemingly safe places. Despite wildfires' unpredictability and the potential to affect large areas, there are many common-sense preparations we can make to minimize our risks and mitigate damage and loss. Studies show that a majority of structures lost might have been saved if some basic fire-safe practices had been followed.

## Before a Wildfire

### Know Your Risk

Objectively evaluate the proximity of your home or business to wildlands. Wildlands are not just forests and undeveloped prairies, but also occur in urban areas in the form of large wild parks, parkways, protected habitat zones, riparian areas, and undeveloped or unmaintained swaths of native land. Because thermal updrafts and wind can carry burning embers a long distance, if your structure is within one mile of wildlands—whether in an urban area or not—you are in a wildfire risk zone. Check with community officials and emergency responders to learn policies and procedures that will be applicable in your specific area.

## Prepare Your House

A fire-defensible house begins with construction methods and materials:

- The roof is the most vulnerable surface for embers to attack. Composition shingles, metal, or tile roofs are most defensible. Wood shingle roofs are the least protective. Make sure all roof vents have a 1/8-inch screen, both those on the roof, and those in the eaves. Make sure the eaves are fully enclosed with soffit and fascia.
- Gutters can collect flammable materials like evergreen needles and deciduous leaves. Keep roof clear, and regularly clean out gutters. Prune tree branches within ten feet of the roof.
- Houses with brick or stucco veneers are most protective; wooden and vinyl siding are least protective.
- Windows can be broken by radiant heat, even if the fire is still at a distance. A broken window is a common entry point for embers. Single-pane, and large windows are most vulnerable. Install a minimum of double-pane windows, with at least one layer of tempered glass. For wildland-facing windows, use noncombustible and non-melting frames.
- Balconies and decks can collect embers. Use heavy timber or non-combustible decking materials. Minimize the amount of combustible material stored on balconies and decks, and keep the underdeck free of weeds, leaves, or other fuels. Move woodpiles away from decks and store propane tanks in the garage.
- Fences that are combustible can lead fire up to the house. Consider replacing the nearest five feet of fencing with non-combustible materials. Keep fence lines clear of weeds, leaves and flammable debris.
- Assure your external garage doors shut tightly to prevent embers from blowing through gaps. Store flammable liquids in fire protection cabinets, and assure clear space around power equipment,

and furnace or water heater installations in the garage. Mount fire extinguishers in easily accessible locations and check/maintain them regularly.

## Prepare Your Landscape

- Pay special attention to the five-foot zone nearest your house. Consider non-combustible landscape materials such as rock mulch. Plant low-height ground covers and succulents for this space. Carefully maintain this space to remove build-up of leaves and other debris, and frequently prune out dead branches and thicker undergrowth. Get rid of scrap lumber piled against the foundation.
- Store firewood and other combustible materials at least thirty feet from the house.
- Prune overhanging trees to at least ten feet from the roof, and frequently remove dead branches. Conscientiously care for trees to make sure they are properly hydrated and free from insects and diseases that make them more flammable.
- Consider landscaping in vegetation "groups" to break up continuous fuel trails in the yard, and minimize "fuel ladders" like intermediate height shrubbery that connects ground plants to tree branches.
- Assess the vulnerability of your property to properties that adjoin yours. A good rule of thumb is to manage defensible space to about a hundred feet from the house. Coordinate fire protection with neighbors. If your property adjoins public property, contact local officials to help manage build-up of fuels.
- Make sure your driveway can accommodate emergency equipment. Help keep hydrants clear and visible. Make sure your address is clearly visible on the house, the curb, and the mailbox.

## Prepare Your Family

- Create a family emergency plan (see Chapter 2). This will include all kinds of possible scenarios, but make sure it includes wildfires if you are vulnerable. This plan should address communications, and evacuation. It should include a family fire plan, escape routes, and reuniting locations. Make sure you understand the policies and emergency plans of schools or daycares. Update yearly.

- Check with local officials about how they will communicate with residents in emergencies and sign up for phone and text alerts if they are on an opt-in basis.
- Keep fresh batteries in a portable radio tuned to a local station. This might be a primary channel for updates and evacuation orders. Evacuation routes and possible shelter locations may also be broadcast.
- Keep the interior of your home fire safe (see chapter 12). Install smoke detectors, carbon monoxide detectors, and fire extinguishers in accordance with manufacturer instructions. If your local fire department holds a fire prevention day, be sure to attend. You might get practice operating a fire extinguisher.
- Inventory (video, photo, or paper) your home belongings and store copies of the inventory with copies of other important papers in a safe-deposit box or other safe, off-site location. Check with your insurance agent to assure your policy is up to date and will cover replacement costs for your home and belongings. You can also check about fire coverage, though if you are in a vulnerable area, it may be difficult and expensive to obtain wildfire insurance. Following several years of extreme damage by wildfires across the nation, many insurance companies are scaling back the coverage and/or increasing the costs of premiums.
- Prepare short-term emergency kits as recommended in chapter 3 to give you resources in a wide variety of emergencies. A key consideration in wildfire scenarios is that the kit must be complete, up-to-date, and stored in an easily accessible place. In wildfires, especially, you may not get an extra minute to grab what you will take.
- Plan for evacuation as discussed in chapter 4. In a wildfire scenario, it is critical to know what evacuation routes might be available to you. Depending on the location and direction of movement of wildfire, some routes may be dangerous or unavailable. Keep a paper map of possible routes, and practice driving them frequently.

## When Wildfire Risk is High

- Revisit and review your family emergency plan with everyone in the family. Make sure they know when to act, what to do, who to tell, and where to go.

- If conditions make wildfire possible or if wildfires are already burning, keep up on the news. Listen for information about evacuation orders, routes, and shelters.
- Check the exterior of your home and the yard, and reduce any risks you may find, such as piles of flammable materials or debris. Clean leaves and needles off roofs and out of gutters. Clean up debris within five feet of the structure.
- Stay close to home in case evacuation orders are issued. Fill containers with water in case it becomes unavailable. A tub full of water can provide washing and flushing water. Dress in practical clothes, including sturdy shoes or boots. Natural fibers are better than synthetic materials.
- Connect with neighbors and friends. Arrange to assist the elderly and neighbors with mobility, health, or strength concerns. Stay hydrated for your own health.
- Put your emergency kits and other valuables you might want to save into the car. Your car will become your evacuation kit. Make sure your gas tank is full. Refresh your memory of the various possible routes. Charge your phone and extra phone power banks. Make sure you have an extra charging cable in your kit. Put extra filter masks in the car but remember these only can reduce smoke particles. They are not designed to replace oxygen or remove any toxic chemicals, like carbon monoxide or other organic compounds. Smoke might also trigger asthma attacks, so keep emergency inhalers close.
- Check in with your out-of-area contact so they know what to expect and how to help.

## During a Wildfire

- Use your best judgment to decide if you should evacuate even before officials make the call. If in doubt, go. If it turns out to be necessary later, you have an early start. If it turns out to be not necessary, no harm done except perhaps some inconvenience. Alert your out-of-area contact.

- Communicate with texts if phone doesn't work. Fires can destroy landlines and cell towers, reducing available resources; texts use less bandwidth.
- If time allows, close windows and doors, and remove curtains and drapes. Move flammable furniture away from windows that might break and allow embers in. Leave exterior lights on to give your house more visibility in smoke. Turn off gas at the meter, recognizing you will need to have the gas company reconnect it upon your return.
- Do *not* leave sprinklers or other water running. Responders will need all the supply that is available.

## Evacuation

- Survival is your first job. Your priority is to save lives, both yours and others you might help. This likely means evacuation and out-prioritizes protection of property and inconvenience. In the Camp Fire of Paradise, California, most deaths were attributed to delayed evacuation, and not because they evacuated into danger.
- If you didn't get an early evacuation start, leave as soon as officials direct. Listen for instructions on routes and shelter locations. The route and direction matters. If you have family and friends outside of the danger zone, you might arrange a "guest visit" to their house. (Pro-tip: make a reciprocal deal with them: they might need to evacuate to your home sometime.)

## Shelter-In-Place

- Because of the speed of the fire and the unpredictability of its direction, you might be prevented from evacuating. If trapped in your home, try to call 911 and let them know where you are. Shelter in your home until the fire passes. Shelter in an interior space away from outside walls, and make sure you have an escape route to the outside if the house catches fire. It might get hot, but if it is hot in the house, the temperatures will be much higher outside. Fill sinks and tubs and other containers with water. (Drink some of it, too, and stay hydrated.) Place wet towels under doors to reduce the smoke coming in. After the fire passes, assess your house, inside and out and put out any fires you find.

- If trapped while evacuating, listen to your radio for instructions on possible community shelters you might reach. During the Camp Fire, some people who couldn't get out of town successfully sheltered in a large parking lot.

## After a Wildfire

- Frequently it takes days for a wildfire to be contained. Exercise patience and wait for official approval to return.
- Approach your property cautiously. Wildfires create tremendous heat and hot spots and still-hot cinders may remain.
- Assess your entire property to get an idea of the scope of damage. Document carefully, both by photo as well as written notes. Your insurance company will need complete and accurate records and reports. Do the documentation early: in some disasters, volunteers frequently arrive to help before insurance adjusters can get to you.
- Protect your own health. First, wear personal protective equipment: sturdy shoes, nitrile gloves, as well as sturdy leather work gloves, long-sleeve pants and work shirts, wide brim hats. Particulate filtration masks may be needed as breezes can stir up ash.
- Go slow, rest often, hydrate obsessively, seek assistance for big tasks: it is just as easy to perish from over-exertion as it is to perish in the fire.
- Be aware that hazardous materials may be a problem. Contaminants released by the things the fire burned—plastics—are particularly bad actors. Fires also concentrate metals, and firefighting water and rainwater can transport them to groundwater and drinking water systems. Hazardous materials could have been released from nearby businesses or even containers stored in garages. Sewage, pesticides, fuels may all be in the environment.
- After a disaster, both repair scams and loan scams abound. Be careful when arranging loans or contracting for repairs.
  - » Be sure you understand and verify your insurance coverage and benefits.
  - » Obtain quotes from multiple sources. Bids should contain all of the assumptions used to make them: what will be done,

what materials will be used, when will the work be completed. Insist on references and diligently check them out. Also check out contractors with Better Business Bureau and other review sites on the Internet.

  - » Insist on written quotes, written contracts, and copies of bonding, insurance coverage, and licenses. Even though contractor help may be scarce, use common sense about contract terms and up front payments. A requirement for a full payment up front is a red flag.
  - » Beware the deal that is too good to be true: immediate repair, low cost, immediate signing discount. Don't sign anything you are not comfortable with.
  - » Only pay with credit card or check. Do not pay with cash, gift card, cryptocurrency, or electronic app. Withhold the last substantial payment until you are satisfied with the job.
  - » Not all difficulties with contractors are scams. If you get into difficulties with a contractor, seek to resolve it directly with the contractor first. Use registered mail with return receipt, and document all calls and conversations. If this doesn't work, there may be help from local consumer protection organizations. Legal assistance may also be required.

- Keep notes on what you learned in the disaster and its aftermath and use this information to update your protections for future disasters.

## Emergency preparedness: Do one thing today

# Technological Emergencies

## Technology Risks

Technology pervades our lives, from the communications and utilities that we use every day to the interdependent systems that keep stores supplied with goods and financial systems working. Technology is responsible for much of the comfort we enjoy. But like anything else, it can go wrong. Technological emergencies are related to those things around us that are manmade, as opposed to natural phenomena such as tornadoes and hurricanes. For example, they may include

- Utility failure (see chapter 17 for a power outage)
- Hazardous materials incidents (see chapter 14 for preparation and response)
- Chemical plant or refinery emergency
- Nuclear power plant emergency
- Widespread computer failure, whether from viruses or from solar storms

### Chemical Plant or Refinery Emergency

There are many locations that produce, handle, or store hazardous materials. Some of them are close to homes and schools. The vast majority of them are regulated and safe. In some cases, though, it is difficult to separate fact from noise to determine whether a real danger exists. How do you know if a facility near you is under control, or is an accident waiting to happen? Federal law provides citizens with the right to know about the dangers in their communities. Learning whether a facility is safe may be as simple as asking a few questions: What hazardous materials are involved? What processes are used? Where else has the process been tested? What happens to the wastes? What are the emergency plans? When are they tested? Who is in charge in an emergency? How are nearby residents alerted? Are there any unresolved legal or enforcement actions? If the answers to any of these questions are unsatisfactory, you can continue to ask them of facility officials or local, state, and federal authorities until you are satisfied with the answers.

Emergencies may consist of a chemical vapor plume mixed with steam or smoke, or a liquid spill that may be transported by sewers; storm drains; or natural creeks, rivers and drainages. As part of preparing for such emergencies, communities may have established local emergency planning committees (LEPCs), who compile appropriate information about hazardous materials producers, transporters, storage facilities, and users in the area. LEPCs may also have prepared plans—including ways to notify the public and actions people must take to deal with such emergencies. Contact your local public safety authorities, such as local governments or fire departments to find out what planning has been done. The information should be public.

In such incidents, you must avoid contact with, or inhalation or ingestion of potentially harmful chemicals. As in other hazardous materials incidents (see chapter 14), the public may be required to evacuate or to shelter in place. Sheltering in place means staying put in your home, and reducing the intake of outside air for a short duration while an airborne plume passes over. Your LEPC or public safety officials will tell you if it is a possibility for you, depending on the proximity of potential sources, and how to do it. You will likely be asked to keep some plastic sheeting, scissors, and duct tape in your emergency kit so you can seal off an interior room in which to stay for a short time, as needed. Other responses to chemical or refinery accidents may include restrictions on sources of fresh fruits, vegetables, livestock, and other foods from the potentially affected areas, depending on the chemical and the amount spilled.

## Nuclear Power Plant Emergency

Nuclear power plants produce about one-fifth of the nation's electricity by converting the heat of fission reactions to steam to turn generator turbines. There are several types and designs of reactors; and design, construction, and operations of nuclear power plants are overseen by the Nuclear Regulatory Commission (NRC). Despite rigorous regulation, extensive monitoring, and an enviable safety record overall, a generation of experience has taught us that accidents can happen, releasing potentially dangerous amounts of radioactivity into our environment. FEMA estimates that about three million Americans live within a ten-mile radius of a nuclear power plant.

The unique hazard with nuclear power plants is exposure to radiation, and the primary transport mechanism of concern to the public is through the air in a plume of steam or smoke. People exposed to the plume might receive radiation directly through the plume or particles that deposit, or "fall out" of the plume, or through inhalation of airborne particles. Of course, there are natural and daily sources of radiation such as dental or medical X-ray machines, or airplane flights, but radiation is cumulative, and a nuclear accident could increase our dose past safe limits.

Protection from radiation is based upon time and distance. The longer a person is exposed to a higher dose of radiation, the more serious the effects; the farther away you can get, the smaller the dose; most forms of radiation drop off sharply after just a short distance. Distance can be effectively enhanced by placing more mass between you and the source, as well. Time also plays a part, since radioactive materials decay over time. Some decay quickly in days or weeks, but there are some radioactive materials that persist for many years.

The key thing to know about nuclear accidents is the NRC requires operators to define two emergency planning zones to focus their response in case of an accident. Federal, state, and local governments all get involved. The first zone covers the area within a ten-mile radius of the reactors, which is at highest risk from direct exposure to radiation. The second zone expands to a fifty-mile radius where radioactive materials could get into the environment, water supplies, and food chain. Plant operators share these plans with State and local officials who then prepare their response plans to protect the public in case of an accident. Regulations require a large-scale practice every two years to make sure the plans stay up-to-date, are workable, and are effective.

In case of an accident, authorities may require evacuation, or they may request you shelter in place. If you live within ten miles of a power plant, you should annually receive emergency preparation information from the power plant or your local emergency officials. These materials will tell you if you might be asked to shelter in place, and how to do it. As with similar emergencies, you will likely be asked to keep some plastic sheeting, scissors, and duct tape in your emergency kit, so you can seal off an interior room in which to stay. Other responses to nuclear accidents may include restrictions on sources of fresh fruits, vegetables, livestock, and other foods from the potentially affected areas. If you have any question, call your local officials or your state's department of public safety.

## Widespread Computer Failure

At the end of 1999, there was much concern about a potentially widespread computer programming glitch where use of two-digit codes to designate years would result in a lot of confused computers when the new year turned over to 1-1-2000 (Year 2000, or "Y2K"), potentially wreaking havoc on our computerized world. There was a flurry of activity to reprogram everything from social security payment computers to coffee machines. In the end, whether because of the preparation or in spite of it, there was not much disruption, not much confusion, and certainly no havoc. But Y2K did highlight how dependent we are on computers and embedded chips, and how thoroughly everything from factory processes to just-in-time transportation systems to medical care could be turned upside down if it all goes wrong at the same time. Although a Y2K glitch is not on the horizon, after almost twenty-five years, our vulnerability to a wide-spread failure of computers is more profound than ever. How might a widespread computer failure be triggered? Hacking and malware (viruses), and—though less-likely—solar flares.

- **Hacking**: For reasons difficult to understand, there are people in the world who try to interrupt, disrupt, and corrupt everyone else's computer through viruses, Trojans, spam attacks, and so on. Many viruses are fairly innocuous and focused more at stealing personal information or hooking your computer into their network of "spambots." But more malignant types of hacking are certainly out there: the hacker extorting ransom payments by holding your data hostage; the hacker that is protesting some real or perceived injustice; the state-sponsored hacker whose job is to incapacitate an enemy's digital infrastructure. Since so much of our existence is tied up with computers and computer-controlled processes, and because we are so thoroughly interconnected, just the wrong pandemic of computer viruses could entangle big parts of our lives.

- **Solar flare**: The surface of the sun is quite active, and frequently has large energy releases with coronal mass ejections. Some years, solar activity is more frequent and more intense, and when the flare/ejection is pointed at the earth, the particles and energy can reach the earth as quickly as fifteen minutes or long as a couple of days later, causing a geomagnetic storm. In 1989, a large geomagnetic storm struck the earth and knocked a Canadian power system offline for nine hours. It interfered with shortwave radio transmissions, and temporarily disabled a weather satellite. Bigger events are possible and might have more impact.

Because computers are entangled in so many parts of our lives, it is difficult to predict possible effects, but we might see disruption of the following:

- **Banks/financial services**: Electronic transfers of funds could be interrupted, ATMs could stop issuing cash, debt payment records could be fouled up. Keep some paper copies of key records like mortgages, loans, insurance policies, and the payments you make against them. Also, keep some cash on hand to make purchases if electronic cash registers and credit card machines stop functioning for a time.
- **Production and distribution of food and consumer products**: Factories may have production problems, and warehousing/transportation companies may have distribution problems. They may be related to inventory shortages, or they may simply be unable to retrieve and fill orders from balky computers. Store a couple of weeks—a couple of months if you can—of food and essential products (think toilet paper). These potential shortages will not last long, but you want the option of not having to fight in store aisles for scarce supplies.
- **Telephones/communication systems**: The communications industry is one of the most technologically advanced, and, therefore, one of the most vulnerable to technological disruptions. For example, if the wrong satellite were to malfunction, millions could be without phones, data, news, or weather observation. On the plus side, the

communications industry also has one of the fastest turnovers for equipment and employs some of the best technical talent to enable it to quickly fix itself.

- **Utilities** (including water, power, natural gas, and sewage systems): Water purification and distribution, power distribution, and sewage processing plants all have electronic control systems, software, and embedded chips and, therefore, some exposure. Could malicious code or a small failure somewhere cascade into the entire system? The best preparation here is to store some water, prepare for a long-term power outage—have some backup plans for key needs.
- **Personal convenience**: Because of the prevalence of embedded and interconnected computer chips in just about everything, there might be further disruption to elevators, temperature controllers, ventilation systems, security systems, coffee makers, entertainment systems, watches, microwaves, ovens, and cars.

## How Do You Prepare?

One of the problems of trying to prepare for a technological emergency is the uncertainty of how widely it could affect an area and how it could affect you personally. Some people will feel no effect, some will have mild effects, some could have severe effects temporarily. This implies that preparing for technological emergencies should be like preparing for any other possible emergency, such as a severe winter storm. Here are things you could do—and should do—anyway:

- Stay informed, stay current, and agitate for community readiness, as well as family readiness.
- Update your readiness. Regularly pull out your short-term emergency kit and replace batteries, outdated food, any water that's not sealed, and clothes that children have outgrown. Take inventory and upgrade the items that aren't as functional as you want. Make sure that your water supply stays fresh, and take a look at the food you have stored. Rotate items that are close to expiring and replace them with fresh. How many days or weeks could you go without a trip to the grocery store? If you decide to buy more bulk food items, remember to only buy what your family normally eats anyway. Then replace it as you use it up. Don't forget to make sure

you have an up-to-date supply of important drugs and other critical medical supplies.

- Have some cash on hand, since an earthquake is just as likely to shake up banks, ATMs and stores as a technological event is. How much you store is a matter of preference. The more you have, the more you could lose to thieves. Some experts recommend from one to four weeks of cash. If you do decide to increase your cash on hand, do so a little at a time all through the year rather than waiting to do it all at once.
- Plan for an alternate source of heat if you live in a colder climate, like you've intended to do anyway. A power outage in the winter—from any source—can become a matter of safety. Also, extended power outages without alternate heating could result in frozen or burst pipes with additional inconvenience or damage.
- Organize your own computer, clean up the files and make a backup copy of important files on a separate device, like an external hard drive.
- Organize your financial records and keep recent paper copies around. Mortgages, deeds, loans, payment schedules, insurance of all kinds—maybe in a three-ring binder?
- Don't go buy a cabin in the woods (unless you were going to anyway . . .), don't buy an arsenal, don't convert all of your money to gold bars, and don't sever all ties with civilization just yet. Prepare for technology emergencies just like you would any other potential emergency.

Emergency preparedness:
Do one thing today.

# EPIDEMICS AND PANDEMICS

The difference between an epidemic and a pandemic is largely one of scale: an epidemic is an outbreak and rapid spread of an infectious disease in a defined area. An epidemic becomes a pandemic when it cannot be contained and spreads to a larger area; pandemics are usually considered global. This is a significant distinction because if there is an epidemic in a small village, outside entities can rally to help. In a pandemic, every location is fighting its own battle, and the sharing of resources may be more difficult. (For later reference, a disease becomes "endemic" when it becomes part of the normal landscape of pathogens that are always with us, like colds and flu.)

Viruses have given us most of the pandemics we've had since 1900, partly because they spread quickly and mutate into a potentially new disease by each passage through a new host; previous immunities may lose effectiveness. We have had worldwide influenza pandemics in 1918-1920 (H1N1, twenty to one hundred million fatalities), 1957-1958 (H2N2, one to four million fatalities), and 1968-1969 (H3N2, one to four million fatalities); and the HIV virus—which produces AIDS—has killed an estimated forty-two million worldwide over more than forty years. AIDS is variously called a pandemic and an epidemic.

The latest pandemic, COVID-19, which has claimed an estimated seven million people worldwide, is actually the third coronavirus that has posed an epidemic threat in the past twenty-five years, including SARS (severe, acute respiratory syndrome) in 2002, and MERS (Middle East Respiratory Syndrome) in about 2012. And there are an estimated 1.6

million other viruses in the world's fauna, about half of which have the ability to jump from animal to human populations. Pandemics could be caused by bacteria, fungi, and parasites, as well. Typhus, for example, is a parasite-borne bacterium that killed two to three million people in Russia in 1918-1922. Experts agree that more epidemics and pandemics are in our future, and maybe even the near future. The clear fact of the matter is that the next pandemic is not a matter of if, but when.

The World Health Organization (WHO) maintains the Global Outbreak Alert and Response Network, which partners with public and research health systems around the world to monitor the emergence and outbreak of diseases, and to assess whether they have the potential to escalate into epidemics and pandemics. In the United States, the Centers for Disease Control and Prevention (CDC) maintain a running list of current outbreaks both domestically and worldwide. They also issue advisories so travelers can be fully informed before travel to potentially impacted regions. As we saw during the COVID-19 pandemic, the CDC was a key participant in gathering and reporting data, conducting studies, and issuing guidance.

## Prepare Before an Epidemic or Pandemic

One of the defining characteristics of the recent COVID-19 pandemic response was the lockdown, a mandated isolation of the populace. Lockdowns occurred in most countries, ranging from rigidly enforced quarantines to moderate reductions of movement and meetings. Most public gatherings were prohibited, schools were closed to in-person education, businesses sent employees home to work remotely, and even stores were required to limit shoppers to the number that could safely stay more than six feet away from each other. Isolation measures were initially expected to last a few days, then weeks, but they occurred on and off for about two years. These quarantines revealed that many people were not able to be self-sufficient for any length of time. There are some preparations we can make to maximize the effectiveness and protection of isolation mandates.

### Supplies

Storing food is addressed in more detail in chapter 7. During the COVID-19 pandemic, restaurants—on which many of us regularly rely—were not open for dine-in service, though many were able to prepare carryout. For emergencies, it is prudent to plan to make your own food until restaurant options return. Food storage might be thought of in tiers:

1. The first tier is perishable foods, like fresh fruits and vegetables, and these may or may not continue to be available in stores, but do not store well. The best strategy here is to not plan on availability, but to look for freeze-dried or frozen substitutes that might be stored and used in familiar recipes. For example, you may not be able to obtain fresh onions, but freeze-dried onions and onion flavorings are available and store well. Then you can be flexible as you watch for fresh products to become available. Be creative with whatever fresh produce appears.

   Fresh milk, cheese, and eggs have short shelf lives, but powdered options exist for recipe use, and some shelf-stable products exist, though you may have to search for them. It is also difficult to stock bread, but you can look for substitutes that store longer, like pitas, tortillas, or crackers to substitute. Consider storing ingredients to make your own breads/tortillas when you cannot buy them.

2. The next tier is storable ingredients for meals you already make. Eating familiar meals may be a source of comfort in a stressful situation. Most families can identify a dozen or two basic meals that they prepare regularly, and can stock supplies merely by buying an extra amount each shopping trip. If you have fourteen meals in rotation, and you have enough supplies to make two rounds of each, you have four weeks where you don't need to brave the germ-laden crowds at the store. This extra amount of food takes some space, and food stores better at cooler temperatures, such as basements. Pay attention to expiration dates on packages and make sure you rotate supplies by consuming the oldest stock first.

3. The next tier is long-term storable foods like freeze-dried meals, which can be purchased from outdoors stores (backpacker meals) and emergency preparedness stores. Some businesses supply multiple days of meals in prepackaged buckets or bins, with expected shelf lives measured in years.

   This long-term tier might also include "basics" such as bulk storage of rice, wheat, oats, beans, sugar, honey, oils, basic spices, and canned goods. This is advanced food storage: wheat, for example, must be processed to use in most recipes, which will require a mill for making flour. Also, switching from your normal diet to one high in whole wheat will require a potentially uncomfortable period for digestive systems to acclimate.

Beyond food, it is necessary to lay in other non-food supplies like soap, detergent, food wraps, parchment, plastic bags, and, as COVID-19 showed, toilet paper. Health-protection items such as nitrile gloves, filtration masks, hand sanitizer and cleaning supplies should be kept on hand because they might not be immediately available. Also to remember storage for your pets. It is inevitable that there will be other spot shortages.

## Technology

Since the objective of preparedness is to reduce your exposure to potential infection sources, a good option is to prepare to do necessary activities remotely if possible. The COVID-19 pandemic resulted in the creation and evolution of many computer tools for remote living. For example, many workplaces converted to on-line work and streaming meetings. Many doctors' offices offered remote "telehealth" consultations, and many churches streamed Sunday services. On-line vendors and doorstep delivery services made shopping for both necessities and luxuries easy and fast.

The effectiveness of these technology-based options depends upon keeping computer resources up-to-date and learning how to use them. Keeping up with the latest version of computers and phones can be expensive, but hardware that may be a little bit older can still be effective. If you do not consider yourself computer-savvy, find someone in your family or circle of friends who can help you assess the status of your hardware and assure that your software is up to date. They might also help you learn the basics of applications that you'll need for remote activities. Currently, phones are eclipsing desktop and laptop computers for accessing many of these remote personal services. Whichever your preference—desktop or handheld— you might need to step out of your comfort zone to learn new skills, and new connections. Consider it emergency preparedness!

Also note, that on-line enterprise usually requires a current credit card. Yes, there are on-line cash transfer options like Venmo, but a credit card is still essential. While a full discussion of the risks and rewards of credit cards is beyond the scope of this chapter, a couple of recommendations may help:

- Pay attention to the credit terms of each card you possess
- Select one card to use for your on-line activities
- Keep track of your expenditures and never spend more in a month than you have budgeted. One way to avoid interest costs is to pay off the balance every month

### Entertainment in Isolation

A long-term lockdown means that you will likely spend more time by yourself or in your small bubble of trusted family and friends. Prepare to entertain yourself by storing board games, cards, rulebooks for different games, and supplies for crafts and hobbies. Sign up for a library card and connect to their digital collection. You will be able to check out books and periodicals in a variety of formats, either for reading on your phone or tablet devices, or for listening.

## During an Epidemic or Pandemic

As in any emergency or disaster, the fundamental priority is to survive; where there is life, there is hope. From the case studies (chapter 11), it becomes clear that the best way to prioritize survival is to listen to and follow authoritative guidance from local and national authorities. During COVID-19, there was some confusion and even some reversal of guidance as the public health infrastructure struggled to understand the character of a novel virus, and to craft protective advice and policy. While the public message was sometimes uneven, it remained the most trustworthy of potential sources for one basic reason: identifying and responding to public health crises is their business. For many public health workers, education and training spans many years—especially for the specialties of epidemiology, immunology, and medicine—and state and national public health workers have much experience across a broad spectrum of crises. A variety of other voices crowded and clouded information channels; some people innocently promoted rumors or unproven treatments, and some purposefully promoted political agendas. Looking back at the COVID-19 experience has enabled us to untangle some of that, but the fact remains that the next pandemic will be experienced in forward gear, and in the fog of easy information, the safest and sanest path is to follow the guidance of the authorities.

## Protect Your Health, Minimize Your Risk

- Learn how the pathogen spreads, and what symptoms to look for.
- Wash hands often with soap and water, following the recommendation of scrubbing for twenty seconds, or the time it takes to sing Happy Birthday to yourself twice. When handwashing is not available, use hand sanitizer with a minimum of 60 percent isopropyl alcohol. Don't touch your eyes, nose, or mouth with unwashed hands.
- Frequently sanitize highly touched surfaces like doorknobs, handrails, light switches and counters.
- Work your food plan, your remote work plan, your remote shopping plan. This may require that you innovate with the resources you have and make do without some conveniences for a time to minimize exposure.
- Stay out of crowds. Especially don't go out if *you* have symptoms or believe you have been exposed. Cover your coughs and sneezes.
- Be realistic about the potential risks extended family and friends pose. They may be exposed to risk through their other activities, and you may need to reduce the frequency or closeness of visits for a while. During COVID-19, there was some talk of creating trusted "bubbles" or "pods" of like-minded people, with the idea that if they are being safe and you are being safe, you could be safe together, but the bigger your circle, the less control there will be and the less protection it will offer.
- When in public, wear a mask, and stay six feet away from others. Highly ventilated indoor spaces are safer in a respiratory epidemic. In COVID-19, outdoor activities were safer than indoor events, presumably because of better air movement. A word about masks: during COVID-19 there was mixed official messaging about wearing masks. A number of studies were conducted—and many more anecdotes were reported—with inconclusive results, but in 2023, The Journal of American Medical Association reviewed all available data and published a study with this conclusion: "Masking in the community to reduce the spread of SARS-CoV-2 (the virus that causes COVID-19) is supported by robust evidence from diverse

settings and populations."[1] This conclusion only applies in situations where pathogen spread is respiratory, but it says that most masks provide some protection, and better masks, such as the N-95 type, provide better protection. The mask must fit snugly and cover the nose and mouth.

- If a vaccine becomes available, consult with your doctor about getting it. Pay close attention to what authorities say about its effects; during COVID-19, a vaccine became available in record time, but it did not completely prevent transmission. While it may have slowed spread, its main effect was to reduce the severity of infection. Vaccines are typically helpful for the majority of people, but there will be some with complicating health issues, allergies, and other conditions who might need further guidance.

## Manage Your Information

- Consciously and deliberately select your news sources. One of the lessons learned from COVID-19 is that it is very easy to fall into the habit of "doom-scrolling," or endlessly surfing the internet for bad news story after bad news story. These are typically not even journalistic stories, but just commentary and speculation and awfulizing. Consider setting limits on news consumption. You can also deliberately select news sources that can be trusted to provide edited, checked, and balanced news. There are several websites that assess and rate news sources according to accuracy and political bias. Choose reputable sources for both instant and deep background news. Some will require a subscription fee, which might be worth it to move from hysteria to dependable news.
- Also stay informed through official media, such as the CDC and local, county, and state public health sites. It is common sense that detailed websites and sources curated by professional immunologists, virologists, doctors, public health experts will be more trustworthy than social media posts by untrained friends and distant acquaintances.

1 Cash-Goldwasser S, Reingold AL, Luby SP, Jackson LA, Frieden TR. Masks During Pandemics Caused by Respiratory Pathogens—Evidence and Implications for Action. JAMA Netw Open. 2023;6(10):e2339443. doi:10.1001/jamanetworkopen.2023.39443

## Manage Your Mental Health

- Any extended emergency that upsets every pattern and routine, and deprives you of your normal stress coping strategies is going to put pressure on the mental and emotional health of individuals, families, and other employment and social groups. A full treatment of anxiety, personal and family stress, and depression is beyond the scope of this book, but psychologists offer a few ideas to cope.
  - » **Routines:** Establish a routine that includes normal schedules for work, sleep, meals, and self-care. Continue with dressing, shaving, and normal hygiene and fitness activities (modified to avoid the crowds and shared equipment at public gyms.) Eat balanced meals at regular times; drink enough to stay hydrated, and limit alcohol and caffeine drinks maybe more than you would normally. Apply limits to naps, snacks, TV, gaming, and social media use. Try to get outside, get some sunshine, some fresh air, and some movement. A walk around the neighborhood checks these boxes.
  - » **Social contact:** Deliberately list and keep in touch with your favorite people: family, friends, coworkers, people from church, clubs, teams, bands. Write down the names and conscientiously reach out to one or more each day. Use the technology that works best for you, from video calls to handwritten letters.
  - » Pay special attention to children, who will also be stressed. Jointly setting goals and writing schedules will help bring some measure of control. Play, read, watch a show, talk, draw, have a puppet show, dress up and write a play. Imaginative play will give an outlet for feelings and stresses. Some behavior issues and emotional outbursts might be expected. Sleeping and eating problems may arise. Be the adult and react with gentleness and patience. It may help to focus on activities and discussions that bring a feeling of safety and security and control. Children take many of their cues from parents. Your doomscrolling could affect them.
  - » Let everyone build a self-care toolbox. Pampering is vital, so focus on small, simple things. This can be a collection of comforting items, activities, foods, and so on, like blankets, plush toys, books, photos, hobbies, or journals. Each person should

identify their own safe retreat space. Maybe you don't have a separate room for each, but even a blanket fort can give a little respite. While creative activities can be fulfilling, be careful to not go overboard on goals to write the Great American Novel, craft new living room furniture, or learn to play the harp.

- Healthy attitudes you can consciously cultivate:
  - Patience: we're all doing the best we can; patience with yourself, too
  - Assume good intent in others
  - Notice the positive, cultivate gratitude for small things
  - Find ways to laugh every day, but not at others' expense
  - Help other people, check in often with neighbors, share shopping duties, recipes, even supplies if needed
  - Look for good stories, lessons, things to remember about this time
  - Ask for help when you need

## After an Epidemic or Pandemic

- Start reentry slowly. The declaration that a pandemic emergency is over does not mean the pathogens no longer are circulating. It most likely means that an arbitrary threshold of cases, or hospitalizations, or deaths was achieved. After COVID-19, the tendency was to try to catch up on all the things missed. Many parties, family reunions, and crowd events became sources of post-pandemic infections.
- Continue protective behaviors like handwashing and staying home when ill, and be cautious of gatherings and crowds. Take baby steps until you are comfortable in public spaces.
- Build your routines back cautiously and deliberately. Ignore pressure to normalize immediately. It is your health, and you get to choose when and how you will re-enter.
- Build or rebuild your emergency preparedness supplies.
- Build or rebuild a rainy-day fund. With studies showing many families cannot withstand a surprise four-hundred-dollar emergency, the best time to start saving is now. Open a new savings or

investment account and discipline yourself to add to it every paycheck even if the amount is small.

- Purposefully rebuild relationships. This takes time and is accomplished one person at a time. Cultivate those that were supportive and helpful during the pandemic. It may be time to let a few toxic relationships fade away, too.
- Did the lockdowns show you that an upgrade in your job or career is needed? Make a plan to get the information, education, or training you need for your target job.
- Evaluate your experiences and update your personal and family preparedness. What did you wish you had done? Watch for books and articles about lessons learned from the pandemic. In addition to expanding your perspective from the narrow view to a wider picture, you may learn about ways to prepare for the next epidemic or pandemic.

Emergency preparedness:
Do one thing today.

# Social Unrest

## When a Crowd Gets out of Control

May 2020, Minneapolis: George Floyd, a 46-year-old black man, died during his arrest while an officer knelt on his neck for more than nine minutes. Only hours later, fueled by phone videos and social media postings, crowds began to gather to protest Floyd's death and other police violence grievances. The crowds protested peacefully for some time until vandalism at a police station triggered a police response of tear gas and rubber bullets. Over the next several days, rallies and protests—both organized and spontaneous—occurred at many locations throughout the city. While most remained non-violent, in several locations, violence between the crowds and police escalated. Arson, property damage, and looting all occurred. The Governor instituted curfews and called in the National Guard, but protests continued for nearly two weeks. Two deaths were attributed to the violence, as well as over five hundred million dollars in property damage. Protests spread to hundreds of other cities in the United States.

July 2012, Anaheim: Two police-involved shootings were being protested by a crowd of about five hundred. Then someone in the crowd pelted police with rocks. When police fought back, the crowd turned ugly. The protests lasted over four days, with Molotov cocktails, smashed windows, looting, injuries, and arrests. Many compared the unrest to the riots of April 1992, when a Los Angeles jury verdict in the Rodney King case was the catalyst for three days of rioting, arson, looting, violence, and murder. In the 1992 riot, curfews were instituted and National Guard troops were deployed before things got under control. When it was over, more than fifty people were dead, over two thousand were injured, and around a billion dollars damage was done, much of it in neighborhoods least able to bear it. Thousands of businesses were torched, looted, or destroyed. It was worse than the five-day riot in Watts in 1965 (thirty-four dead), and the racial riots in Detroit in 1967 (forty-three dead).

February 2012: Thousands of soccer fans stormed the field to celebrate an upset victory in Port Said, Egypt. Police fired tear gas, and fans stampeded the exits only to find several locked and chained. Seventy-nine people died in the crush, sparking additional riots around the country. Soccer (and other sports) riots are reported frequently every year.

Riots occur frequently in our society. They occur when a great injustice is perceived to have occurred. They occur on college campuses, usually accompanied by great quantities of beer. They occur when strikers demonstrate. Or when police try to control demonstrators, like the Occupy Wall Street protesters. They occur at sporting events, sometimes because of a loss, sometimes because of a win. They occur in small cities as well as large urban areas.

Riots are similar to other types of emergencies—there is little or no warning, although in some instances, signs of escalation are apparent. There is no way to know how severe or long-lasting they will be. They impact different neighborhoods in different ways, confounding a one-size-fits-all response: in some cases, staying put is best; in some cases, evacuation is best. In all cases, a little preparation and forethought can affect your outcome.

## What Is a Riot?

A riot is the coordinated violent and destructive actions of a large number of people. The first ingredient in the mix is a crowd. An event or well-publicized signal—like an assassination, or a national/international sports victory—occurs, and crowds spontaneously gather in prominent places without recruitment. In many cases, the crowd is recruited through social media. In order for a riot to start, a significant fraction of the crowd must believe the crowd will become violent. The fact that they stay means they desire it to become violent. If the crowd is big enough, then individuals in the crowd feel immune to arrest or punishment. All it takes after that is a catalyzing event, like a rock through a window, to trigger violence and looting. Another catalyzing event could be a first strike or a rumored first strike by a policeman, even if he is using crowd control and nonlethal technologies, like beanbag bullets, or pepper spray. The crowd acts as a mass, typically overwhelming police or even troops. The crowd commits looting, arson, vandalism, even violence. Armed rioters can become deadly. Some opportunists take advantage of the general anarchy to attack icons of long-standing tension. In Los Angeles in 1992, for example, although the jury decision acquitted white police officers of criminal behavior in beating a black man, much of the violence was focused on Korean-run grocery stores. In locations away from the riots, snipers ambushed police officers and fired on firemen responding to emergency calls.

Witnesses and survivors of riots describe fires, looting, beatings, shootings. Vandalism consists of arson, broken windows, and overturned cars. When the police are overwhelmed and retreat, the witnesses realize they are alone, and no one can help them. The looting can become so intense that cars of the looters can cause traffic jams in the looted neighborhood. Business owners intent on defending their shops might arm themselves, adding to the possibility of lethal violence. In intense encounters, police fire tear gas and nonlethal—and sometimes lethal—weapons into the riotous crowds. Secondary effects of several days of widespread rioting include runs on banks, long lines at stores, and lines at gas stations. Public services may be temporarily halted.

## Preparing to Survive a Riot

The first rule of riot survival is to stay out of riots. Avoid riot-prone situations. It is not necessary to avoid all public gatherings, although it would seem wise to stay out of large intoxicated crowds. Pay attention to the mood of the crowd. Get out before it gets ugly; you will frequently have warning that things are edging towards violence. This goes for city council meetings as well as World Cup soccer games. If you can't get out, get to the edges where you can use your surroundings to protect you.

You may not be in the riot when it starts, but you may blunder into it, or it may overtake your neighborhood, or transportation route. As in any emergency situation, the more you know from reliable sources, the better. Listen to the most reliable news sources you can find in tense situations. Ignore unsubstantiated rumors. If violence breaks out, completely avoid the areas where it is reported. Give the riots a wide berth, knowing that action hot spots could spread. Once the violence gets started, it could break out in other places as well, so for the duration of the riots, it would be wise to avoid prominent public places. Sightseeing is completely out, unless you think that the one blurry snapshot you'll get of the riot is worth your life.

Prepare to hunker down in your house or office. This is where it is handy to have three to four days of self-sufficiency in the form of a kit. You may need to take care of your family's needs—even in the absence of utilities—for several days in order to avoid going out into the streets. If you work in an urban center, you may have to ride out a riot in your office. Prepare a short-term emergency kit for your office and keep it at your desk. If it is in your car, you may be exposed if you have to retrieve it. Even if you are away from the reported violence, you may want to avoid the crowds and lines at stores and gas stations anyway. If your family is separated and you cannot communicate directly for any reason, call or text your out-of-state contact. Check on neighbors, especially the elderly and infirm, if you can do so safely.

Prepare to leave your house if it becomes necessary. If there is a chance that the violence could progress to your area, you should leave immediately. The first step is to know where you are going. There may be public shelters, or you may have family or friends out of the area you can go to. As soon as your decision is made, contact separated members of your family or call your out-of-state contact. Let them know what time you expect to arrive at your destination. Assure that your evacuation path will not take you through the areas of violence. Take your emergency kits and the extra things that you have room and time for. Make sure that you have a current inventory of household goods to document any insurance claims you may have to make. Do not load up the car with belongings that would advertise you as a refugee. Take your less mobile neighbors if they will go with you.

## What to Do If Caught in a Riot

- If driving, keep moving. Get through the danger areas quickly. Most riots, even widespread ones have areas of less intense action. You may be able to drive out of a riot area within a few blocks.
- If on foot, try to get to a public building, hospital, or hotel, unless that is the direction the crowd is flowing. If so, move away from the crowd. You may be able to walk away from the most violent areas within a block or two.
- If the riot begins in your neighborhood, or surrounds your apartment, residence, or place of work, your best course of action may

be to stay put. Only you can decide if you want to try to escape during a lull in the violence. In many riots, a dusk-to-dawn curfew is imposed and enforced by troops.

- Stay out of sight from the street and stay below window level. Stray and not-stray bullets could be a danger.
- Because arson is so common in riots, post a fire watch: someone should stay awake to alert the rest if your building is set on fire.
- Listen to the news on your battery-powered radio if the electricity is off. Believe your own eyes and ears in preference to the news: if the media reports the violence diminishing, but you do not believe it is safe to go out, then stay put.
- Believe the news in preference to rumors you may hear from neighbors. Distortions and fabrications can run rampant during a period of violence.

## Other Crowd Scenes

Of course, there are other crowd scenes that can get out of control. Every year there are numerous reports of stampedes in clubs, holiday parties, theaters, and stadiums where people are crushed, suffocated, or trampled. In these cases, your brain is your only tool, don't lose it to panic. When you go into a public place like a theater or a stadium, note where *all* of the exits are. Try to notice how you would be able to find each exit in total darkness. If a stampede develops, try to stay out of it. You'll have better luck if you can stay put until the crowd subsides, and then choose an uncrowded exit. If a fire is causing the panic, get close to the ground while waiting for the panic to subside. If you are unavoidably caught up in the rush, try to move to edges, but don't try to counter the flow. Your best bet may be to "surf" the flow and concentrate on keeping your feet beneath you.

If you have teenagers attending concerts, advise them to avoid the largely uncontrolled, frequently overcrowded "mosh pit" area in front of the stage. In recent years, several kids have died as non-violent crowds surged and asphyxiated them.

Many of our favorite experiences are more fun because there is a crowd: athletic events, concerts, movies, clubs. Not many types of crowds are dangerous. But if you find yourself in an unruly crowd, plan now to keep your head; it is your best protection.

Emergency preparedness:
Do one thing today.

# Terrorism

## No Special Preparation for Terrorism

Although it has been over two decades since the 9/11 attacks, terrorism is still on our minds and a big part of our lives. And we worry about the possible shape of future attacks. What might someone intent only upon disruption and damage do to us? What if we don't know what it will be? Is there something we should do to prepare for terrorism? Is there anything we can do?

Yes, preparation for terrorism amounts to doing what we know we need to do anyway. In the end, the world has not changed as much as our perception of it. There have always been people who wish to destroy others. There have always been people who hated Americans or our institutions. There have always been terrorists. There have always been vulnerabilities, and perhaps there always will. The difference is we now see what we didn't before. Do we need to drastically overhaul our preparedness to be ready for the different possibilities of terrorism? Probably not. Let's look at the risks.

- **Transportation disruption:** The airport part of this is easiest to imagine because we live with it. But terrorists could also halt road, rail, and harbor operations with easily imagined acts. Is this a new threat? Not really. We have always been dependent upon others to bring items produced in other locations to us. Natural causes disrupt transportation, too, such as earthquakes, severe storms, or flooding. If transport ceased for a period of time, existing local supplies of food and fuel would be consumed quickly. It seems likely, however, that even a major terrorist disruption would only last several days, or maybe a week or two. Preparation, then, consists of storing supplies to carry you through two weeks with no grocery store trips. Store what you already eat, rather than something completely foreign. List your menu for two weeks and calculate the quantities required. Now buy double of each item, as steadily as your budget allows. Over the course of several shopping trips, you will be able to lay in everything you need (see chapter 7).

- **Power disruption:** Power generation and distribution systems are somewhat vulnerable to terrorism because they are public, aging, and fragile. If plants or transmission systems are damaged in an attack, then we could have rationing or even lose power completely for some time. But is this a new threat? Not really. Many natural causes, such as earthquakes or severe storms—think of Superstorm Sandy—could impact our power at any time. Preparation consists of identifying alternative sources of heat and light, and alternative methods of cooking food. You probably have an outdoor stove of some kind that will provide alternate cooking for several days. If you have a charcoal barbeque, you can store solid fuel as an option. Safety first: don't cook indoors or heat your home with charcoal; it produces toxic carbon monoxide. Try to have battery-powered light sources available for emergencies, but if candles or kerosene lanterns are your alternate lighting, an adult should oversee every open flame for safety (see chapter 17).
- **Water supply disruption:** We don't even need to imagine terrorists; only a few years ago, a dead raccoon contaminated a small suburban city's water system for nearly a week. Could someone intentionally cause disruption? Probably, but once again, preparation consists of doing what you ought to do anyway. Store a gallon of water per person, per day for two weeks. For some luxury, like laundry or baths, store more. Water heaters contain forty to fifty gallons. A fifty-five-gallon drum will meet the needs of a family of four. Make sure the drum is new or has only stored food grade materials; fuel or chemicals could leach into the water. Clean the drum thoroughly before filling, and add bleach, eight drops per gallon. Water in spas, pools and waterbeds is not drinkable. Replace stored water every six to twelve months (see chapter 6).

- **Illness/germ terrorism:** Annual flu and virus season shows us every year that we are vulnerable to biological terrorism. Is this a new threat? Not really; anyone who spends time with other people has always been vulnerable to catching a virulent strain of something contagious. Consider that over fifty million people worldwide died from a natural flu epidemic in 1918-1920. Stockpiling antibiotics is not recommended. Antibiotics have a limited shelf life, and self-diagnosis/medication is dangerous. Instead, prepare to be self-sufficient for several days or several weeks so you can avoid contact with infected people (see chapter 22).
- **Chemical terrorism:** This threat seems like a bona fide new concern, but it is just like the risk from any hazardous chemical spill. Any incident will be in a limited area for a limited duration. The only difference is that accidents are random, and terrorists will target crowds. Preparation is the same: prepare to evacuate from a hazardous area to a safe one. If you are in a crowd, don't panic; the risk from crowd crush is probably higher than the risk of poisoning. If you are in a building or neighborhood that is asked to evacuate, grab your short-term emergency kit and follow recommended routes to safety. The communications plan you already have will tell you how to contact other members of your family. Should you get a gas mask? Only you can decide, but consider that gas masks must be sized and fitted to each face, and they must be maintained and tested regularly. As children grow, they will need new masks. You also need to have the right (and functioning) filter cartridge for the specific chemical. And it must be with you when you need it: are you really going to take it to the big game? (See chapter 14.)
- **Nuclear terrorism:** For those that grew up in the duck-and-cover 1960's, this is not a new threat. In today's environment we could look at sabotaged nuclear power plants and improvised "dirty bomb" nuclear weapons. But the threat is limited: it may hit somewhere, but it won't hit everywhere. What should our preparation be? By now you can work this out: preparation for natural disasters will give the most options in a nuclear scenario (see chapter 21).
- **Product tampering:** A few well-publicized cases of product tampering could undermine our confidence in products at the grocery store, denying access to food and supplies. But product tampering

has been around much longer than even organized terrorists and is something we must be aware of anyway. In addition to being cautious consumers, and paying attention to recalls and warnings, we can store some extra food that will see us safely through a supply crisis. Once again, the things we do to prepare for other emergencies will serve us here, as well (see chapter 7).

- **Economic impact:** In the long term, it seems that widespread economic downturn will be the most likely and the most impactful result of terrorism. Unemployment may rise and production may decline. But we know what to do here, too, because as individuals we have always had the risk of lay-offs or serious illness or accident: live frugally within your income; stay out of debt; put aside emergency funds; store some food and supplies (see chapter 25).

• • •

The chances of terrorism directly impacting us are small, maybe even smaller than the threat of earthquake, or tornado; the chances we could be impacted by the larger reaction to a distant terrorist attack are much higher. But we don't need to do more or different things; we only need to do what we know to do anyway.

Emergency preparedness:
Do one thing today
(that you should be doing anyway).

# Financial Emergencies

## Preparing for Financial Disasters

Sometimes it is easy to take our personal and national economic systems for granted: how much we get paid, where our money is kept, how we can trade it for goods and services, how much things cost. But given the fragility of our personal financial lives, it makes sense to evaluate the kinds of financial disasters that could impact us and look at the measures we might take to mitigate them.

### Personal Financial Disaster

This type of disaster can come about for a variety of reasons: perhaps you were "down-sized" out of your job, or an injury or illness caused the family's primary wage earner to miss work. Think about it: how many paychecks in a row could you afford to miss? A legal judgment against you or high medical bills not covered by insurance could also cause personal financial crisis, as could the failure of the bank or savings institution that stores your money. To mitigate the effects of any of these occurrences, consider the following:

- Maintain appropriate insurance. A primary wage earner with dependents should have several types of insurance: homeowner's or renter's (make sure the policy is for replacement value of home and possessions, and make sure you have some liability coverage); auto insurance; life insurance (an agent will help you calculate the amount necessary), health insurance (at least some sort of catastrophic coverage) and disability insurance. In all cases, you should seek advice from a trusted insurance agent. In most cases, insurance is not intended as a ladder to higher prosperity, but as a safety net to prevent complete financial destitution.

- Maximize your education. Income studies show that the best paying, most stable jobs in our society are held by those best educated. More education typically means more money and more stability. Take advantage of every educational opportunity at your disposal. If you were not able to finish that college degree years ago, start back now with night classes, or home-study or on-line courses. If you have the skills but not the class work to nail down that certificate or license, there is no better time than the present. Community colleges, trade schools, and universities all have programs to accommodate the working person, and many companies offer tuition reimbursement to reduce your out-of-pocket costs. Also take advantage of every skills training course offered by your employer. These continuing education courses are usually free or at a greatly reduced cost and will enhance your current skills or expose you to other new and interesting areas. Read books and periodicals both in your field, and in related or even totally new ones.
- Be employable. In your current job, be on time, dependable, honest, hardworking, pleasant, and creative. Try to improve the breadth and depth of your own skills. Also try to understand your job in the larger context of the overall company. Try to learn about jobs of the others around you. Those who are flexible and versatile and easy to work with are usually not the first ones laid off.
- Get out of debt and stay out of debt. There are a number of good programs available to assist you if your debt is out of control. Stop charging anything you cannot pay off on the next credit card statement. Cut up all of your credit cards except one for emergencies. Be careful about refinancing consumer debt into your house mortgage. Pay close attention to the terms of any loans and be especially wary of home equity loans that can put your house at risk.
- Practice saving. Pay yourself the first ten percent of every paycheck. After you have saved up a month or two of living expenses—in an account separate from your household account, and maybe in a different institution—put this money into a long-term savings account; don't use it to finance the boat upgrade or the extravagant

vacation. The more you invest early in your life, the sooner you can assure your financial independence. If your company has a 401K program with matching contributions, get into it as soon as possible and contribute enough to get the maximum match.

- Develop other marketable skills. Explore other skills you might be interested in: real estate, investing, electronics, computers, writing, sewing, crafts. Explore them as hobbies at first, but try to determine if there is any moneymaking potential in them. Who is making money in these fields? How are they doing it? Are there any certifications that you need? Any special equipment? How could you use this skill if you needed to fall back on it? Don't neglect the talents/skills of both spouses. While one spouse can be a primary wage earner, the other could be going to school to enhance earning potential. A part-time job could keep less-employed spouses current in their skills, even if they spend most of their time as the primary caregiver of children.
- Put away some food storage. Pick a cool, dry location in your house, and build some sturdy shelves. Then watch for sales of items your family eats anyway and buy in bulk. You can put away food gradually that will last you for weeks or months, which might be all you need to tide you over an unexpected job change or financial hardship. Be sure you mark each food storage item with the date of purchase so you can rotate it to prevent spoilage.
- Spread your savings around. Try to keep your emergency liquid account—a month or two of living expenses—in a different bank or savings and loan than your primary household account. This will prevent troubles in a single financial institution from completely devastating your family.
- Practice frugality. Remember the old rhyme: Use it up, wear it out, make it do, or do without. Learn how to maintain and repair your home and items in your home. There are many do-it-yourself videos on every aspect of home maintenance freely available on the Internet. Learning these skills will not only enable you to live more frugally but may also be marketable skills themselves in a financial crisis. Resist the urge to buy more *stuff* just because it is there. Simplify your life and get by with less. Do you really need all of the clothes in your closet now? Or all of the personal grooming

chemistry? Or all of the mechanical or electronic gadgets and toys? Every new thing you buy is something else that will require time and maintenance, further complicating your life. Simplify.

## Financial Complications following Another Emergency

An earthquake, extensive flooding, severe storm pattern, or even social unrest could make money in banks and ATMs inaccessible for some period. Here are some things you can do in advance:

- Store some cash in your emergency kits. While it is not wise to store large amounts of cash, several hundred dollars in small bills (store some coins, too) will give you some flexibility in any purchases you need to make before the area's financial resources are restored.
- Food storage is useful in any emergency. Consider storing some goods you could use to trade and barter. In a short-term emergency, seemingly common items like toilet paper, candles, matches, charcoal, or drink flavoring might be in demand. Convenience foods like meal-in-a-can items might also be useful for barter.
- Don't go it alone. Check on your neighbors and pool resources. Others may have what you lack.

## Global Financial Turmoil

A global financial crisis, while a remote possibility, could develop if the right (or wrong) conditions were present. Global inflation or depression could develop, literally changing all of the rules. In this sort of situation, no amount of preparation will ready you for all of the conditions that could arise, but the following could help.

- Put away some food storage.
- Depending on the nature of the crisis, money may or may not have value. In some circumstances, for example, hyperinflation renders legal tender useless. Some observers recommend putting some emergency funds away in gold or silver. This has its advantages like giving you some stable purchasing power under a variety of conditions. It also has some disadvantages, chief of which is the vulnerability to theft. Additionally, gold and silver may not be negotiable, and it would be difficult to store small enough denominations to be useful. Be aware that homeowner's insurance policies do not cover theft of any significant amount of cash.

- If the crisis is deep and widespread, then your first priority is to provide the basics for your family: shelter, food, water, medical care, sanitation. Whatever society does not or cannot provide, you must create yourself. But don't go it alone. Team up with your neighbors and neighborhood to create a community. Pool your skills, your resources, and your energy. A group is more likely to thrive under difficult circumstances than a single family. In a long-term, widespread financial emergency, a trade-and-barter economy may develop. Consider storing some goods that store well and could be in demand—soap/shampoo, detergent, spices, candles, sanitation supplies. Skills are also useful commodities to trade. If you have some valuable skills, make sure you have supplies on hand to enable you to ply your trade in an emergency.

• • •

Financial crises can strike us without warning, whether they are individual or global in nature. Take some steps now to reduce their impact on your family's lives.

## Insurance: An Important Part of Financial Emergency Preparedness

Buying insurance is a classic example of preparing for an emergency. In the case of homeowner's or property insurance, you are assuring your financial recovery from many kinds of disasters. Here are a few insurance tips from a veteran claims adjuster and insurance agent:

1. Know what your policy covers and what its limits are. Excavate your policy from that pile of papers and read it. You'll probably understand a lot more of it than you think. Your insurance agent can help if you have questions; he or she wants you to know your policy, too. Don't hesitate to request an insurance review with your agent whenever you feel like your coverage may be too much or too little. When you are done reading it, make a copy to keep, and put your policy in a safe place with other important papers. You'll want to make sure you know exactly where it is in an emergency.

   Many homeowners have a type of insurance called a "special form" policy. This type usually covers a wide variety of specific disasters (high winds, winter storms, vandalism, theft, fire, and so on) except those explicitly excluded. Common exclusions are earthquake, flooding, and wildfire. The special form policy also usually guarantees replacement of the structure, which means that inflation is accounted for.

If you have a policy with a replacement value specified ("face value"), you'll need to upgrade every few years to make sure you could rebuild your home, if required. If you have any question about your type of insurance or its coverage and limits, read your policy; it's all in there.

2. Evaluate your deductible level. The deductible is the amount you would have to pay following a disaster before your insurance coverage takes over. The deductible will be stated in your policy. You could consider increasing the deductible to lower the premium.

3. Add earthquake, flood, and wildfire insurance to your policy, as needed. A standard homeowner's policy does NOT cover earthquakes. Earthquake endorsements are additions to your policy to reimburse you for earthquake damage. Remember that earthquake endorsements have a separate deductible (typically five to ten percent of the face value) and have a maximum reimbursement limit specified. This means that if you have a one-hundred-thousand-dollar face value and a five percent deductible, the insurance company will reimburse you ninety-five thousand dollars after you pay the first five thousand dollars. You should review the face value of an earthquake endorsement every few years to make sure that your coverage will enable you to replace your home, if necessary. Common claims after an earthquake relate to damaged brickwork, cracking of walls and ceilings, and collapsing chimneys. This kind of damage can be expensive to repair.

   Homeowner's policies usually cover flooding from internal sources, such as broken pipes, leaky fixtures, and so on. A standard homeowner's policy typically does not cover flooding when the water comes from outside of the house. When you see your agent about flood coverage, he or she will consult a FEMA flood map to determine the risk zone your home is in. This is a standard flood map prepared by the government and defines drainage and groundwater risks. The cost of your flood insurance will depend upon the flood risks to which you are exposed. You can also buy a disaster policy that covers both earthquake and flood, often at a competitive price. Ask your agent.

4. Review your business insurance needs. If you own a business, you may have unique insurance needs, depending on the type and size of business. You may need property insurance and liability insurance. You may need professional liability or "errors and omissions" insurance. You should review your specialized business insurance needs with your agent.

• • •

Even though insurance can't prevent a disaster, it can give you the peace of mind that you can get back on your feet quickly following an emergency. In fact, after a disaster, insurance companies send out extra claims adjusters to the disaster site for prompt processing and payout of claims so clients can rebuild immediately. Your objective should be to make sure that your insurance coverage matches your needs.

Emergency preparedness:
Do one thing today.

# Existential Threats

This book attempts to identify reasonably anticipated risks to our safety, health, and well-being, and to craft common-sense responses to prepare for both the disaster and its aftermath. The most common possible emergencies are those that are most personal, and perhaps even individual. For example, more people will experience a house fire, car accident, or personal unemployment than will experience a volcanic eruption or magnitude 7 earthquake. In general, the larger the scale of disaster, the smaller the probability of occurrence. Accordingly, this book has not focused the largest potential events: disasters large and heinous enough to potentially end life on earth. Academics call these events existential threats because of the possibility of ending human existence. These end-of-the-world scenarios range from laugh-out-loud absurdities to credible possibilities. Informed analyses indicate extremely low probabilities of occurrence, but "extremely low" is not "zero." Existential threats include, but are not limited to:

- **Runaway Climate Change.** Many people study the increase of global temperatures, the causes, the effects, and the responses to human-caused climate change. Most of the scenarios indicate gradual increases in sea levels, increased severity of extreme weather events, risk of famine and pestilence, collapse of food sources, and so on. The existential risk is that previously stable environmental systems—the atmosphere, the oceans, meteorological events—will get caught in positive feedback loops and run away to the near-extinction of humans.
- **World War III.** Humanity has not yet found a way to prevent war, but historic wars were fought with relatively primitive and

short-distance weapons, requiring combatants to be close to the enemy. Not many hundred years ago, war might impact local and regional populations, but human existence was not threatened. Until, that is, the escalation of war technology—particularly the development of nuclear and thermonuclear weapons—made it possible for mankind to eliminate itself. Toss in a few deranged dictators with their own nuclear arsenals, and the threat to existence doesn't seem too far-fetched.

- **Alien Invasion.** The prospect of the arrival of an intelligent, hostile, colonizing alien species is almost a science fiction cliché. Of course, sober and intelligent people don't need to worry about that. Until a first contact proves that we do. An imperialistic alien race may need pesky humans out of their way, and if they have the technology to find us and come here, then wiping us out should be easy. On the other hand, the ETs may be benevolent and wish to share knowledge and technology that will enable a peaceful leap forward. But it is easier to make a summer blockbuster movie out of the evil kind.
- **Planet-killer Asteroid.** Speaking of things from space, we live in a hazardous universe that was constructed through violent and explosive forces, some of which flung big chunks of rocks and ice into space. Some of these are gravitationally drawn to the mass of our sun, which brings their paths near earth's orbit. International space agencies work hard to identify and characterize such objects, and several creative ideas (and not a few far-fetched ones) have been proposed to deflect small chunks before they get too close. Scientists estimate that considering both the impact and the dust-induced winter that would follow, an asteroid of about one kilometer in diameter would be enough to end all life on the earth. An asteroid this big would be easy to see afar off, but difficult to divert.
- **Natural or Bioengineered Pandemic.** With the COVID-19 pandemic we learned that in an interconnected world, an illness does not take long to spread to virtually everyone. A more virulent pathogen with a high fatality rate may emerge. It is not hard to imagine the evolution of a natural germ, because we have just lived through it, but many nations purposefully develop or enhance germs for use in war. Gene-manipulation technologies may augment these efforts. A miscalculation—or worse, an intentional release—could exterminate humanity.

- **AI and Robot Technology Run Amok.** The recent emergence of large language models and generative artificial intelligence (AI) programs have triggered alarmed responses. Scenarios revolve around the possibility that computers will develop sentience, the ability to think and reason for themselves. Add in the ability to design and fabricate robotic systems for every type of task, and then put the two together. Could AI-controlled robots decide that humans were bugs that must eliminated? Could thinking machines, not encumbered with the weight of conscience or moral codes decide to "cure" the world of the cancer that is the human race? Science fiction writers, and a concerning number of current pundits worry.
- **Supervolcano.** Paleoclimatologists tell us that in the earth's long past, cataclysmic volcanos have erupted, spewing hundreds of cubic miles of rocks and ash into the atmosphere. Beyond the immediate explosive effects and destruction by tsunami of everything nearby, all of that ash would obscure the sunlight and plunge the entire globe into a decades-long winter. Geologists and vulcanologists have cataloged about twenty or so possible supervolcano regions, though much is still unknown about the volcanic risks of long stretches of tectonic plate boundaries.
- **Acts of God.** Many of the religions of the world cite scriptural texts that prophesy the end of the world according to God's plan and timing. In most of these scenarios, the end of the world is a widespread destruction of many plagues and crises all at once; the "wicked" will be destroyed and the "righteous" saved. Will God use natural or man-made means to destroy the earth and those who have it coming, or will there be as-yet-unconsidered extraordinary disasters to accomplish the end? In either case, we likely will not have to worry about preparing for this one: the wicked will perish and nothing will save them; the righteous will be protected. No need to store food if a benevolent God will feed you.
- **The "Black Swan" Event.** This is best described as the scenario that you don't know that you don't know. The thinking goes that you can plan for scenarios you can imagine and watch for, but a black swan event is the thing you didn't know could happen until it did. By definition, if you don't know, there is nothing you can do for the specific event. But as long as we are considering long shots, we might just as well include it here.

There are variations, of course, on all of these ideas. Dystopian and science fiction writers have long explored each of them and are more likely to have useful (and frightening) insights about how these events might impact survivors than even high-powered think tanks. Finding these speculative fictions is an exercise left to the interested reader. But what should we do about existential events? Most of the end-of-the-world scenarios described would result in the collapse of society as we know it, so all bets are off. Few of the principles contained in this book would likely apply, but here are a few observations.

1. If you are interested in—or obsessed with—any of these ideas, go ahead and prepare for them. One of the principles that DOES apply: anything you do is better than nothing. It is also true that almost everything you do (minus the silver bullets for vampires and the pricey Geiger counter) will help you be prepared for most of the other disaster risks in this book. So go ahead and store the toilet paper, canned beans, and battlefield first aid supplies, knowing that your preparation for earthquakes and floods is improved.
2. Similarly, even though most of our risks are in the small/individual category, the things we might do to reduce risks in the existential category will improve survivability in the more common crises. For example, if you anticipate running from the zombie hordes, then you'll want to be as healthy as possible. Coincidentally, being healthy improves your outcomes in more mundane situations, too. So, eat a balanced and moderate diet, maintain a healthy weight, exercise for cardiovascular health, as well as strength and flexibility. Remove things from your life that are unhealthy (i.e. alcohol, tobacco, drugs), and add things in that are health-promoting (sleep, exercise, stress management). Practice good hygiene, get necessary healthcare and well-care advice from qualified professionals, and protect yourself from pathogens. (In general, the majority of vaccines have served the human race very well.) Cultivate healthy relationships and social interactions, build networks of support. Drive aware and undistracted; wear a seatbelt. Wear sunscreen. Floss. You get the idea.
3. Cultivate the survivor's mindset. Many commenters in the preparedness field note that survival in extreme situations depends more on attitude than on supplies or equipment. Of course, it all

starts with staying calm, but this is largely dependent on your confidence that you can adapt, improvise, and survive. You will always carry the knowledge and training you have, even if you are separated from the gear you have stored. This means you should learn all you can about as many diverse topics as you can imagine. Take a first aid course. Camp out for a night or a week; even better, go backpacking to get into the mindset of minimizing your gear. Learn wilderness survival skills. Learn about water safety and purification. Practice various types of cooking: stove, open fire, utensilless. If you do focus on gear, look for proven equipment that is sturdy, reliable, and might have multiple applications.

• • •

In short, there is little reason to focus on the extreme scenarios that have extreme unlikeliness, but neither do you have to ignore them in your preparations. Another principle that still works in the realm of existential threats?

Emergency preparedness:
Do one thing today.

# Part 3

# EMERGENCY PREPAREDNESS AS A WAY OF LIFE

# Get Started: Ten Easy Things To Do

Maybe you have read straight through this book. Or maybe you have flipped back and forth and looked at things that are interesting. Or maybe you have come back to it, after some major event in the world—or your neighborhood—has jolted you. In any of these cases, you may still be scratching your head saying, "Where do I start?" Here are ten ideas. If you just want to get started simply, do the basic list. If you have more ambition (plus time, money, and energy), move to the deluxe list.

## 1. Family Plan

- **Basic**: Make an emergency contact plan. Identify a friend or relative outside of the immediate area (preferably outside the state) that everyone in the family can call or text to relay messages. In an emergency, it may be easier to make long distance calls than local ones. Put important phone numbers on a card for everyone in the family.
- **Deluxe**: Add a get-together plan. Where do you spend your time? Work, school, friends' houses? Discuss how you will get from each location to home in an emergency, and the routes you will take. Select a primary reunion location, like your home; then select a secondary reunion location out of the immediate area, in case you are not able to get home. Don't forget to consider the emergency plans and policies that schools have in place.

## 2. The No-Kidding Emergency Flashlight

- **Basic**: Buy a good, solid flashlight with a wide and bright beam. Buy extra batteries and bulbs. Declare this the no-kidding emergency light. Threaten severe consequences to anyone who even thinks about using it for some other project or game. Put it in an easy-to-get-to, easy-to-find location that you can find by touch.
- **Deluxe**: Buy some extra inexpensive flashlights and a battery lantern. Have a lights-out practice one evening where you turn off all of the lights and don't do anything that requires electricity. Have a reading night or a board game night. You may have to plan ahead for electricity-less snacks.

## 3. Utilities

- **Basic**: Find out where the gas, water, and electricity shutoffs are.
- **Deluxe**: Teach everyone in your family where they are and when/how to turn them off. Put the proper tools in a known place.

## 4. Fire Safety

- **Basic**: Identify two escape routes out of every room. Pick a spot outside your home to get back together. Have a family council and talk about getting out of the house, and how to stop, drop and roll.
- **Deluxe**: Walk through your house with a paper and pen and look for fire safety problems: overloaded sockets; worn wires; clutter near the furnace or water heater; expired fire extinguishers; fire hazards around space heaters, fireplaces, and stoves; battery-less or broken smoke detectors or carbon monoxide detectors. Then fix things that need to be fixed.

## 5. Short-term Emergency Kits

- **Basic**: Get a large box, or a plastic tote, and get the list in chapter 3. Spend fifteen minutes collecting as many things on the list as you already have hanging around the house. You'll be surprised at how much you already have.
- **Deluxe**: Make a shopping list of all of the things you don't have and go get them. Finish the kit and put it—in a portable container or

duffle—in an easy place to find if you need to grab it and go with no warning.

## 6. Water

- **Basic**: Store a couple of gallons per person in 2-liter plastic soda bottles.
- **Deluxe**: Calculate how much water you need if everyone in the family gets a gallon a day for two weeks. Find the right bulk container and get that water stored.

## 7. Food

- **Basic**: Buy extra groceries, enough to make three to five of your regular meals. Store these meals.
- **Deluxe**: Actually make a list and a plan to acquire supplies for a couple of week's—or even a month's—meals.

## 8. First Aid

- **Basic**: Collect all of the first-aid supplies you have in your house right now into a box or a bin. Compare it to the list in chapter 5. Go shopping.
- **Deluxe**: Get online, call your local fire department, or ask your supervisor at work and find a first-aid and CPR class and get signed up.

## 9. Neighbor Networks

- **Basic**: Pick one neighbor to be your preparedness buddy. This is someone who will check on you, and you will check on them in an emergency. Have that first discussion. You may find it motivational to have someone else to work with.
- **Deluxe**: Look into CERT (Community Emergency Response Team) classes and organize your whole block to work together in an emergency.

## 10. Information

- **Basic**: Gather all of the information you've been collecting—articles, books, and clippings—into one place.

- **Deluxe:** Organize your files by topic and put them in a three-ring binder. You may actually have to read some of them.

• • •

The most important thing to remember if you are just starting out is to do one thing today. And then do another thing tomorrow.

Emergency preparedness:
Do one thing today.

# Life Preparedness: Sharing Information

It happens. Sometimes it's natural and expected. Sometimes it's sudden and tragic. It's always disruptive. Within hours of the death of someone you depend on, you will have to answer important questions and make decisions without their help. In the days and weeks following their passing, you will be required to shoulder their responsibilities: childcare, house and car maintenance, bills, taxes. Imagine how difficult daily life would be if your spouse died. Now imagine how difficult daily life would be for your spouse if you died. Getting your life in order now could spare your loved ones unpleasant surprises and the burden of trying to organize a mess after you are gone. Here are some principles to use in organizing your life:

## Gather Information into a Single Location

Gather all you can find right now. Every time you find a new piece of information, put it with the rest. Use a three-ring binder and pocket dividers to organize the papers, including:

- Deeds to real estate, titles to automobiles or other property
- Mortgages, loan agreements
- Insurance policies
- Investment papers and reports
- Retirement and pension plan information
- Savings and bank accounts
- Medical history, records, consent forms

- Important certificates: birth, death, marriage
- Military papers
- Divorce papers or records of other legal proceedings
- Income tax records
- Wills, living wills, advanced medical directives, organ donor papers

## Protect Important Papers

Make copies of important, irreplaceable papers, and put originals in a fire-proof, theft-proof location. Some people buy a safe for their home. Others are better off renting a safe deposit box at a bank. You and your spouse both need to know which bank the box is in and where the key is. It's a good idea to inform a third person, in case something happens to both of you at the same time.

## Share Financial Information

Both of you should understand the regular and the long-term finances, including budget, debts/loans and monthly bills. Keep a complete list of bank and investment accounts, and make sure that more than one can sign on each of them. Keep a list of credit cards (also handy if you lose your wallet or purse). Check deeds and mortgages; ownership should be in both names ("joint tenants"), or you'll need to otherwise ensure that death will not make assets unavailable to the survivor. You both should know the terms and conditions of all loans and mortgages. Make sure that you both understand what retirement benefits you are entitled to and whom to contact.

## Make Sure You Are Protected

Consult an insurance agent about the type and amount of life insurance you have. Insurance needs evolve as obligations come and go. Make sure your beneficiary information is up-to-date, especially if you are married. Keep all records together. Seek competent legal advice about creating a simple will and estate plan. It needn't be complicated nor expensive; your goal is to ensure that your family is not legally or financially stranded if you die. Record your desires for the distribution of personal effects as a part of the will or make a separate list. Write it all down; no one can remember that much.

It is also important to dictate the medical care you wish to receive if you cannot make your own decisions. Some people want no heroic (and expensive) or artificial measures taken if they have no reasonable chance of recovery. Seek legal advice if you want to create a binding document. If you want to be an organ donor, make sure you have the correct paperwork, and tell your family members; they will be the ones asked to sign the donor forms at a critical emotional time.

## Learn Each Other's Jobs

After years of living together, most couples fall into comfortable roles. One may take care of the finances and household while the other takes care of house, yard, and car maintenance. If your spouse passed away, would you know how to do what they do? Trade household roles for a month or six. Learn what your spouse does, and then help him or her learn your jobs. Besides learning how to keep the household running, you also get to spend time together and get a fresh perspective on your relationship. After the trade you won't take your spouse for granted again.

Or try this exercise: write the instructions that you would give to a babysitter/house sitter if you were going on a two-week vacation. (It would even be more fun if you then took the two-week vacation.) Don't forget kids' schedules, household routines, pets, alarms, and so on. You get the picture. You may already have done something like this. Decide if the instructions change depending on the season. Now add instructions you might give to someone who will live in your house while the whole family tours Europe (or choose your fantasy) for six months. Include things like winterizing the house, the sprinkler system, the RVs, water and electricity shutoff, yard maintenance, and car upkeep. Does your house or car have little quirks that might alarm or confuse someone new to them? Include your tricks. Don't worry about capturing every detail of your life—you'll know when it's enough. The question to ask is: could my spouse do this if I were gone?

## Make Plans Now

Whom do you want (or need) to be notified when you die? What aspects of your life would you want in your obituary? (Be frugal with the words, long obits can be expensive.) Where would you like to be buried? Do you own a burial plot? Where, exactly? Do you want cremation? Who should speak (or not speak) at your funeral? Do you want flowers or contributions to a charity? If you have wishes, write them down (memory fades) and give them to the people who will be responsible for making decisions when you are gone. Be considerate: your loved ones may find comfort in fulfilling your wishes, but they may also suffer guilt if you give instructions that are impractical.

### List the Experts in Your Lives

Doctor, dentist, orthodontist, mechanic, plumber, furnace repairman, lawyer, accountant, pharmacist, lawn care expert, alarm company, stock broker, insurance agent, banker, and so on—these people know your situation and are in the best position to help you keep your life together.

### Businesses Require Special Attention

If you own a business or income properties, you have more information to gather. What are the debts? What contracts do you have? Who is dependent upon the business? Could it function without you? Who best knows how to run it? Who could liquidate the business most effectively? If you want your business to survive you, it might be worth your while to invest either time or money in a detailed contingency plan.

• • •

Putting your life in order is a gift to your loved ones. Putting your life in order doesn't mean that trouble will come any sooner. It doesn't mean that trouble will be prevented. It does, however, mean that your family will have less confusion and worry should the unexpected happen. And that is what emergency preparedness is all about.

Emergency preparedness:
Do one thing today.

# Neighbors Help Each Other

In the 1944 Alfred Hitchcock movie, *Lifeboat*, survivors of a torpedoed boat are thrown together and must make the best of the situation. In an emergency, we could find ourselves in a similar situation with the people in our neighborhood. Imagine a large earthquake, for example. Utilities are damaged, communications are out, roads are damaged, and supplies cannot get into the area. Movement within the damaged zone is severely restricted. Emergency services are overwhelmed—everyone is on their own. Or are they? In emergency preparedness, we strive for self-sufficiency, yet that ignores a vital part of the equation: none of us is truly alone if we live in a neighborhood. As individuals, we are vulnerable to almost everything, yet there is almost nothing that a neighborhood can't face together. Why? Because each of us has different resources and skills to contribute.

What is a neighborhood? Although we may define it geographically—everyone within certain boundaries—a neighborhood is best defined as a collection of like-minded people who know and help each other. Do the people have to be demographically homogeneous for a neighborhood to work? No, all ages, races, sexes, religions, and economic classes have something to offer each other in times of emergency. Some may have medical skills, some may have construction skills, and some may have communications skills. Others may contribute supplies or equipment. But when these people put their best effort together in a common cause, no emergency situation is too daunting.

## Creating a Cooperative Neighborhood

So how do you create a neighborhood that helps each other? Neighborhood cooperation begins with neighbors knowing neighbors, and it has to be rooted in understanding and respect. This process can start small: get to know your next-door neighbors. Go introduce yourself and your family. If you are embarrassed, take over a plate of cookies as an excuse. Or plan your introduction to coincide with a holiday or a celebration so it seems less forced. Once you do it, you'll find that it's not as hard as you think. It takes time to get to know someone, so plan on spending some time doing things with them: go to dinner or a community event, or have a barbecue in your yard. Get to know their children's names.

Once you know a few neighbors, getting to know others is easier. Get to know the parents of your children's friends—you probably have a lot in common with them. Is there someone who is the social ringleader of the area? Get to know them and you'll have ready-made introductions to your other neighbors. Walk around your neighborhood when the weather is good. Wave to people when you see them. Stop and introduce yourselves to people in their yards. If there is any kind of block party or neighborhood gathering, go to it. Be a little outgoing as you try to get know others. It takes effort to establish an open and friendly atmosphere.

If you are the long-term residents, be inclusive of the new family. Meet them when they move in and invite them to neighborhood gatherings. Help them feel part of the group. As you get to know your neighbors, you'll be in a better position to identify others who may be receptive to working together on neighborhood projects like emergency preparedness or neighborhood watch programs.

## What Organized Neighborhoods Can Do

A neighborhood that acts together can be a powerful force:

- Neighbors can look after each other on a day-to-day basis. Neighbors with special needs such as health problems or reduced mobility can receive help from those who live close to them. These relationships can be supportive when situations changes, as they surely will. Neighbors can assist each other on a day-to-day basis and can make sure that the special needs are met even in an emergency. Who can respond faster or with better understanding than a neighbor who knows his neighbor's needs?

- Neighborhoods can form neighborhood watch programs in conjunction with their local police or sheriff's department. Although each law enforcement jurisdiction has its own program, they have many similarities: they raise citizen awareness of burglaries, vandalism, and other crimes in the neighborhood through an information program; they instruct and assist neighborhoods in better property protection through property marking and home security instruction; and they foster neighborhood action programs where neighbors watch each other's property and record and report suspicious activities. Although law enforcement departments can provide the information and the training, the basic organization is set up by the neighborhood. One metropolitan neighborhood banded together to get rid of people that were selling drugs from a nearby residence. The neighborhood set up a surveillance of the excessive and odd-hour traffic and presented local authorities with a database listing all of the cars, license plate numbers, descriptions of visitors, and details of odd goings-on. With eyewitnesses and complete and organized information, authorities were able to conduct arrests that shut down the dealers and removed users from the neighborhood.
- Neighborhoods can organize for emergency preparation and response. Some neighborhoods band together to purchase bulk supplies at discount, and to distribute preparedness information. Some neighborhoods organize into blocks and create plans so neighbors will check on and assist each other in an emergency.
- Sometimes it takes an emergency to get neighbors together. In a local contaminated water incident, it was discovered that the best way to disseminate accurate information was by neighbors going door-to-door. And in any kind of evacuation situation, what better, faster, more complete way to notify people than neighbors going door-to-door? In an organized neighborhood, no one would be left out: neighbors know where basement or garage apartments are, and neighbors know who is home and who needs extra help.
- Neighborhoods can be social units with regular social functions like barbecues or block parties or even family outings to recreational areas.

- Neighborhoods can organize as political units. Often the political actions carried out have to do with local issues such as planning and zoning, or neighborhood safety.

## It Takes a Leader

The clear message is that people can create the kinds of neighborhoods they want to live in. But be aware: if you think that any of this is a good idea, you may have to step up to be the leader—many people will contribute to a good idea, but often it takes a single individual with a vision and some gumption to get it started and keep it rolling. If you wait for someone else to pick up your broad hints, you might have a long wait. Being a leader will take some of your time, but you could consider it an investment in making your corner of the world a nicer place to live. Who wouldn't want to live in a place where people knew, cared about and supported each other? You can live in such a place, but it may be up to you to get the ball rolling. Like other aspects of emergency preparedness, you have to take some personal responsibility to make it happen.

Emergency preparedness:
Meet one neighbor today.

# Share Emergency Preparation Information in a Fair

An important part of emergency preparedness is gathering and sharing information with neighbors and friends. It motivates you and them, and opens doors to creating that caring neighborhood. One way to share information is through a preparedness fair. Anyone—church groups, civic organizations, clubs, Scouts, or even a neighborhood group—can organize a preparedness fair or workshop. For example, a local church group held an emergency preparedness fair. Leaders and members of the group gathered many available resources into a single, information-packed morning. Here are a few lessons they learned.

## Pick a Date and a Location

Give yourself four to six weeks to pull everything together. "We made the decision to have the fair about four weeks in advance, but some of our people would have liked more time," said the fair director. The location determines how many and what type of topics you can cover. You may want a single large room for displays, or several smaller rooms for workshops. Some outdoor space gives you flexibility to have cooking demonstrations. This church group had about twenty exhibits in their building, and occupied the main hall, the back parking lot, and three or four other rooms. If you don't have a large hall, consider a smaller, single topic fair. Or if you are a neighbor group, try a "progressive fair" and move from home to home for each topic.

## Divide and Conquer

Everyone is an expert at something, or can learn to be. Let individuals or groups (like Scouts, or youth groups) create a display on their area of expertise. You'll be surprised at what comes out. Or simply assign topics and watch everyone become experts in their areas.

## Use Available Resources

Here is a list of some of the organizations this group utilized in their fair. Most have free information and brochures they are happy to have you distribute. Some will lend you hardware to display, or videos to show. Although the organizations listed here are specific to a locale with both rural and metropolitan areas, other locations should have similar resources. Call the public relations department and start asking questions.

- The gas company has brochures on gas safety in general and earthquake preparedness specifically. One favorite is the scratch-and-sniff card to teach kids the smell of gas. They have a model gas meter so people can practice turning off a real gas valve. They also have a small model of a water heater, so you can show how to restrain it against tipping.
- The power company can provide brochures and videos on electrical safety for both kids and adults. One of their pamphlets tells what to do in a power outage.
- Departments of environmental health and public health can provide information about water purification and safe drinking water.
- Since the Red Cross mission includes community education, they publish many free pamphlets on family emergency preparation. They can also schedule classes (First Aid, CPR, and such) for your group, although some of these may require a fee.
- FEMA has many topics they might be able to help with, either through handouts and brochures, or even direct participation.
- The local fire department is active in community education and cooperative about helping you distribute fire safety and first aid information. If you schedule far enough in advance, the local station may even send someone to help you demonstrate some of these

concepts. They have information on fire safety, fire extinguishers, tips for older folks, and coloring books for kids.

- Local extension services may help disseminate information about gardening, food preparation, and preservation. Printed materials may have a nominal cost.
- The local police or sheriff's department can provide information on child safety, phone safety, latchkey kids, child identification programs, street safety, stranger danger, and so on. They have pamphlets to distribute and videos to loan.
- There are a number of local vendors of emergency preparation supplies. These people usually have lots of good information, but they also have products they are trying to sell. Only you can decide if you want the commercial flavor in your fair.

## Focus on Your Group's Own Special Needs

The church group had a number of displays wholly prepared and staffed by their own members and tailored to their own needs. Their personalized displays included information on short-term emergency kits, cooking in an emergency, car kits, family disaster plans, long-term food storage, protection of valuable papers, and emotional/spiritual preparation. Other ways to focus on your group's needs include inviting an expert to speak about a specific topic; organizing your fair around a theme; presenting mini-classes, and so on.

## Don't Forget Follow-Up Activities

If you have enough interest expressed by the group, follow-up by scheduling Red Cross CPR and first aid training courses. Have a local enthusiast schedule a HAM radio class to certify more people in your area. If you have twenty-five to thirty people interested you can even schedule a CERT (community emergency response team) class with the fire department. In seven sessions you will learn disaster preparedness, fire suppression techniques, first aid, light search and rescue, and team organization/psychology. The class is intended to teach citizens basic skills to respond to emergencies before authorities arrive, and it ends with a disaster simulation.

Whatever your approach, a preparedness fair has many benefits. "Our objective was to educate as many people as possible in emergency preparedness skills," said the fair director. "Those who participated certainly learned a lot." Learning the information, however, is only a first step. The most important thing is to put it into practice.

Emergency preparedness:
Do one thing today.

# Networking and the Experts in Your Lives

Recently a friend had trouble with the heating system in her new house. She repeatedly took hours off work to meet with electricians, plumbers, and repairmen, each of whom used different diagnostic tools and gave her different answers. After the last round of confusing advice, she said in frustration, "I wish I lived in a neighborhood!"

What she meant was that she wished she had a network of friends and neighbors to whom she could turn for help and advice: people that she trusted, people who had skills and knowledge. In fact, all of us need just such a network, day in and day out. Whether it is a personal emergency like house flooding, or heating system breakdown, or whether it is widespread like an earthquake or severe storm, none of us need face it alone. Here are some suggestions for building a network to help out in emergencies:

## 1. Be Part of Your Neighborhood.

Get to know your next-door neighbors. Introduce yourself. Walk around your neighborhood, wave to people. Stop and talk to people in their yards. If there is a block party or neighborhood gathering, go to it. Be a little outgoing.

## 2. Network in All of Your Circles

No matter who you are, you participate in a variety of groups ready-made for networking: social circles, work groups, clubs, organizations, church. Actively participate in each of these groups. Be genuinely interested in others, their lives, families, skills, and problem-solving network. When you have a problem—like trying to find a reliable furnace repairman—ask opinions. Others may have had the same situation and developed trusted contacts.

## 3. Help and Be Helped

In your network, sometimes it is your turn to help and sometimes it is your turn to be helped. Accept both roles graciously. When it is your turn, actively try to help people. Is a neighbor trying to start a car repair business? Steer some of your other friends that direction. Does a friend have the same difficulty with a child that you had? Share the information you collected. Does a co-worker need the same house repairs you just made? They might appreciate a recommendation from someone they know.

Don't think that you have to possess specialized knowledge to help. Taking pizza and cold drinks to a moving neighbor can be a huge help. Watching a neighbor's children or pets during a critical time can be sanity-saving for them. And your skill set is always changing, based on work opportunities, service in church, or even hobbies. Offer them unselfishly when a neighbor or friend needs them.

When it is your turn to be helped, swallow hard and allow it. People would rather network with someone who both gives and takes because it feels more like a community where everyone benefits from each other. When others help you, they become more connected to you, more likely to let you help them, and even more likely to help you again. It is a definitely a circle, but it is the opposite of vicious.

## 4. Develop Appropriate Loyalty with Experts

Building a network is often about repeated contacts with the same people. If you find a car repairman that is proficient, friendly, and reasonably priced, make it a point to take your business there. Frequent the same business establishments when they meet your needs. Of course, this does not mean that you should blindly support someone who is dishonest, unpleasant, or high-priced. It only means that you may tolerate minor inconveniences and even mistakes if the service is generally acceptable the rest of the time. Offer compliments when they are deserved and suggestions when you have them. Good businesses desire honest feedback.

## 5. Thank Those Who Help You

One of the most powerful network tools is the thank-you note. When someone helps you out, no matter how small, be sure to thank them. For some situations include a gift. This needn't be pricey or elaborate: a plate of cookies or freshly baked bread shows that you recognize that the other person's help came at some sacrifice and that you appreciate it.

• • •

In the end, the woman with the heating problem realized that she did, indeed, have friends and family who could help her sort out the situation: a brother explained the diagnostic devices, and a repairman she had previously identified helped sort out the advice and provide a path. It takes a lifetime to collect family, friends, neighbors, and associates who can help us through life. And whether you're in an emergency or not, this network makes life easier and more rewarding.

Emergency preparedness:
Do one thing today.

# Emergency Preparation for Businesses

Do you own or operate a business? What events would challenge your ability to function? How would a fire or earthquake disrupt operations? In a disaster, you have two main objectives: protect the safety of staff and customers, and protect your ability to stay in business. After 9/11, it is estimated that thousands of businesses in Manhattan closed.

## Basic Principles

- In a business, everything starts at the top; if the boss doesn't value the activity, it won't get done. Also, there will be costs that the boss must approve.
- The leader's job is to watch for threats and decide which emergencies you will prepare for.
- Preparedness will be more thorough and effective if you involve your staff. They will buy into the activity and will better understand what is required of them.

## Prevent What Can Be Prevented

Make sure that the disaster doesn't originate in your workplace. Start by walking through and identifying hazards. Bring a pad of paper—you will find more hazards than you think. Write them all down so you can prioritize them for fixing.

- For fire safety, note cluttered workspaces, and piles of boxes and papers. Check electrical equipment and look for worn cords, overloaded sockets and circuits, or wires that snake under carpets. Look for portable heaters, coffee machines, and other electrical devices at workstations. If you are required to use hazardous and flammable materials, OSHA Hazard Communication Program requirements may apply in their storage, labeling, and disposal. If materials are not needed, dispose of them properly. Check smoke and carbon monoxide alarms. Replace or recharge old fire extinguishers.

- For employee health and safety, note cluttered workspaces, and slip, trip, and fall hazards. Pay special attention to break rooms and kitchens. Make sure that employees who work with power tools, or knives, or chemicals have proper safety equipment, in addition to a controlled workspace and adequate tools and lighting. Although it's beyond the scope of this book, now might also be a good time to do an ergonomic analysis for each process in your business. Like emergency preparedness, employee well-being is an on-going process that requires continual support and encouragement. And an injured key employee can be a disaster for a business.
- Determine if your office is in any danger from external flooding. If you are in a flood plain, as shown on FEMA maps, seriously consider moving your operation. Note that there can also be flood hazards from malfunctioning irrigation or water supply systems. And don't overlook the possibility of in-building flooding. Where do water pipes run? What will be affected if they freeze and break, or if a sink upstairs runs all night?
- Look for earthquake hazards. Check hanging fixtures and art. Examine tall furniture. Where will bookshelves fall? Will computer equipment fly off the tables? Will falling furniture block exits? There are relatively simple fixes for each of these things.
- Examine the physical security of your office. Do you need to invest in a security system? How would you be affected if you were the victim of theft or vandalism?

After the hazards walk-through, prioritize the hazards, find the budget, and fix the hazards you found.

## Mitigate What Cannot Be Prevented

Many businesses are required by OSHA to have a written emergency action plan. The OSHA requirements (from www.osha.gov;

search for "emergency action plan") include:

- Procedures for reporting a fire or other emergency
- Procedures for emergency evacuation, including type of evacuation and exit route assignments
- Procedures to be followed by employees who remain to operate critical plant operations before they evacuate
- Procedures to account for all employees after evacuation
- Procedures to be followed by employees performing rescue or medical duties
- The name or job title of every employee who may be contacted by employees who need more information about the plan or an explanation of their duties under the plan
- Employee alarm system. An employer must have and maintain an employee alarm system. The employee alarm system must use a distinctive signal for each purpose and comply with OSHA requirements
- Training. An employer must designate and train employees to assist in a safe and orderly evacuation of other employees
- Review of emergency action plan. An employer must review the emergency action plan with each employee covered by the plan when the plan is developed, or the employee is assigned initially to a job; when the employee's responsibilities under the plan change; and when the plan is changed.

Simpler is better: a short summary of procedures is more useful than a fat binder that never gets read. In addition to the above, you may need to consider

- Special responsibilities: protecting data, securing hazardous operations or equipment
- Special needs employees (consider a buddy system)
- Emergency supplies, and materials (establishing and maintaining)
- Data backup. Most businesses rely on computer data. Computing needs may include financial and accounting information, materials planning and ordering, shipping and transportation, and client lists. Some high-tech companies also have expensive specialty software.

Establish a data back-up plan that makes copies of this information on a regular basis (daily, weekly, monthly, or some combination) and store back-up data offsite. This may require the purchase of a back-up storage device and/or software, but many effective options are inexpensive. As part of your data back-up plan, consider what paper documents are important, and make copies to store offsite or in a fireproof safe. Don't forget a complete inventory of equipment and materials

- Relocation plan. Gather your key personnel for a brainstorming session: if your present place of business were suddenly unavailable, how would you stay in business? One small company suffered a fire one night, but by the end of the next day, they had rented temporary space, recovered data, and were functioning at a bare bones level. What are your core functions? What are the critical data sources? Where could you move, and at what cost? You may never have to implement the plan, but the exercise may identify areas to focus on in your planning.

## Prepare to Recover Quickly

- **Insurance**: One key part of your disaster preparedness is insurance. Review existing policies with your agent and learn exactly what coverage you currently have. Determine if you need other kinds of insurance. In addition to property (be sure you have replacement value) and liability, consider loss-of-business insurance. Offices within residences have special insurance considerations. Some homeowner's policies have limitations on coverage that a business might need. Review your needs with your agent.
- **Communications**: After a disaster affects you, you will need to figure out how it affects your suppliers, and how it may affect your clients. Quick personal contact to both sides of the equation will take the uncertainty out of the situation and will significantly reduce your—and their—stress. Decide whom you would need to call and keep a paper copy of the list handy, because your electronic databases may be inoperative for the first few hours or days. Include owners, partners, banks, debtors, and creditors, as well. Many businesses also find it difficult to get the word out after a disaster that they are open for business. Consider how you generate clients: if

you depend on street traffic, a sign may be best. If you have business clients, consider a phone campaign to contact and assure them.

- **Response**: After a disaster strikes, keep breathing. Experts warn that the shock of a disaster will affect even the most stoic. Take a few deep breaths, gather your team, and begin to assess and plan. When cleaning up after a disaster, avoid physically overdoing it. There may be a million things to do, but they will be more difficult if you have a heart attack. Take pictures, make notes, and keep receipts of everything you do related to recovery. If the government declares a disaster, you may be eligible for assistance of some kind. The records will also help when dealing with insurance adjusters.

• • •

An emergency doesn't have to mean the end of your business—that would be a disaster indeed.

Emergency preparedness:
Do one thing today.

# Communications in an Emergency

Communities, first responders, and rescue organizations constantly practice emergency response skills. Sometimes they practice around a table. Sometimes they practice with other emergency organizations. Sometimes they practice full-scale, with volunteer victims and fake injuries. In all cases, the main thing they are practicing is communications. Of course, we are talking about organizations that use widely different communication equipment and different frequencies and protocols. But the lesson is still clear for us: effective response to emergencies is all about communications. Here are a few ideas about keeping information flowing in an emergency.

## Personal Communications

Every short-term emergency kit should have a battery-powered AM/FM radio, with fresh batteries. Better if it is also powered by solar cells or hand crank. The radio will keep you in touch with the most reliable sources of news and leave you less susceptible to rumors. It is useful to also have a list of local radio stations. Check the internet for a listing by format and dial location, print a copy and store it with the radio.

Another useful item for your emergency kit is a collection of recent family photos. If you need the authorities to help you locate a lost member of your family, a photo with a physical description may hasten the search.

## Family Communications

In any emergency, you want to check on your own family and then let them know you are okay. Many disasters, such as earthquakes or power outages, may make it difficult for you to contact each other directly. Identify a friend or relative outside of the immediate area (preferably outside the state) that everyone in the family can call or text to relay messages. This out-of-state contact person can act as a message board and write down where the caller is, what time they called, where they are going, what route they will use, when they will call again, and so on. Make sure everyone in the family has a copy of key phone numbers and knows when and how to use them.

## Neighborhood Communications

In a larger emergency, neighborhoods will likely band together to help each other. Communicating in this larger area, however, requires different tools. Before an emergency, some neighborhoods have established phone trees to help get the word out. In these systems, one person calls two people, who each call two more, and so on until everyone has been alerted. While useful in many situations, phone trees are vulnerable to single-point failures: if someone in the line is not home or neglects to make their calls, others down the line may not get the message. Be sure to build some flexibility into your phone tree if you choose this method.

During a disaster, the most reliable neighborhood approach is the old-fashioned "sneakernet:" written messages transmitted by runners. This system works at the neighborhood scale, even when roads are impassable. To reduce the possibility of miscommunications, make sure all messages are written clearly and legibly. Keep a small pad of paper and a pencil in your emergency kit. (If you store a pen, be sure to replace it often to keep it from drying out.)

If cell phones are inoperative, as they were for wide areas right after Superstorm Sandy, you can still use local-area radios, known as FRS radios. For a modest investment, you can have a walkie-talkie with a radius of several blocks. Radios by a number of different manufacturers share the same frequency ranges, so coordinating with others in your neighborhood requires that you select a common frequency that everyone can remember and use. Remember that FRS radios all share a frequency range and do not provide private or secure communications. These radios are also useful in neighborhood searches or watches.

## Communications with Authorities

Obviously, if the phone system works, calls for assistance can be made on the 911 system. If telephones are not functional, emergency responders, like the fire department, sheriff's office, and police departments, all have radio systems to communicate with each other. As noted above, they practice frequently to make sure they can coordinate. Less well known is a network of licensed amateur HAM radio operators who are also organized and constantly training to assist in case an emergency disables standard communications. In Hurricane Katrina, sometimes the only functional communications were through HAM radio operators, who even functioned as 911 dispatchers. HAM operators may be attached to city emergency operations centers, various emergency organizations and other public services, such as shelters. Amateur radio organizations welcome new members, and many clubs even sponsor training to help the new member qualify for a license. Amateur radio organizations frequently participate in large-area disaster drills to improve their effectiveness in a real emergency.

• • •

One last note about communications: information is only as useful as it is accurate. If you have a message that needs to be transmitted, it may be helpful to include your source: "I heard on the radio WABC that . . . ," or "The mayor just reported that . . . ," or "the fire department recommends . . ." That way, the recipient can evaluate the information, and pursue additional confirmation, if warranted.

Emergency preparedness:
Do one thing today.

# Camping: A Great Preparedness Hobby

No electricity. No running water. No flushing toilet. You carry everything and depend on yourself. You find water, but you dare not drink until you purify it. With no place to buy food, you make a one-pot casserole from your meager stores. It's okay, the simpler the meal, the less fuel you use. Night comes on; you'll need shelter against the cold, or maybe a storm. You protect your food from animals and judge that you have enough for an evening treat. Cradling a hot drink, you revel in another gorgeous sunset and wonder if you should start a fire tonight.

No, this is not the description of an end-of-the-world scenario. I'm describing a campout. Few family activities are as useful for practicing emergency preparedness skills as camping. Backpacking is even better. Here's why:

## Camping Fosters Preparedness Attitudes

When you camp you develop attitudes and perspectives that are different from a comfortable life at home. For example, you must get used to thinking ahead. Wilderness is usually far from the supermarket. You have to think through your trip and get supplies beforehand. Inevitably you will forget something, or an unforeseen situation will arise, so you must also develop an attitude of improvising—make do with what you have. And often you discover that not as many things are necessary to your life as you thought, which is another good preparedness attitude. In fact, camping helps distinguish between basics and luxuries. Other beneficial attitudes you develop while camping include self-reliance, discipline, and the concept that you can do without constant comfort or immediate gratification.

## Camping Develops Preparedness Skills

People who camp develop skills that are useful in emergencies. Backpacking is especially good because of the total separation from civilization. Campers learn to estimate types of supplies and necessary quantities. You learn to minimize excess and waste. One key skill is to see which compromises will save weight or complexity. Extreme example: backpackers who save pounds of stoves and gear by planning only no-cook meals. Frequent campers also learn how to conserve fuel, minimize messes, use less water, and ration personal energy to get everything done.

Other skills include cooking with dried foods, one-pan cooking, spicing up bland or repetitive meals, water purification, and pest avoidance. Skills like choosing a campsite, seeking shelter, and organizing a camp could be handy if you were displaced from home. Building a fire with a variety of fuels and tools—and only one match—is harder than it looks. And learning methods of reducing your exposure to severe weather could literally be lifesaving.

## Camping Gets You Equipped

Accumulating great equipment is a key preparedness benefit of camping. All camping gear is emergency gear. The equipment gets the most benefit out of the smallest volume or weight. Be careful, you can spend a lot on equipment that is not right for your family or camping style. Define your needs before shopping. Are you going to camp from a car? Then weight and bulk are not as important. Are you going to camp at undeveloped sites? Then you'll need to take water and sanitation into account. Are you going to camp yearly or weekly? Shop around and be patient. Discontinued styles or last year's models have extra discounts, and if they were good enough last year, they'll be fine this year. With research (outdoors magazines usually have primers on buying gear . . .) you can identify the features you need and pick up some great gear. Here are some additional tips:

- Tents: You don't need to buy a blizzard-resistant model (expensive), but the rain fly should cover the tent and be waterproof, not just water-resistant. Best buy: a three-season tent. Climb in before you buy, not all two-man tents fit two men. Other handy features are a freestanding design and a large vestibule. Make sure it's easy to set up in the dark, and that it is sturdy: breaking a tent pole on a rainy night is not fun.

- **Sleeping bags**: Rectangular bags are roomier. Mummy bags are usually warmer. Get one that fits: if it is too big, you will be cold; if it is too small you'll be uncomfortable. Temperature ratings are only a guideline, not a guarantee. Down fill is warmer (and more expensive) but synthetic fibers insulate even when wet. Don't forget a sleeping pad, it will not only ease the hardness of the ground, it will also insulate for more warmth. Closed-cell foam pads are cheap and light; self-inflating pads are comfy and don't take much space.
- **Clothes**: Clothes should be worn in layers. In cold weather, wear synthetic materials next to your skin; cotton stays wet, and you'll get chilled. Synthetic fleece is good for a middle insulating layer since it is light and insulates even when wet, like wool. The outer layer should be waterproof, not just water-resistant. Don't forget a knit cap, and remember that cheap mittens (fleece works well) are warmer than expensive gloves.
- **Cooking gear, stove**: Spending a lot on stoves is easy, and most veteran campers try several types before finding a favorite, so ask your friends. The varieties are mostly based on type of fuel and adjustability of the flame. A versatile cook kit contains a couple of pots, a lid/frying pan, and a handle. Add some insulated plastic mugs, spoons, and a pocketknife.
- **Water purification**: No stream or lake is guaranteed to be drinkable. Purify by heat (bring to a rolling boil), chlorine (eight drops unscented Clorox per gallon), iodine tablets, or filters. If you pick a filter, don't skimp; get one guaranteed to remove giardia. A carbon add-on filter will help it taste better, too.

## Camping for Better Emergency Preparedness

If you have camped before, try it again. If you haven't, start slow. First go to a developed campsite with toilets and water. After you are comfortable creating your own light, heat, and shelter, try a "dry camp" where you take your own water and sanitary arrangements. If you want even more challenge, camp in the wilderness. Safety advice: don't try summer desert camping or winter mountain camping without instruction and proper equipment. Be sure to practice low-impact camping: camp two hundred feet away from water; use established campsites and fire rings; bring your own firewood; don't trench around tents; don't cut live trees; try to stay off vegetation; and leave each campsite and trail cleaner than you found it.

Chances are that your first camping trip will have surprises, so go with an attitude of adventure. You probably know some accomplished campers; learn from the experts. But the best advice for learning preparedness skills is to camp, camp, camp.

Emergency preparedness:
Do one thing today.

# Adaptability: Lessons of a Bandanna

## 103 Uses for a Bandanna

In virtually all lists of emergency kits of all kinds in this book, a bandanna is listed as a key item. The reason for this is simple: the bandanna is cheap, versatile, and adaptable. In everyday life as well as emergency situations, the common cotton bandanna is unrivaled in the number and type of functions: medical, personal hygiene, survival, food preparation, clothing, repair, and so on. One hundred and three uses are listed here, but the list could surely go on and on. The bandanna demonstrates a key survival principle: resourcefulness. You may not have all of the things you want on hand, but if you can adapt a little and be creative with what you do have—like bandannas—you can probably make a go of it.

When buying bandannas, look for 100% cotton, get a color that isn't embarrassing to you, and look for the larger sizes. Buy several and place them in your cars, short-term emergency kits, coat pockets, desk drawers at work, first aid kits, camping gear, fanny packs, school backpacks, lockers, boats, campers, trailers, and so on.

### First Aid

1. **Bandage**: use as a compress on a bleeding wound.
2. **Tie**: hold a pressure bandage in place.
3. **Sling**: tie opposite corners together, sling over neck, and insert arm. Use two more bandannas tied end-to-end to immobilize sling against chest.

4. **Finger splint**: tape or tie folded bandanna around injured finger to immobilize.
5. **Splint tie**: rip into strips to secure splints against limbs.
6. **Poultice**: fill with clean, cool mud or damp sand for bug bite or minor burn relief.
7. **Tourniquet tie**: use only if life is in immediate danger.
8. **Snake bite band**: tie two to four inches above bite to slow the spread of venom.
9. **Ankle wrap**: tie a snug crossing pattern around the ankle and over the shoe to give support to twisted ankle.
10. **Wrist brace**: wrap around wrist joint for extra support.
11. **Sponge**: use to clean around wounds.
12. **Face cloth**: dampen and use to relieve fever or swelling.
13. **Hot pack**: dip in warm water and apply to skin.
14. **Cold pack**: fill with ice and apply to injury.

## Clothing

15. **Hat**: make a sun cover for head, pirate style. Soak with water to cool.
16. **Ear muffs**: tie as a wide headband and pull down over ears.
17. **Mittens**: wrap around fingers to protect from wind chill.
18. **Work gloves**: wrap around the hands to minimize blisters.
19. **Winter scarf**: tie loosely around neck to slow heat flow out of parka.
20. **Summer scarf**: tie around neck to prevent sunburn.
21. **Belt**: tie end-to-end. Some waists may need two or three bandannas.
22. **Sweatband**: tie around forehead or wrists.
23. **Dust mask**: make a "train robber" mask. Also works in winter to warm face.
24. **Sock**: wrap around foot and insert into shoe.

25. **Shoelaces**: rip into strips and roll up.
26. **Patches**: subdivide to patch several holes in clothing.
27. **Boot padding**: stuff in toe of oversize shoe or boot.
28. **Strap padding**: use folded bandannas to provide extra padding under backpack straps and such.
29. **Knee pad**: tie or tape folded bandannas to knees for canoeing and such.
30. **Insulation**: fold up and lay inside bottom of each boot for extra warmth.
31. **Sunglasses**: poke small holes and tie across face to reduce the glare of sun on snow.
32. **Glasses strap**: tie one end to each earpiece.
33. **Purse**: wrap personal valuables.
34. **Watchband**: rip a strip and tie around band pins to replace a broken band.
35. **Hair tie**: you'll feel better when you look better.

## Food Preparation and Cleanup

36. **Dishcloth**: fold several times to use as a scrubber. Add some sand to increase effectiveness.
37. **Dish towel**: dry dishes directly, or lay out flat to lay clean utensils on.
38. **Apron**: tuck in the front of waistband.
39. **Hot pad**: fold several times to insulate fingers from hot pans.
40. **Tablecloth**: lay bandanna out flat to prepare food on.
41. **Seat cover**: lay bandanna out flat to sit on.
42. **Steamer**: stretch over top of pan containing a small amount of water and place vegetables on cloth and lid on top of that.
43. **Strainer**: use to drain water from vegetables, pasta, and so on.
44. **Food wrap**: wrap up bread or other food temporarily.
45. **Bug cover**: lay over dishes of food to keep insects off until serving time.

46. **Bib**: tie loosely around neck.

47. **Napkin/wipe**: for messes on hands and faces.

48. **Tea bag**: use to mull spices or teas.

49. **Trash container**: wrap up scraps and garbage until you get to a real can.

50. **Water strainer**: will not purify water but will remove large contaminants.

51. **Sterilizer**: wrap baby bottle nipples and such in bandanna and dip into boiling water.

52. **Wick clarifier**: clarifies (does not purify) murky or silty water by wicking from a high container to a lower one.

## Personal Hygiene

53. **Washcloth**: if used for personal hygiene, don't use for food preparation.

54. **Towel**: to dry off. May need to wring it out several times.

55. **Handkerchief**: like it was designed!

56. **Diaper**: dispose after use.

57. **Toilet paper**: rip into small pieces. Dispose after use.

58. **Feminine hygiene**: if out of supplies.

59. **Toothbrush**: dab a corner in water and scrub teeth.

## Survival

60. **Shade**: protect tender skin from sunburn.

61. **Fire windscreen**: rig to protect a match or infant fire.

62. **Fire starter**: shred to provide dry tinder.

63. **Fire wick**: twist a small piece into string and use with wax to make a candle.

64. **Cord/rope**: rip into strips and tie end to end.

65. **Lashing**: rip into strips to lash sticks into tools and utensils.

66. **Small-game snare**: lay it over a small pit trap and cover with leaves, or make a fling snare.

67. **Sling**: make a primitive slingshot, David-and-Goliath-style.
68. **Pack**: wrap up items and tie to a stick, hobo-style.
69. **Stuff sack**: keep small personal items together in pack or container.
70. **Signal**: display against contrasting background.
71. **Flashlight cover**: put different colors over flashlight to send colored signals.
72. **Trail marker**: put small bits on the tops of rock cairns to show the way you went.
73. **Notepaper**: light colors work to leave notes if you use ink.
74. **Tie**: repair tents, packs, clothes, gear, and so on.
75. **Tie down**: lash gear to pack or canoe.
76. **Bear bag**: suspend food in one or more bandannas to keep animals out.
77. **Throwing weight**: fill with dirt or rocks, tie to one end of bear bag rope, and throw over a sturdy branch to anchor the bag.

## Miscellaneous

78. **Pillow**: lay a clean cover over other stuff.
79. **Earplugs**: for sleeping in noisy public shelters.
80. **Kite tail**: you never know when this will be a sanity saver.
81. **Blindfold**: use to sleep in a lighted shelter or play games.
82. **Parachute toy**: tie corners to a small weight, roll up, and toss.
83. **Windsock**: tie corners together to make a drag chute.
84. **Magic tricks**: use to distract bored children.
85. **Puppet**: use rubber bands to create features.
86. **Doll clothes**: you never know when you'll need this distraction.
87. **Game pieces**: tear some pieces to play checkers, for example.
88. **Ball or Hacky Sack**: fill with stuffing and tie tightly.
89. **Car antenna marker**: tie to radio antenna in a large parking lot.
90. **Bookmark**: use a single thread.

91. **Glasses cleaner**: sometimes you just need a clean, soft cloth.
92. **Specimen holder**: wrap up shells, leaves, pinecones, rocks, or whatever is being collected.
93. **Baby pacifier**: soak a corner in water or juice and let baby suck on it.
94. **Applicator**: use to apply paint, stain, grease, and so on.
95. **Broom**: use to sweep up a small floor area.
96. **Dustpan**: hold down the front edge and sweep dirt up onto the bandanna.
97. **Mop**: dampen, fold, and wipe a floor area.
98. **Burp cloth**: what parent hasn't needed an extra one of these?
99. **Window wipe**: clean grime, smudges, or fog off the inside of car windows.
100. **Car window shade**: close the window on one side of the bandanna. Be sure not to obscure driver's view.
101. **Plumb bob**: fill with sand or dirt, tie ends together, and suspend from string.
102. **Pet collar**: be careful not to tie too tightly.
103. **Gift wrap**: give a bandanna to someone you know as the wrapping for another gift.

• • •

The bandanna is a versatile tool, the uses of which are limited only by your resourcefulness.

Emergency preparedness:
Buy one bandanna today.

# Emergency Preparedness Gift Ideas

Gift holidays, like Christmas and birthdays, are a great time to augment your emergency preparedness. For you early holiday planners, here are some gift ideas for just about everyone:

## Dutch Ovens

Everyone loves a Dutch oven meal, in any season. Dutch ovens also increase your cooking options in an emergency. With a little charcoal, or a wood fire, you can cook a variety of outdoor meals easily (never use charcoal indoors). Some Dutch oven supplies that make great gifts include:

- **Dutch oven:** don't scrimp here. Buy a good cast-iron oven with uniform wall thickness, well-fitting lid with a lip on the top, sturdy legs, and handle. The size you choose depends upon the size of crowd you want to cook for. Four to six hungry people can eat from a twelve-to-fourteen-inch oven.
- **Tools**: Dutch oven cooking is made easier with the right tools, including a charcoal starter; a small shovel; coal tongs; heavy leather gloves; lid lifter; lid rest; and outdoor cooking box with spatulas, spoons, oven mitts, spices, paper towels, and so on.
- **Cookbooks**: Even the most experienced Dutch oven cook is always looking for new recipes. Choose from the basic to the exotic among the many Dutch oven cookbooks on the market. See Additional Resources for some Dutch oven cookbook recommendations.

- **Other**: A Dutch oven hearth and windbreak are also useful. Buy a commercial charcoal holder/windbreak, or make your own.

## Camping Gear

Any camping gear adds to your family preparedness. A lot of camping gear is also lightweight for backpackers, which makes it more versatile in your preparedness inventory.

- Backpacks/day packs (carry emergency gear)
- Tents (emergency shelter)
- Sleeping bags/pads/camp pillows (a good night's sleep in an emergency is invaluable)
- Water filters (make an emergency water source drinkable)
- Stoves/cooking kits (emergency cooking)
- Warm, versatile clothing (emergencies don't always happen on sunny spring days . . .)
- Flashlights and battery lanterns (emergency lighting)

## Emergency Kits

You can assemble a variety of kits for emergency preparedness. An advantage to this type of gift is you can buy individual items as you find them on sale, and you can tailor the gift to your budget.

- Short-term emergency kit: see chapter 3
- Car kit: tools and emergency supplies that you might need if you broke down or were stranded
- Office kit: a mini emergency kit for that extra drawer in your office
- First aid kit: this can range from a small pocket kit for hikes to a fully equipped home or car kit to cover a wide range of emergencies

## Service Gift Certificates

Homemade gift certificates are always a fun idea and can be inexpensive. Try certificates for:

- Quarterly smoke detector checks; function and battery
- Water supply rotation
- Water heater tie-down

- Lights-out practice and candle-lit dinner
- Emergency preparedness files organizing

## Stocking Stuffers

For a limited budget, you can also get some emergency preparedness stocking stuffers for Christmas:

- Space blanket/bag for car or pocket kit
- Signaling whistle
- Pocket heat packs
- Emergency radio, powered by battery, hand crank, or solar
- Light sticks
- Inexpensive flashlight
- Pocketknife
- Emergency gloves, hat, or socks

## Other

Other gift ideas include:

- Good LED lantern, battery-powered
- High-quality, heavy-duty, no-kidding emergency flashlight (and batteries)
- Anything for the food preserver in your family: pressure canner; juicer; applesauce maker; food dryer; vacuum sealer; jar lifter, and so on
- Multipurpose pliers/tools. Be sure to get a good quality tool; many cheap brands don't fit together well and won't last long
- Emergency preparedness books: any bookstore or emergency preparedness specialty store will carry a good selection. See Additional Resources

• • •

A little imagination can result in useful and much appreciated gifts. The possibilities are endless.

Emergency preparedness:
Do one thing today.

# Conclusion

## No-Cost Emergency Preparedness Tips

Too many people think of emergency preparedness as overwhelming, complex, difficult and time-consuming. We think we are so busy that we don't have time; we think we are living so close to the edge that we don't have the money. But there are a huge number of things you can do—today!—that are free, simple and helpful. Some of them don't even take much time. Here are fifteen:

1. Wear your seat belt—everybody, every trip. This may not prevent an earthquake, but it could reduce a car accident to a mere inconvenience.
2. Stop smoking, eat right, exercise, and get enough sleep. Don't underestimate the effect your health can have on you and your family. A healthy person is able to weather the stresses of other kinds of crises.
3. Do a hazards hunt in your home. Take a pencil and paper and walk through your house noting conditions that may be unsafe. Check for fire hazards; hazardous materials; unsafe or unstable furniture; and access to medicines, chemicals, dangerous tools, or paints and solvents. Most household hazards can be corrected with some simple cleaning or rearranging.
4. Create a fire evacuation plan. Pick two ways to get out of every room. Make sure there are tools for safely opening (or breaking) windows, and ladders if required. Designate a location to gather outside of the house. Teach everyone how to call 911, and when. Teach kids how to test for fire beyond a door; how to crawl to a window; how to stop, drop and roll. Practice your evacuation.

5. Teach utility shutoff skills. Teach everyone old enough where to turn off the electricity, water, and gas. Teach them *when* to turn it off and when not. Practice, but don't really turn off the gas since a plumber or gas company employee will have to come and turn it back on and light the pilot lights.

6. Practice flame safety. Never leave candles burning unattended. Don't let children play with matches or candles. Put away matches and lighters. Consciously teach fire safety to kids.

7. Create a family plan. Write down your out-of-state contact, the person everyone will call in an emergency. Write down other emergency numbers and make a copy for each member of the family. Figure out how and where you'll all get together after an emergency. Don't forget to designate a second place outside of your neighborhood in case your house is inaccessible. Plan out what other things you would like to do to get ready, including short-term emergency kits, food and water storage, and emergency and first aid training.

8. Learn your children's school emergency response plan. Learn your workplace emergency response plan.

9. Network with your neighbors. A neighborhood is an awesome resource, but you must work out how you can cooperate with and watch out for each other. Getting to know your neighbors is the first thing to do. Agreeing to something as simple as checking each other's utilities, or pets in an emergency is a real step forward.

10. Sleep with a flashlight and pair of shoes next to your bed. Even a mild earthquake can knock out the power and create serious hazards for bare feet.

11. Learn something new about some aspect of emergency preparedness you are especially worried about or interested in. Libraries have books on the shelves and other books available by requesting transfers from other libraries. The Internet has many sites, some better than others, chock-full of good information. Try the American Red Cross site, or ready.gov, or search for "emergency preparedness" (see Additional Resources).

12. Practice. Eat a meal out of your short-term emergency kit. How does it taste? Have a lights-out practice. Do you really know where

that flashlight is? Does it work? How will you entertain yourself and the kids without electricity?

13. Organize and protect your important papers: deeds, titles, insurance policies, contracts, mortgages, and so on.
14. Learn to make your own non-technological fun. Learn to play simple games with few pieces or parts. Collect instructions for card games and parlor games. Store dice, playing cards, pencil and paper and other items that support a variety of different games.
15. When staying in a hotel, read the evacuation plan fixed to the door. In restaurants and bars note where the closest doors are. When you go to public places or events, get into the habit of mentally choosing a primary and backup exit in case of emergency.

These are just a few of the many things you can do to get ready for an emergency that don't take a lot of time and don't cost a lot of money. After you do one of them, choose another one to do tomorrow; emergency preparedness is an on-going process.

## Four Principles to Keep You Going

Understanding four key principles of emergency preparedness can us keep going when obstacles like apathy, confusion, and discouragement get in our way. Keeping these principles in mind will help you avoid distorting emergency preparedness, getting distracted from your objectives, or even overdoing it.

### Principle #1

***The objective of preparation is to keep bad situations from becoming worse.*** Preparing is about giving yourself options in a bad situation. This changes your attitude from victim to survivor. The knowledge that you have not used the last of the tricks in your bag can stave off panic. Almost no situation gets better if you panic; hysteria is not our friend. Two examples:

- A retired couple exploring back roads of southern Utah late one autumn encountered some difficulty on a dirt road. They stayed with the car for several days but finally decided to walk for it. The strain was too much for the man and he died of a heart attack before help arrived. A bad situation got worse.

- One January, a mother dropped her car off for maintenance and walked several blocks to the school to pick up a child. The sun was shining, the air calm. It felt like spring. She met the child and started back just as a stiff breeze kicked up and the sun disappeared. In an instant, spring returned to winter. They were not dressed for it. The child got cold and refused to walk. They were blocks away from the car and it was cold. A now-frightened mother picked up the child and ran, walked, and finally limped back to the car. This story ended happily. But a bad situation could have become worse.

Many bad situations could get worse, ranging from personal emergencies, like house fires and becoming lost or stranded, to neighborhood or wide-area emergencies like floods, storms, chemical spills, or earthquakes. Sometimes it seems like the world is a minefield and we're doing the polka in snowshoes, but if you remind yourself that these are bad situations that you may not be able to prevent, all you really have to do is ask yourself what you could do now to prevent them from going from bad to worse.

## Principle #2

***Any preparation is better than no preparation. It doesn't have to be perfect.*** Here's why: you can't possibly know everything to prepare for, and there is no way to know what perfect is. Further, each family will not be alone, even in the worst scenario. We live in neighborhoods and communities. We will still be able to trade, barter, and help each other. So, armed with the knowledge that all you are trying to do is keep bad things from getting worse, and now realizing that it doesn't have to be perfect, you're probably already better off than you think. Anything you do is right. Anything you prepare, including knowledge, pushes you forward. Here are some things to keep in mind:

- Tailor your preparedness to your own family—have a meeting or informal discussion. You probably already know what you need to work on next. If you are just starting out, try discussing fire safety and develop an escape plan. Learn where utility shutoffs are located. If you are more advanced, test yourselves and your preparation with a practice.
- Prepare to have some comfort and some fun, too. It actually doesn't take too much to survive. It takes a bit more to survive without

whining. Most of our preparation turns out to be creating comfort and convenience. Think about what it would take to have your family regard an emergency less like an ordeal and more like an adventure. It is good advice to store a game or two, and to store fewer sawdust cookies and more pudding cups.

- Since you can't prepare for everything, you've got to be flexible; go for multiple solutions. You can prepare several kinds of light sources, for example, or several ways to cook your food.

## Principle #3

***Less can sometimes be more.*** Don't overdo it. Especially don't overplan it. Having an imperfect grab-and-go box is better than having a plan for a perfect, color-coordinated short-term emergency kit. Having one flashlight that works is better than having a dozen in various states of disrepair. You get the idea.

## Principle #4

***Do one thing today.*** As trite as it sounds, and as tired of it as you may be by now, this is the most potent emergency preparedness advice in this book. It counters distraction by letting you focus on one thing, no matter what it is, and doing it every day. Preparedness means not procrastinating. And key to not procrastinating is to get started, no matter how small the step. Involve everyone and return to it often.

• • •

Besides getting prepared, there are other rewards. Emergency preparedness gives us perspective: we acknowledge that nothing is permanent; things can change. And things change not only for the worse but also the better—when things are bad we know that "this too shall pass." If we involve our families, preparedness can teach our children to put something away for a rainy day. This is a worthwhile lesson considering that advertisers constantly howl at them to seek immediate gratification. Finally, emergency preparedness gives us confidence that can spill over into other parts of our lives.

Emergency preparedness:
Do one thing today.

# Additional Resources

This book is not meant to be comprehensive. For those interested, a number of additional resources are available from which advanced information can be obtained. Public organizations as well as published literature are all available. In all cases remember: caveat emptor, "let the buyer beware." This is because information sources can be outdated or inaccurate. With preparedness information, you must constantly update and expand.

## Websites

- https://www.ready.gov (US Department of Homeland Security)
- https://preparecenter.org (American Red Cross)
- https://emergency.cdc.gov (Centers for Disease Control)
- https://beready.utah.gov (Utah Division of Emergency Management)
- https://www.usgs.gov (US Geological Survey)
- https://www.usda.gov/topics/disaster-resource-center (US Department of Agriculture)
- https://www.nrc.gov/about-nrc/emerg-preparedness/protect-public.html (Nuclear Regulatory Commission)
- https://www.aarp.org (search for "emergency preparedness")

## Books


- Bouwman, Fred, *The Practical Camp Cook*, Cedar Fort Publishing, 2005.

- *Boy Scout Handbook*, 14th ed., Boy Scouts of America, 2023.
- *Fieldbook: The BSA's Manual of Advanced Skills for Outdoor Travel, Adventure, and Caring for the Land*, 4th ed., Boy Scouts of America, 2004.
- Briscoe, Alan K., *Your Guide to Emergency Home Storage*, Cedar Fort Publishing, 2009.
- Dickey, Esther, *Skills for Survival: How Families Can Prepare*, Cedar Fort Publishing, 2009.
- FEMA, *Are You Ready?*, US Department of Homeland Security, 2023
- Hansen, Mark, *Stop, Drop and Cook: Everyday Dutch Oven Cooking with Food Storage,* Hobble Creek Press, 2015
- Jaynes, Blair D., *Emergency Survival Packs: How to Prepare a Fourteen-Day Evacuation Kit*, Horizon Publishers, 1982.
- Jones, Kylene and Jonathan, *The Provident Prepper,* Cedar Fort Publishing, 2014
- Lee, Brent, *Living for Tomorrow*, Cedar Fort Publishing, 2009.
- Martin, Dale, *Every Man's Guide to Outdoor Survival*, Horizon Publishing, 2011
- Mason, Rosalie, *The Beginner's Guide to Family Preparedness,* Horizon Publishers, 2009
- Rawlings, Marla, *The Beginner's Guide to Dutch Oven Cooking*, Cedar Fort Publishing, 2012.
- Read, Teena, *Family Emergency Preparedness Plan*, Cedar Fort Publishing, 2008.
- Ririe, Robert L., *Doin' Dutch Oven*, Cedar Fort Publishing, 2012.
- Salsbury, Barbara, *It's Time to Plan, Not Panic*, Cedar Fort Publishing, 2006.
- Salsbury, Barbara, *Preparedness Principles: The Complete Personal Preparedness Resource Guide for Any Emergency Situation*, Cedar Fort Publishing, 2006.
- Schimelpfenig, Todd, *NOLS Wilderness Medicine*, 7th ed., Stack pole Books, 2021.

- South, J. Allan, *The Sense of Survival,* Timpanogos Publishers, 1986.
- Spencer, Sam, *Caught Prepared,* Hobble Creek Press, 2015
- Utah Geological Survey, P*utting Down Roots in Earthquake Country,* 2nd ed., Utah Seismic Safety Commission, 2022
- Wells, Larry; and Giles, Roger, *You Can Stay Alive,* Cedar Fort Publishing, 2007

## Other

- County extension service: Information about growing and preserving food.
- Electrical utility: Information about electrical safety.
- Fire department: Fire safety and prevention, hazmat response.
- Gas utility: Gas safety, water heater tips, shutoff info.
- Insurance agent: Insurance coverage and needs.
- Local government: Community preparedness plans, LEPC.
- Public safety (police/sheriff): Street safety, neighborhood watch.
- State health department: Water purification, epidemics.
- Water utility: Water quality, shutoff info.

• • •

There are additional resources for any topic of interest. Search in your local library, in your favorite bookstore, or on the Internet using keywords like "emergency," "disaster," "survival," "food storage," "prepare." Or do a search on your area of specific interest: hurricanes, earthquakes, tornadoes, and so on. Emergency preparedness is all about information.

Emergency preparedness:
Do one thing today.

# Index

## SYMBOLS



## A



## B



## C



## D



## E

## F



## G



## H



## I



## K



## L



## M



## N



## O



## P



## R



## S

## T



## U



## V



## W



## Y

# About the Author

**EVAN GABRIELSEN** started collecting information and writing articles on emergency preparedness to counter misconceptions and provide accurate and helpful advice for friends and neighbors. He has presented preparedness concepts to numerous groups and organizations. As he researched the various topics, he became convinced of the need for a balanced, accurate, common-sense resource for families, and this book was born. He wanted to compile basic information for families seeking self-reliance without panic or extremism. The result is a book that is easily read, motivating, and able to help any family get just a little better prepared for the disasters that will surely come to all.

Gabe received a bachelor's degree in mechanical engineering from Brigham Young University in 1983, and has worked on booster rockets, demilitarization, advanced materials, and environmental cleanup projects before retiring.

He and his wife are the parents of two children and grandparents of eight. He enjoys reading, writing, camping, stargazing, and traveling, especially to see the grandchildren.